Books & Software

Get in-depth information. Nolo publishes hundreds of great books and software programs for consumers and business owners. They're all available in print or as downloads at Nolo.com.

Legal Encyclopedia

Free at Nolo.com. Here are more than 1,400 free articles and answers to common questions about everyday legal issues including wills, bankruptcy, small business formation, divorce, patents, employment and much more.

Plain-English Legal Dictionary

Free at Nolo.com. Stumped by jargon? Look it up in America's most up-to-date source for definitions of legal terms.

Online Legal Documents

Create documents at your computer. Go online to make a will or living trust, form an LLC or corporation or obtain a trademark or provisional patent at Nolo.com. For simpler matters, download one of our hundreds of high-quality legal forms, including bills of sale, promissory notes, nondisclosure agreements and many more.

Lawyer Directory

Find an attorney at Nolo.com. Nolo's unique lawyer directory provides in-depth profiles of lawyers all over America. From fees and experience to legal philosophy, education and special expertise, you'll find all the information you need to pick a lawyer who's a good fit.

Free Legal Updates

Keep up to date. Check for free updates at Nolo.com. Under "Products," find this book and click "Legal Updates." You can also sign up for our free e-newsletters at Nolo.com/newsletters/index.html.

1st edition

Healthy Employees, Healthy Business

Easy, Affordable Ways to Promote Workplace Wellness

By Ilona Bray

FIRST EDITION   OCTOBER 2009

Cover Design   SUSAN PUTNEY

Book Design   TERRI HEARSH

CD-ROM Preparation   ELLEN BITTER

Proofreading   SUSAN CARLSON GREENE

Index   MEDEA MINNICH

Printing   DELTA PRINTING SOLUTIONS, INC.

Bray, Ilona M., 1962-
    Healthy employees, healthy business : easy, affordable ways to promote workplace wellness
/ by Ilona Bray. -- 1st ed.
        p. ; cm.
    ISBN-13: 978-1-4133-1074-0 (pbk.)
    ISBN-10: 1-4133-1074-5 (pbk.)
    1. Employee health promotion. I. Title.
    [DNLM: 1. Health Promotion. 2. Occupational Health Services. 3. Preventive Health
Services. WA 412 B827h 2009]
    RC969.H43B73 2009
    658.3'82--dc22
                                2009021420

Please note

We believe accurate, plain-English legal information should help you solve many of
your own legal problems. But this text is not a substitute for personalized advice from a
knowledgeable lawyer. If you want the help of a trained professional—and we'll always
point out situations in which we think that's a good idea—consult an attorney licensed
to practice in your state.

Acknowledgments

I've been known to exaggerate (just a bit) in the interests of a good story, but let me say that if any of what follows sounds like hyperbole—it's not. This book was a major team effort. It wouldn't have been possible without the time, effort, wisdom, and patience of the people named here.

First, I'd like to thank our advisory board members, who generously drew on their years of medical, workplace wellness, legal, and life experience to make valuable contributions to this book. Even in this age of instant information, some insights can only be gained by talking to people who know their stuff. I appreciate the many hours each adviser spent on the phone with me, hammering out both overarching concepts and fine details. You'll meet our advisers in the coming pages—and you can hear their podcasts on the included CD-ROM. The advisory board includes, in order of their profiles in this book: Dr. Kenneth R. Pelletier; Rae Lee Olson; Dr. Douglas Metz; Dr. Charles Gerba; Dr. Preston Maring; Dr. Robert Sallis; Dr. Albert Ray; Jonathan Foulds, M.A., M.App.Sci., Ph.D.; Renee Brown, M.A., LMFT; Lisa Molbert; Trina Histon, Ph.D.; Dr. Janet Greenhut; Matthew Sears, CEBS, CMS; and Kelly Kuglitsch, Esq.

Thanks, also, to those at Kaiser Permanente who helped conceive this project and bring the book to fruition. They include Janet Venturino, Paul Van Voorhis, Tom Carter, Marla Kaufman, and Melanie Fields.

Maurice Levich, Bruce Licht, and Janet Thiry of Poster Compliance Center, in Lafayette, California, helped with initial brainstorming and were important early proponents of the book.

A number of businesspeople and workplace wellness experts across the United States were kind enough to share stories and ideas. They include: Kara Parker, vice president of finance and human resources at Buffalo Supply in Lafayette, Colorado; Patty Frett, account executive at Frett Barrington Ltd, in Pewaukee, Wisconsin; Theresa Islo, director of operations at the Wellness Council of Wisconsin (in Milwaukee); Joline Woodward, assistant to the

Council of Small Business Executives at the Metropolitan Milwaukee Association of Commerce; and Debby Tappan and Jackie Grabin, co-presidents of Arrow Exterminating Company, Lynbrook, New York.

Marcia Stewart, Nolo's acquisitions editor, championed this book from the very beginning and performed tireless outreach in lining up our team of advisers. Also at Nolo, I owe a huge debt to Stan Jacobsen, who scoured the University of California library system for the latest, greatest, and, in some cases, most academically arcane research on workplace wellness and health. Sigrid Metson and Tom Silva of Nolo's business division were also important early advocates of the book. Lisa Guerin contributed crucial insights on employment policies and legal matters. Rich Stim helped define the book's structure and added audio wizardry by recording interviews with the members of our advisory board. Shae Irving edited, and in some cases wrestled the manuscript to a state of completion, with a wise and graceful balance of prodding and encouragement. She also offered many substantive ideas and developed several of the forms on the CD-ROM. Barbara Kate Repa, one of Nolo's most experienced authors, contributed material regarding stress in the workplace. And thanks, finally, to Nolo's production and applications development departments, including Jaleh Doane, Emma Cofod, Terri Hearsh, Susan Putney, and Ellen Bitter.

About the Author

Ilona Bray is an author and editor at Nolo and a former attorney. She has written on a wide range of topics, from real estate to immigration law to nonprofit fundraising. She is the author of *Effective Fundraising for Nonprofits: Real World Strategies That Work* and *Becoming a U.S. Citizen: A Guide to the Law, Exam & Interview,* and coauthor of the popular *Nolo's Essential Guide to Buying Your First Home.*

Ilona's working background includes solo legal practice, nonprofit, and corporate stints. She received her law degree and a Masters degree in East Asian (Chinese) Studies from the University of Washington, and a degree in philosophy from Bryn Mawr College. A health and fitness buff, Ilona enjoys cooking healthy (and gluten-free) foods, hiking, swimming, and yoga.

Healthy Employees, Healthy Business
Board of Advisers

 **Dr. Kenneth R. Pelletier**, clinical professor of medicine at the University of Arizona as well as at the University of California School of Medicine, San Francisco (UCSF), in both the Department of Family and Community Medicine and the Department of Psychiatry.

 **Rae Lee Olson**, principal with Vita Benefits Group, an employee benefits brokerage and consulting firm in Mountain View, California.

 **Dr. Douglas Metz**, Chief Health Services Officer and Executive Vice President at American Specialty Health (ASH) and its subsidiary, Healthyroads, located in San Diego, California.

 **Charles P. Gerba, Ph.D.**, professor at the University of Arizona and author of many books, including *The Germ Freak's Guide to Outwitting Colds and Flu: Guerilla Tactics to Keep Yourself Healthy at Home, at Work and in the World*, cowritten with Allison Janse.

 **Dr. Preston Maring**, a primary care physician at Kaiser Permanente in Northern California and founder of the Friday farmers' markets outside Kaiser Permanente medical facility locations.

 **Dr. Robert Sallis**, a Board-certified family physician at Kaiser Permanente in Southern California and leader of the international "Exercise Is Medicine" initiative.

 **Dr. Albert Ray**, Physician Director for Patient Education and Health Promotion at Kaiser Permanente in Southern California, as well as Regional Assistant Medical Director of Business Management and Physician Director at Positive Choice Wellness Center in San Diego.

 **Jonathan Foulds, M.A., M.App.Sci., Ph.D.**, Professor and Director, University of Medicine & Dentistry of New Jersey School of Public Health, Tobacco Dependence Program.

 **Renee Brown, M.A., LMFT**, Executive and Clinical Director at Sequoia Center, a drug and alcohol treatment and recovery center located in the San Francisco Bay Area.

 **Lisa Molbert**, Assessment Director and Interventionist at Sequoia Center.

 **Trina Histon, Ph.D.**, Senior Manager of Weight Management and Director of the Weight Management Initiative at Kaiser Permanente's Care Management Institute in Oakland, California.

 **Dr. Janet Greenhut**, Senior Medical Consultant at HealthMedia, a provider of online health and wellness coaching programs in Ann Arbor, Michigan.

 **Matthew T. Sears, CEBS, CMS**, Executive Vice President, the Jenkins Insurance Group, in Concord, California.

 **Kelly Kuglitsch**, attorney in the Employee Benefits & Executive Compensation Practice Group at Drinker, Biddle, & Reath in Milwaukee, Wisconsin.

Table of Contents

Appendix

Files on the CD-ROM

Wellness Plan Worksheet

Wellness Program Waiver and Release of Liability

Checklist for a Successful Wellness Program

Wellness Program Interest Survey

Wellness Program Announcement Letter

Wellness Program Newsletter Announcement

Your Wellness Program's Baseline Data

Treatment Center Evaluation Form

Food and Exercise Diary

Why Create a Wellness Program?

Wellness Program Incentives

Wellness Program—Walking

Your Workplace Wellness Companion

You may have heard media buzz lately about "workplace wellness." But given what it takes to run a business these days, when your to-do list is already too long and your balance sheet may be anything but balanced, you may have simply tuned it out.

This book shows you why it pays to pay attention. An affordable, simple workplace wellness program can actually boost your business by making your employees healthier, happier, and much more productive. Instead of cigarette breaks, your employees may start taking walking breaks—returning reenergized and more alert. Instead of reaching for the communal candy jar—and complaining about weight gain—when stress levels rise, they may compete to eat the five recommended daily servings of fruit and vegetables. Add up lots of little changes like these, and you've got a more vibrant and efficient workforce.

To help you understand how a wellness program works and how it can benefit your particular business, we've brought together a team of experts on topics like medicine, fitness, nutrition, health insurance benefits, workplace laws, and more. And because we know you're busy, we've packed a lot into this easy-to-digest resource, which will show you:

- why healthy employees are essential to the financial success—and in some cases, the survival—of your business
- how you can help improve employee health by providing not only basic health insurance, but support for better fitness and nutrition, stress management, and other keys to well being
- how to design a wellness program that fits your budget—one that will let you recoup your investment and then some, and
- how to comply with the relevant employment or disability laws.

If you don't know where to start when it comes to a workplace wellness program, don't worry. We'll help you evaluate the unique needs of your business and give you lots of ideas and program activities to choose from. This book is organized so that you can pick and choose among various wellness topics, selecting those that best fit your employees. For example, some highly successful programs have started by focusing solely on employee fitness and nutrition, saying "maybe next year" to programs that tackle stress or chronic illness.

We think you'll like what you see after implementing a wellness program—in both bottom-line financial terms and employee morale. A workforce that gets healthy together often has a load of fun doing it, spurred by friendly competition and mutual support. New relationships and trust levels build around shared goals and achievements. Workers are absent fewer days and illnesses like the common cold are less likely to plague your worksite. Bodies are stronger, brains are sharper, everyone's happier—and business is better as a result.

Why You Need a Healthy Workplace

Meet Your Adviser

 **Dr. Kenneth R. Pelletier,** clinical professor of medicine at the University of Arizona as well as at the University of California School of Medicine, San Francisco (UCSF), in both the Department of Family and Community Medicine and the Department of Psychiatry. Dr. Pelletier is also director of the Corporate Health Improvement Program (CHIP) and chairman of the American Health Association.

What he does: In addition to teaching, Dr. Pelletier is a prolific author, whose books include the international bestseller *Mind as Healer, Mind as Slayer* (Delacorte and Delta) as well as *Holistic Medicine: From Stress to Optimum Health* (Delacorte and Delta); *Healthy People in Unhealthy Places: Stress and Fitness at Work* (Delacorte, Delta, and Doubleday); *Sound Mind, Sound Body: A New Model for Lifelong Health* (Simon & Schuster); *The Best Alternative Medicine: What Works? What Does Not?* (Simon & Schuster); and *Stress Free for Good: 10 Scientifically Proven Life Skills for Health and Happiness* (Harper Collins). At CHIP, Dr. Pelletier conducts research with Fortune 500 companies to develop and evaluate innovative health and medical programs and cost outcomes in the workplace, with an emphasis on integrative health, combining traditional and alternative medical approaches.

Favorite healthy food: "As a lifelong vegetarian but also an avid open-ocean sailor, my favorite foods are virtually every fruit and vegetable (even broccoli), as well as salmon, cod, and Dungeness crab."

Top tip for staying fit and healthy: "My daily exercise varies between running, swimming, and an elliptical trainer, since I honestly find the same physical workouts to be just boring. Also, I do have a daily meditation which I developed in my undergraduate years and have sustained and deepened every year since—wonderful for stress management and food for my soul."

A s a small business owner or manager, you've got a lot on your plate. It's tough to keep profits up and costs down, especially when so many factors are beyond your control, like consumer preferences, the national or regional economy, reductions in employee productivity due to illness or medical problems, and the rising costs of health insurance benefits.

But wait: Is there something you can do about those last two costs? Many employers are discovering that, by actively promoting employee wellness, they can improve employee productivity *and* keep their health insurance expenditures stable—for a net profit on every dollar they spend.

To gain these advantages, you don't have to be a giant corporation that can build its own gym, serve fancy salads in the employee lunchroom, and create an on-site employee clinic complete with nurses, acupuncturists, and massage therapists. Comprehensive programs like these do attract the media spotlight. But your business, whatever its size, can make health-related changes that deliver significant results.

In this book, we'll show you how a small business can, with creativity and smart planning, create a workplace wellness program that achieves both better health for its employees and an improved bottom line. This chapter gets started by:

- laying out the trends in health-related costs for employers
- exploring the potential benefits of employer-sponsored wellness programs
- examining how much a good program costs, and
- summarizing the potential for a positive return on your health dollar investment.

Health Concerns: What Do They Cost Your Business?

Your employees' health impacts your business's bottom line in two important ways:

- You're probably paying to provide employees with health insurance benefits.
- Your business may be losing productivity due to employee health problems.

We'll focus on each of these separately.

The Rising Costs of Health Care Coverage

Employers provide health coverage to the majority of U.S. workers below retirement age—over 60% at last count. Although no law requires them to do it—and employers are more frequently shifting some of the costs to employees—these employers form the backbone of the American health care system. And for many workers, provision of health benefits is a central concern when looking for a job.

If you provide health coverage, however, you know how expensive it is. Between 2001 and 2008, annual average U.S. health care premium costs per employee nearly doubled, from $4,336 to $8,331. Early reports for 2009 saw a jump to $8,863 per employee. You may already be paying even more, and further increases are predicted. In a 2007 Business Roundtable survey, CEOs pointed to the cost of health care as the single biggest threat to their company profits. No wonder almost half of all small businesses have decided they can't provide health insurance.

Why do these costs keep going up? While part of the cause is the ever-increasing cost of medical care, another part may be a direct result of your own employees' usage levels and health conditions. In other words, when your company's health insurance policies are up for renewal, the insurer may look at how much each employee is costing it to cover, and then adjust the overall rates accordingly. (Insurers are not allowed, under federal law, to create separate rates for each employee, but this doesn't prevent them from taking individual health factors into account when setting an aggregate rate.)

For example, if Bob had a heart attack last year and Jan's soda addiction launched a case of diabetes, these alone may, in a small shop, be enough to raise your rates. Chronic conditions like heart disease, diabetes, arthritis, allergies, kidney disease, multiple sclerosis, and cancer are the most likely culprits, accounting for about 75% of U.S. health care costs.

Employee health may also factor into the amount you pay for workers' compensation insurance. Although state regulators typically set the base premium rate, insurers can adjust this based on what's called an "experience modifier," or your workplace's claims history. The more claims submitted by your employees every year, the more you'll likely have to pay at renewal time. And while some on-the-job injuries are random, many can be traced back to underlying health troubles. For example, Karen's alcohol addiction may account for her slip-up with machinery, while Raymond's lack of physical conditioning and poor posture may contribute to his developing carpal tunnel syndrome.

It's even possible that the amount you pay for life insurance benefits could be affected by employee health. Depending on your insurer and how much coverage you offer, your employees may be required to undergo a health exam as a condition to coverage. More often, however, you'll offer a simple group life policy in which individual medical conditions are not taken into account when setting your premiums. But larger employers—those with roughly 1,000 or more employees—may face an extra hurdle. Even with a group life policy, an unusually high rate of claims coming out of one workplace may drive premiums higher.

Behind the Scenes Costs: Absences and Lost Productivity

In tough economic times, when you may have already cut your staffing to its leanest possible levels, every employee is crucial and needs to be working at maximum efficiency. Both absenteeism and "presenteeism"— that is, showing up to work despite feeling under the weather, stressed, or distracted—can hurt your bottom line. And it can damage your relationship with customers—for example, if a supervisor or lead chef is absent, or the receptionist or cashier is sneezing and unfriendly.

Your workforce may also be aging, especially because so many baby boomers who thought they'd be retiring soon are discovering—with their investment portfolios hit hard or in tatters—that they can no longer afford to do so. You may have employees working well into their 70s. Advanced years don't inevitably mean serious medical troubles, but the importance of screening and preventive care certainly goes up. And for those who have a lifetime ignoring their body's health, nutrition, and fitness needs, the outlook could be troublesome.

Absenteeism. Health problems cause the average employee to miss five days of work each year. And the "average" person doesn't really exist. While some of your employees may almost never take sick days, others will probably be away for more than five days—many more, if they have serious or chronic illnesses.

Who Takes the Most Sick Leave?

- Overall, the biggest users of sick leave are young, less-skilled employees.
- Women take more sick leave than men.
- Elder employees use more sick leave than middle-aged employees.
- People with minor health problems are more likely to be out on cold and rainy days.
- People with drinking problems tend to be out on Mondays and Fridays.

Source: "Planning Wellness; Getting Off to a Good Start," *Absolute Advantage; The Workplace Wellness Magazine*, Volume 5, Number 6.

Absenteeism may affect your business's profitability in more ways than you realize. It's not just about losing the value of a worker's activity for a period of time. Depending on your business, you may lose revenue that can't be earned back—for example, if you have to turn away walk-in or one-time customers during the absence. The resulting delay may also interrupt team members' progress on a larger task, or you might need to pay a replacement worker who doesn't perform as efficiently. The smaller your company, the more dramatic the impact—if two out of your eight employees are out sick, that's 25% of your workforce. In fact, one study found that, on average, the business cost of an absence is 28% higher than the worker's actual wage. (See Sean Nicholson, et. al., "How to Present the Business Case for Health Care Quality to Employers,"

Knowledge@Wharton (2005). Available at http://knowledge.wharton. upenn.edu/papers/1303.pdf.)

Presenteeism. What about those employees who show up for work every day? Are they really giving their all or are some just struggling through despite an emotional or physical health problem? (These troubles could include anything from the common cold to worry about a sick child or spouse to chronic depression.) Studies show that three out of ten working people admit that health problems lower their productivity at work. The problem tends to get worse in a down economy, when people are concerned that if they don't show up every day, they may be among the first laid off.

It's hard to measure the exact productivity difference caused by working while under the weather, but we all know how, on a good day, we may feel sharp, quick, creative, or responsive, while on a bad day, we may feel like we're moving through molasses, grumpily waiting for the day to end. It's easy to see that more can be achieved, and more mistakes can be avoided, by workers who have more good days.

More than one study has concluded that companies would be far better off if sick workers just stayed home. For one thing, the strategy of coming to work while feeling sick tends to backfire, as workers who do so take more sick days than other workers in the long run. Productivity has been shown to drop only 28% when employees stayed home sick compared to a 72% drop when they tried to gut it out and keep working. And, according to industry expert Ron Goetzel, between 20% and 60% of the total health-related costs faced by employers can be traced to on-the-job productivity losses. (See Ron Goetzel, et. al., "Health, Absence, Disability, and Presenteeism Cost Estimates of Certain Physical and Mental Health Conditions Affecting U.S. Employers," *Journal of Occupational and Environmental Medicine*, (2004) Vol. 46, No. 4.)

Of course, the exact numbers depend partly on what type of business you're running and what you expect of your workers. But the effects of working while sick cut across many types of jobs. Managers and data entry workers need to be able to think clearly; air traffic controllers and bus drivers need to stay alert; cashiers need to remain patient and friendly; and construction workers need to be strong and coordinated. All of these can be affected by illness or poor health.

Are productivity losses inevitable? To some extent, worker illness is just a cost of doing business. Between genetics, bad luck, and the occasional flu bug so virulent that not even the vaccine creators predicted it, getting sick is, in some ways, a natural part of life. But not in every way. The toll that personal lifestyle and behavior choices take on Americans' health—particularly when it comes to chronic conditions—is staggering. An estimated 70% of all U.S. deaths are linked to chronic conditions that may be traced back to poor nutrition, physical inactivity, smoking, and mental illness that's gone untreated.

Let's look, for example, at the impact that excess weight has on American workers, as shown in the table below. Keep in mind that around one-third of the U.S. population is classified as not merely overweight, but obese. And the trend is toward further weight gain: While 28 U.S. states had obesity rates below 20% in the year 2000, by 2007 the obesity rates in 49 out of the 50 U.S. states had topped 20%. The resulting total cost to employers is estimated at $45 billion per year.

Workdays Missed Each Year		
	Normal Weight	Obese (30 to 60 lbs. overweight)
Men	3.0	5.0
Women	3.4	5.2
Source: RTI International, Center for Disease Control and Prevention, 2005.		

Weight isn't the only problem that leads to poor health and missed workdays. The table below shows many of the chronic conditions that cause people to miss work—all of which can be either reduced in severity, cured, or forestalled with the right prevention, early diagnosis, or behavioral changes.

Workdays Lost to Chronic Conditions	
Condition	Average Number of Days Absent
Depression/sadness/mental illness	25.6
Cancer (any kind)	16.9
Respiratory disorders	14.7
Asthma	12
Migraine/headache	10.7
Allergies	8.2
Heart disease	6.8
Arthritis	5.9
Diabetes	2.0
Hypertension	0.9
Source: Ron Goetzel, et. al., "Health, Absence, Disability, and Presenteeism Cost Estimates of Certain Physical and Mental Health Conditions Affecting U.S. Employers."	

Clearly there's a lot to be gained by having a healthy workforce. But can an employer really bring about meaningful change? Let's take a closer look.

TIP

Hiring only healthy workers isn't the answer. The Americans with Disabilities Act (ADA) forbids making inquiries into a job applicant's health. When making a job offer, you can ask only about how the applicant would perform the essential functions of the job—those duties that are fundamental to the position. Once you extend a job offer, you can require applicants to take a medical examination, but only if you require all applicants to do so.

How Can a Wellness Program Help Your Bottom Line?

You can't wave a magic wand and make all your employees healthy, nor can you force them to change their behaviors overnight. If you already provide health benefits, that's a good start; it will help make sure your employees don't ignore health problems until they've turned life threatening.

But you've probably observed the limits of what doctors can do to promote overall wellness. (Believe us, the doctors are frustrated, too.) Your workers most likely visit their doctors when they've got big or obvious problems, but soon forget the doctors' advice for ongoing lifestyle or behavioral changes. In fact, some people may use the very availability of treatments like high blood pressure medication as a way to avoid making fundamental lifestyle changes.

Yet you've got an advantage in this game: As an employer, you have communication channels to your employees that almost no one else shares. Your employees may throw out their newspapers, tune out their mothers, and see their doctors only when they can't ignore problems any longer. But you're harder to tune out. Whether it's via company emails, memos, or meetings, you can use your unique access to convey health information and create a health-minded company culture.

For all these reasons, many employers—nearly 80% of them, at last count—are turning to new initiatives for promoting employee health and well-being. Numerous examples of employee wellness programs have appeared in the media, with companies offering on-site health screenings, exercise equipment, and meditation classes, switching from junk food to healthy food in their employee cafeterias, giving bonuses to workers who lose weight or reduce their cholesterol, paying for smoking-cessation and other treatment programs, and much more.

You don't have to do all these things, especially as a small business. The basic idea is to respond to your employees' most pressing health needs by providing a select menu of fitness and behavioral activities, plus some education and guidance toward more specialized health treatments or programs. We'll get into the details in subsequent chapters.

But first, let's fast forward to the potential results. A good, comprehensive workplace wellness program can, over time, produce the following benefits:

- fewer absences
- greater on-the-job productivity
- improved worker satisfaction and retention, and
- fewer dollars spent on health insurance.

Here's why all four advantages are possible and worth aiming for.

Fewer Absences

The science is clear on one thing: People who are physically healthy miss fewer days of work. With workplace wellness programs, employers have been able to greatly reduce absenteeism. Just getting people to exercise can make a big difference: Those who regularly get moderate exercise miss 18% fewer workdays, while strenuous exercisers miss 32% fewer workdays. (See Emmett B. Keelor, et. al., "The External Costs of a Sedentary Life-Style," *American Journal of Public Health,* (1989) Vol. 79, No. 8, 975–980.)

CAUTION

Skimping on allotted sick leave isn't the answer. Sure, workers who aren't allowed much sick leave are more likely to show up at work no matter how they feel—but that just leads to presenteeim, the risks of which we described earlier in this chapter.

Of course, if your office policy is to lump sick time and vacation time into general paid time off or PTO (as is increasingly common among U.S. employers), you probably won't see a difference. But at least your employees will be having a better time on their days away from the office, and hopefully come back relaxed, refreshed, and ready to get back to work.

Improved Productivity on the Job

All the research suggests that employee productivity is where workplace wellness programs yield the greatest returns. This makes sense when you consider that almost every worker, whether or not prone to serious medical conditions, can improve in overall health and fitness to some degree. And with better health comes greater energy and productivity. In a 2002 survey of CFOs performed by the Integrated Benefits Institute, 61% said they believe there's a "strong link" between employee health and productivity.

Imagine what a functional, maybe even fun, workplace you could have if your employees were more fit and healthy. An Australian study found that healthy workers are 3.1 times more productive than others. Healthy employees not only function better at work, but bounce back faster if they do get sick or injured. You might save yourself having to hire more staff in order to make up for the less healthy and productive ones.

Numbers alone can never tell the whole story. Your employees probably don't work in isolation, but either cooperate as teams, advise each other on work, or hold the classic watercooler conversations. The value of each worker extends far beyond any immediate day's outcome. An employee with a positive attitude, vital physical state, and optimal physical and mental effort can boost the morale, drive, and productivity of the entire office.

Worker Satisfaction and Retention

Ask any CEO to name the keys to business success, and retention of the best employees will come up high, if not tops, on the list. Given the cost of recruiting and training a new employee, the benefits of keeping someone who has years of knowledge and experience may be incalculable. Unfortunately, the very employees you most want to keep will inevitably have the most opportunities to find a job elsewhere— perhaps one that offers better health benefits or a lower-stress, more functional office environment.

You might feel that your best employees already take good care of their health, without your help. But that would miss part of the point.

Will a top employee be happy (to take an extreme example) carrying the extra load for an unhealthy workforce and dealing with the germs, depressed state, or slowness of their less healthy coworkers? Probably not.

On the other side of the coin, workplace wellness programs have been shown to bring employees together in important ways. Your employees are probably already forming office friendships or mutual support networks. It's only a small step for them to start influencing each other's health behavior, perhaps by exercising at the same time or competing toward a goal like regular consumption of five daily servings of fruits and vegetables.

Employees at small or medium-size businesses with wellness programs consistently report that they're working harder, performing better, and are motivated to stay with the company. Managers report that wellness programs improve workplace morale, possibly stemming from the fact that their employees are feeling better all around and sense that their employer is interested in them as individuals.

Reduced Health Insurance Costs

Many employers that have instituted workplace health promotion and wellness programs have been able to significantly reduce their costs of health insurance as well as workers' compensation insurance, with some studies reporting reductions of up to 30%.

Most experts agree, however, that not every employer should expect to see dramatic results and that reductions in health care costs shouldn't be your number one motivator for instituting a workplace wellness program. Your health insurance carrier, for example, isn't simply going to say, "Oh, they've started a wellness program, let's lower their rates." The rate determination process (called underwriting) involves looking at numerous variables, such as the average age of your workforce and the cost of delivery of health care. Still, in the long run, a healthier group of employees may successfully drive down both insurance rates and workers' compensation claims for your business.

The trend may be toward even greater possible savings—or at least minimized rate increases—based on wellness programs. Adviser Matt Sears predicts:

Based on my conversations with insurance company executives, health plans may start pushing employers to adopt some more wellness components in their workplace. Some of the insurers are starting to agree with the notion that, if they set up a standard five or six things that employers must do in order to either be allowed to purchase a different or better health plan, or get a rate discount—perhaps a smoking cessation or exercise program, or having employees do screenings or health risk assessments—it will be worth their while.

Dr. Doug Metz (an adviser whom you'll meet in Chapter 3) echoes the possibility of savings, stating that wellness programs may also help lower workers' comp costs:

There are workers' compensation carriers that are looking at the question of how wellness programs will improve workers' physical conditioning, stress management skills, and levels of presenteeism— improvements which may all potentially reduce workplace injuries. Someone who is fit is less likely to have a back injury. Someone who manages their stress well is less likely to be distracted and cut a finger or otherwise get hurt. So, intuitively, there are very good reasons why a wellness program, beyond traditional safety programs, could work to reduce workers' comp claims.

TIP

You can create an effective wellness program without offering health insurance. We recommend offering health benefits to your employees— good medical care is fundamental to their health. (We'll discuss choosing the right plans in Chapter 12, including a focus on how certain health insurance organizations, health maintenance organizations (HMOs) in particular, can provide resources and assistance to augment your wellness program.) Nevertheless, if providing health benefits is way out of your reach, you can still take important steps to promote employee wellness. In fact, if your employees are paying for their own medical coverage, they've got a vested interest in maintaining their health in order to keep their premiums down. Read on for suggestions about what you can do and how much it will cost.

How Much Will It Cost?

An effective wellness program will require investment of both time and money, but it doesn't have to break the bank.

There's a lot you can do that's absolutely free, such as holding regular stretch breaks, organizing a walking program (often named by employees as their favorite workplace wellness activity), instituting policies against smoking at work, putting healthy snack choices in your vending machines, and organizing potluck lunches featuring healthy foods. (We'll expand on all of these possibilities in later chapters.)

Take a look at what on-site assets and advantages your workplace already offers, such as a nearby walking trail or a large conference room suitable for classes, and plan to make the most of those. Beyond what you have on-site, allowing employees to telecommute or use flex-time schedules to participate in wellness activities is also free and a positive way to support employees' efforts.

If you want to bring in guest speakers (discussed in Chapter 2), some might not cost you anything at all. Adviser Dr. Kenneth R. Pelletier suggests:

> Hospitals and universities are terrific sources of speakers available at no or low cost. Check their speaker registries, which may list staff, faculty, or graduate students. And if your employees would be interested in hearing from providers of alternative care like acupuncture, naturopathy, or Chinese medicine, I don't believe those folks get many invitations to speak to workplaces—they'd probably be happy to accept.

Of course, for anyone offering their services in hopes of referrals, you'll need to be clear in advance that you don't expect them to spend much time on business promotion.

As much as you can do for free, some crucial elements of a workplace wellness program will inevitably cost money. It's recommended, for example, that you begin your program by asking all employees to fill out a health risk assessment (HRA), with the help of an outside provider. HRAs usually cost between $5 and $25 per person. (Chapter 3 contains further discussion of administering HRAs.)

For additional—in many cases, small—cash outlays, you can add other useful elements to your program. Subscribing to a printed health newsletter to be distributed (usually quarterly) to your employees should cost between $.35 and $2 per copy, per employee.

Some companies give participating employees cash incentives or purchase incentive gifts, like pedometers or walking shoes, as encouragement to count their steps toward a regular walking goal. Others install a refrigerator on-site so that people can bring healthy lunches instead of relying on local fast food joints. And some stock up on fruit for the break room to head off less healthy snacking.

Not surprisingly, the sky's the limit on how much you could spend. Estimates of what's "normal" range from $0 to $450 per employee per year (including internal staffing costs), but it will depend partly on the size of your office and the program elements and incentives you choose. The biggest costs tend to be for incentives, equipment, or outside service providers like consultants, counselors, and gyms. And some speakers do charge a bundle, in the range of $150 to $300 per hour.

Decide on a budget amount in advance, and then see what you can do within that budget. Sharing certain costs with employees is a popular strategy among small businesses, particularly for things like classes and memberships. You can also protect yourself, where appropriate, by requiring your employees to prove that they actually used the service in question, and then to repay part of the fee if they didn't.

RESOURCE

You aren't alone. Local nonprofit or government health agencies, colleges, and even your own health insurers can be great sources of free health information, low-cost supplies, or screening services. For example, your insurer or a health-focused nonprofit might offer regular health newsletters that you can pass on to your employees. Sharing ideas and resources with other small businesses in your area—including holding joint classes or seminars—can also keep costs down. You can start at www.healthfinder.gov (click "Find Services & Information").

On-Site Gyms: The Ultimate Benefit or a Waste of Money?

On-site gyms come up a lot in discussions of workplace wellness, making many small employers feel instantly guilty that they can't afford to provide one.

But that guilt may be misplaced. In a survey of 509 employees conducted by BlueCross BlueShield of North Carolina, the surveyors were surprised to find that little more than a third of them used an on-site gym even when it was offered.

If your employees are really clamoring for a gym—for example, if your business is located in an area with freezing winters and the nearest gym is 25 miles away—another option is to share the costs. If the employees agree to foot part of the bill, and perhaps have their family members pay a fee to use the equipment, everyone might win. (And they'll appreciate how expensive this stuff really is.) But talk to your lawyers and insurance carrier about liability issues first.

Will Your Investment Pay Off?

No matter how much it costs to institute a wellness program, it will be worthwhile if the returns are high enough. Good news: Based on other employers' experience, your chances of coming out ahead look good. Numerous studies have found a positive return on investment (ROI) for employers instituting wellness programs—anywhere from $1 to $13 gained (in improved productivity and reduced insurance costs) for every $1 spent. The median return is currently said to be $3.14. Only a small minority of companies fail to break even—and that's often because their initial investment of time and money was too low.

Still, some experts caution against overoptimism. They note that you're not likely to see high results within the first year, and that many of the studies were based on large companies or measured results only for participating employees, not for the entire workforce. They also note that certain types of industries get better results than others—those with high employee turnover, for example, have less of a shot at changing their employees' behaviors or of reaping long-term rewards from any changes.

Nevertheless, says Dr. Kenneth R. Pelletier, "Having reviewed many of the recent studies in this area, I'd say the evidence that workplace wellness programs are both clinically and cost effective is getting more and more compelling." And even if your wellness program merely breaks even—with a $1 return for each $1 spent—you'll come out ahead. You'll have offered your employees a workplace benefit that was essentially free. Along the way, you'll probably have boosted morale, reduced the odds of unpleasant interactions between sick or unhappy employees, and given your employees a chance to make changes that will benefit them for their entire life. And who knows what fresh ideas or initiatives will come out of a healthy, energized workforce? All in all, it's a low-cost way to do the right thing for your employees and your business.

Another bit of good news: You don't have to turn all your employees into super-athletes addicted only to blueberry smoothies in order for your investment to pay off. Studies have found that a small reduction in your workforce's health risks—even as little as 1.7%—will let you break even within ten years.

The important thing is that, once you start your program, you follow through for a year or more. Results won't happen overnight and, if you don't make a real commitment, your employees won't either. They also won't believe your efforts are genuine if you try to restart them later.

RESOURCE

Ready to run some numbers? A variety of calculators have been developed to help you estimate the likely ROI at your actual workplace, letting you input actual facts about your company's health care costs, how many of your employees are obese or smoke, and more. None of these calculators are perfect predictors, but trying them out and comparing results can be instructive. See, for example, www.ncqacalculator.com/Index.asp and www.wellsteps.com.

Strategies for a Successful Wellness Program

Meet Your Adviser

 **Rae Lee Olson,** principal with Vita Benefits Group, a small, but nationally recognized, employee benefits brokerage and consulting firm located in Mountain View, California (www.vitacompanies. com).

What she does: With more than 24 years of experience developing practical solutions to employee benefit challenges, Rae Lee Olson helps clients with everything from strategic plan design to contract negotiation, from comprehensive compliance solutions to innovative wellness initiatives, and more. She and her team provide ongoing education and direct assistance to employees to help them navigate the health plans their employers chose.

Favorite healthy food: "My lunchtime salad, with lettuce, carrots, radishes, mushrooms, cottage cheese, and almond slivers, all from the company-stocked lunch fridge."

Top tip for staying fit and healthy: "Sign up for an event or a race and train toward a goal ... try a triathlon!"

What exactly is a workplace wellness program? Can you pass out a few newsletters, hide the ashtrays, and call it a day? Probably not.

Experts agree that piecemeal, uncoordinated measures aren't likely to be effective. But that doesn't mean you need to start looking for places to build a gym and hold Pilates classes or fire employees who smoke. You can find a balanced approach to creating a comprehensive wellness program.

Your work environment ("culture") and employee mix will help determine the elements of your plan, including:

- the best program design
- the most effective activities
- how you communicate with employees, and
- other elements that will have the greatest impact at your workplace.

Ultimately it will be up to you, as the employer, to examine your workforce's needs and make appropriate program choices. That's where the rest of this book comes in. It's dedicated to providing tools and strategies for making these important decisions. It will give you specific ideas on program components and tips on tailoring them to your workplace.

 FORM

Keep track of your favorite ideas. You'll find a Wellness Plan Worksheet on the CD-ROM at the back of this book. It will help you note and make plans for the elements you'd like to include in your program.

Where do you start? In this chapter, we'll address the key principles to planning a wellness program. Our experts agree that the best way to reach the greatest number of employees with the best return is to create a comprehensive, total health program. That means a program that addresses a broad range of health needs in a variety of ways, while taking into account your workplace culture and communications preferences as well as an understanding of basic human behavior.

Deciding Who Your Program Is For

For reasons of both cost and common sense, one of the first things to consider is exactly who, within your employee population, you're implementing a wellness program for. If your workforce is like most, it includes people with a mix of health risks and profiles: Let's imagine, Anna, 47 years old, who jogs 20 miles a week, grows organic vegetables, and reminds all the other women to get regular mammograms; Charles, who at age 25 eats mostly pizza, soda, and chips but never gains weight and has enough energy to work late every night; Bob, who at age 56 hates walking farther than the distance from his door to his car, gets heart palpitations and breaks into a sweat after climbing the stairs, and has developed diabetes; and Yolanda, who's been a chain smoker for the past 25 years, catches every cold and other bug that passes through, and just laughs off any suggestions that she quit.

Anna and Charles probably aren't affecting your health premiums right now, though, if he doesn't change his habits, Charles will eventually. Bob and Yolanda are part of that small portion of the insured workforce (5% to 20%) that accounts for the majority (approximately 75% to 85%) of your employee health claims costs, with accompanying absenteeism and lost productivity. Does that mean you should focus your efforts on the health concerns of Bob, Yolanda, and other employees exhibiting the most obvious or serious health risks? Not entirely.

While we encourage you to evaluate the greatest needs among your employees (we'll show you how to do so in Chapter 3) and to develop strategies for targeting individual issues, you shouldn't overlook the potential for long-term savings among employees who are currently in moderate to good health. Charles, for example, may look healthy now, but eating whatever he wants and working too hard may catch up with him—and therefore his employer—in the long run.

Helping employees like Charles lower their health risks, nip developing problems in the bud, and settle into good habits for the future, will help your company save money in the years ahead—and make Charles more likely to stick around. Employees like Anna, meanwhile, are likely to join in some of your group activities and can be a great resource for motivating others, or even for helping to plan and implement your program. (Just be careful that the Annas in your population don't overwhelm and drive others away. As Rae Lee Olson points out, "You don't want to make your office's fitness freak, for whom it all seems easy, a major spokesperson for your program—it's better to choose someone who has struggled with health or wellness issues. Real people working to take healthy steps are a better motivation for the average person.") The more activities that everyone wants to take part in, the more mutual support will be created among employees.

Don't get us wrong: We're not saying that all of your wellness program activities should serve your entire population. In fact, one of the best ways to make your program cost-effective is, in the words of our adviser and wellness expert Dr. Douglas Metz (you'll meet him in Chapter 3), "to carefully assess the population to which the program is being addressed and then target interventions appropriately." As we'll discuss in the next section, that essentially means creating some program options that are open to all employees and others that are made available only to those in need.

Deciding What Health Issues and Behaviors Your Program Will Address

Closely connected to the issue of who will benefit from your program is what health risks and behaviors your program will address. You can roughly divide these into two categories:

- program elements that promote a healthy lifestyle, and
- targeted program responses to actual health risks and conditions.

Both are important, since living a fit and healthy life will improve practically every other health risk or condition—but some conditions inevitably need more treatment than simple lifestyle changes can provide.

Promoting a Healthy Lifestyle for All

All of your employees, whether they need to maintain or improve their health, will benefit from programs that address the subjects below. (Each is discussed in detail in future chapters of this book.) These topics work not only to improve health, but to boost employee morale and inject group energy into your wellness program. They should be made available to all employees, based on their own self-referral—though that shouldn't stop you from providing incentives to get them interested.

- Prevention practices (Chapter 4)
- Good nutrition and healthy eating (Chapter 5)
- Regular activity and fitness (Chapter 6)
- Stress management (Chapter 7).

TIP

What if you can't do it all? Don't wait to implement basic health promotion measures. Although we strongly recommend planning a comprehensive, individually tailored wellness program, adviser Rae Lee Olson says, "If you can't do everything, at least do something. The fact that your business lacks the time or financial resources to implement a perfect wellness plan shouldn't stop it from doing something well."

Targeting Known Employee Health Risks and Conditions

Depending on your employee population, your program may need to increase its reach by including activities or options to address some or all of the issues below. These wouldn't necessarily be made available to all employees, but offered to those whose health risk assessments or other indicators showed a specific need.

- Tobacco use (Chapter 8)
- Obesity (Chapter 10)
- Addiction, primarily to drugs or alcohol (Chapter 9)

- Chronic illness, for example diabetes, heart disease, asthma, or depression (Chapter 11).

Creating a Program for Total Health

How will you tie together these various offerings to give everyone a sense of actively participating in an ongoing, inspiring program? The best way is to structure your wellness program so that it includes six basic ingredients:

- initial health screenings and assessments of workplace health needs
- effective and fun health education, information, and self-help tools
- organized group wellness and fitness activities or help making individual health and fitness changes
- options for individual treatment or coaching, where appropriate
- incentives and rewards for participating or reaching goals, and
- a supportive workplace environment, in which a carefully planned wellness program becomes part of the workplace's core culture, with buy-in at every level of management.

You don't have to go all out with any one of these program ingredients, and you don't have to roll them all out at once. For example, at Frett Barrington Ltd., a ten-person insurance brokerage firm in Pewaukee, Wisconsin, account executive Patty Frett explains:

> *Our first year, aside from doing HRAs, our program activities simply focused on nutrition and eating well. The second year, we added fitness, and the third year, we added stress management.*

Our adviser Kelly Kuglitsch, an attorney (introduced in Chapter 13), has found that among her clients:

> *It's very common that employers will start small, test the waters, and try out a few things. Later, they'll ramp up the program. Incentives, for example—other than small items like free T-shirts—are usually not given in the first stage.*

But your goal should be to eventually put all these ingredients into the mix, so that each supports the others. For example, it's not good to hold a morning seminar on healthy eating and then pass out doughnuts at the company meeting that afternoon. The same goes for holding health screenings or distributing newsletters that get people worried about how little they exercise or the fact that they smoke, but then failing to provide meaningful options, incentives, or support for changing these habits.

Another promising aspect of "total health" is to look beyond traditional Western medical or pharmaceutical approaches. As our adviser Dr. Kenneth R. Pelletier explains:

> *We're finding that certain forms of alternative treatment stand up well to rigorous, evidence-based study, and can make all the difference in changing some people's behavior or health outcomes. The very fact that not all of these require going into a doctor's office—such as the use of guided imagery to lower stress, over-the-counter nutritional supplements and herbs, various forms of yoga and meditation, as well as physical activity in the form of martial arts or tai chi—makes them ideal for inclusion in the on-site portions of a workplace wellness program.*

RESOURCE

More information about alternative medicine. If you want to learn more about distinguishing the proven from the unproven in the realm of complementary medicine, see Dr. Pelletier's book, *The Best Alternative Medicine: What Works? What Does Not?* (Simon & Schuster).

TIP

Keep your program in line with your office culture. This is one of the most important program design principles, according to Dr. Metz, who explains, "If, for example, your company always uses printed text inserted in pay stub envelopes to communicate important information such as promotions and big announcements, suddenly switching to a high-end e-communication wellness program will not work. The program must align with the culture of the worksite, including employee needs and interests, as well as company communication style and methods."

Ingredient #1: Health Screenings

To kick off your program, it's helpful to establish a baseline measurement of your employees' current state of health and a picture of their health-related behaviors. Two useful tools have been developed for this:

- health risk assessments (HRAs), and
- worksite biometric screenings.

HRAs. The HRA is usually a confidential form, prepared and administered by an outside vendor, that employees fill out online or on paper. It asks about employee lifestyle and health-related behaviors—everything from whether they wear seatbelts to whether they exercise regularly, smoke, and so forth.

After the HRAs are done, an employee will be given a personal (and private) report, summarizing the results and making recommendations for improved health. When potential problems are revealed, such as a regular smoker mentioning that exercise is too difficult because of constant tiredness and coughing, the HRA won't attempt to deliver diagnoses. What the report will do is to encourage every employee to get preventive health services, and then possibly make individual recommendations to see a doctor if someone's symptoms suggest a health problem.

The result is that the employee gains both motivation for improvement and guidance in seeking medical treatment or signing up for wellness program activities. And the HRAs can be a direct tie-in to program follow-up—for example, triggering calls from program coaches.

You, the employer, will also get a summary report aggregating the employees' HRA data. It won't include names; it may be presented, for example, in pie chart form. The report will help you further plan your program. Having gained information about your employees' health status, you'll be able to focus your planning on particular medical issues and determine whether the numbers justify offering activities on a group basis or only to affected individuals.

Biometric testing. For more detailed health status results, many employers bring in a nurse or other qualified health professional to collect so-called "biometrics"—test results for weight, blood pressure, body fat percentage, bone density, cholesterol levels, heart rate, blood pressure, and risk factors for various health conditions. This information is gathered via various physical measurements as well as a blood draw.

Though biometric tests are not diagnostic (employees must see their M.D. for that), they're very effective at motivating employees to get necessary medical attention or sign up for health-related activities to improve their biometric results. And again, you'll receive summary results that help you plan.

While biometric testing is more expensive than an HRA, Rae Lee Olson says, "The detailed health and physical information it provides can give an employer an advantage in designing a program that's truly targeted for its specific employee population."

We'll discuss arranging for HRAs and biometrics in Chapter 3.

Ingredient #2: Health Education, Information, and Self-Help Tools

Health education is important to every wellness program. Although there's plenty of information publicly available, you can help make sure your employees get the most accurate, up-to-date health news plus positive messages about how to make beneficial life changes. You'll help them understand what they're working toward and dispel confusion and misperceptions. (There are still people out there who think potato chips count as a vegetable.)

To deliver information, you'll probably want to use a combination of many formats to get people's attention. Popular choices include targeted emails or websites, payroll envelope "stuffers," printed newsletters (mailed to the employee's home so that the whole family benefits), short seminars (or "lunch-and-learns") with guest speakers, health fairs, or multiweek classes. The idea is to give people lots of ways to encounter your health messages and plenty of opportunities to do so throughout the year. As Dr. Metz explains, "People are willing to accept information about change in different ways at different times."

CAUTION

Choose your speakers carefully. Any speaker you bring in needs to be knowledgeable and charismatic; if they're not, employees will start going out of their way to avoid, not attend, your events.

No matter how small your office, it helps to establish a physical location dedicated to wellness. This could be as little as a bookshelf containing educational materials, with a bulletin board for announcements above it. If you have a whole room to spare, it could become the gathering place for classes, activities, and seminars, as well.

As far as subject matter, your health education program might provide, for instance, information about how to set up and maintain an exercise program, recommendations on target heart rates and water consumption, summaries of reports and studies—for example, those linking smoking and obesity to certain diseases—healthy recipes, and much more.

There's no need to stick to straight health topics, either. Spiritual approaches to stress reduction, discussions about living a balanced life, and tips on dealing with financial difficulties or conflicts are also relevant to total wellness, and may be included depending on your worksite culture.

You can get creative, by tailoring information to your employees and your place of business. Some employers, for example, have passed out nutritional information about food served by local restaurants and fast food chains. After your program gets underway, it's wise to ask your employees for input on what they'd like to learn about in the future.

Some companies take information delivery one step farther—for example, by offering individual nutritional and other health counseling or coaching, or access to health advice services. As Dr. Metz explains:

> *People aren't always eager to sign up for coaching, and in some cases might only do so to get a financial reward they've been offered. But they often find that the coach turns out to be a real asset who helps motivate them to get healthy.*

There's No Need to Write Your Own Newsletter

Various wellness program consultants and providers offer health newsletters you can distribute to employees. (If you've got a choice between electronic and old-fashioned paper, note that many people still prefer the latter.) Subscription newsletters can be a handy way to keep one aspect of your program on a steady schedule and to keep everyone up to date on health news.

Before you sign up, compare several newsletters to find one that's interesting, authoritative, and easy to read. Also realize, as Rae Lee Olson explains:

> *Shorter, more frequent messages will grab people's attention better than longer, less frequent communications. Think of the number of times that the same 30-second commercial is played on TV in order to influence buying decisions—that's the standard way that Americans receive information now. And that's the sort of messaging your wellness program needs to compete with.*

A cover letter can't hurt either, reminding your employees that you've subscribed because you care about their health and hope they will read it and share it with their family at home. By way of follow-up, some employers develop a little quiz based on the contents of newsletter, with prize drawings for those who answer.

TIP

Keep your educational materials simple. Most Americans understand information written at an 8th-grade level, while health information jumps up to 11th-grade vocabulary pretty quickly. The more options you can give people for receiving information, such as video presentations or phone consultations, the better the chances you'll reach everyone.

Some of your employees will have medical conditions that need more than basic information, such as how to manage diabetes or asthma.

Below, we'll discuss how to make sure your plan can deliver what they need. (See "Ingredient #4: Individual Follow-Up and Treatment.")

Ingredient #3: Organized Activities

Most wellness programs include some visible activities—often on-site—that employees can actively join, such as group walking or back-safety classes. Some employers have even brought in comedians to relieve daily stress. Dr. Kenneth R. Pelletier adds:

> *Individual and group stress management, yoga, meditation, changing to a more 'Mediterranean' or even vegetarian diet, or basic ergonomics exercises are all programs used successfully in many small to large companies.*

Obviously there's some overlap between this and the education component, but as Dr. Metz explains:

> *These activities bring action to the message, motivating people to get out of their chairs and not just think about the communication, but to actually participate.*

Some off-site or individual activities can also be valuable program components, however. For example, you can offer to subsidize employees' gym memberships or give program points for taking part in other activities away from work.

Ask Participants to Sign a Waiver

With proper planning, your wellness program won't pose a significant risk of injury. Accidents can happen, however, whether it's a broken nose on the soccer field, a mild burn during a cooking class, or an inappropriate choice of exercise activities at home.

Lawsuits are even less common than accidents, but it's still a good idea to be prepared. As adviser and attorney Kelly Kuglitsch notes:

> *So far, there hasn't been nearly as much litigation around wellness programs as one might expect. But there may be more in the future, after employees and their attorneys fully grasp the tangle of laws that*

apply. One case that employers should know about was brought by a widow in Ohio whose late husband's HRA blood test results showed a very low hemoglobin level, but was given no explanation as to what that might mean, because the employer was just looking at cholesterol and other such factors. Two months later, the man died from a very aggressive form of colon cancer, and it turns out that the blood results would have been a marker if they had been trying to diagnose him.

Assuming you take all appropriate safety measures, the next best thing you can do is require all participants to sign a waiver of liability before they start the program, promising not to sue you—or any teachers you bring in—for injuries, and stating their understanding that the employer's provision of HRAs, coaching, or other wellness program-related advice is for limited, nondiagnostic purposes.

We provide a sample waiver you can use; you'll find it below and on the CD-ROM.

Why a Waiver Isn't a Solid Shield

A waiver form, such as the one below, is intended to relieve your company from lawsuits or similar claims brought by injured employees who participate in the program. But it's important to understand that no waiver form can act as a complete shield from legal claims.

Lawyers have found various ways to attack or invalidate waiver forms. Here are the most common:

- **Gross negligence.** In some states—for example, California—a signed waiver will not shield your company from wellness program injuries resulting from your company's "gross negligence," no matter what it says. Gross negligence is activity that demonstrates an extreme departure from the ordinary standard of conduct—for example, an intoxicated personal trainer failing to monitor a participant. A lawyer may bring a lawsuit alleging gross negligence if he or she thinks you'd rather settle for some amount than bear the expenses of a lawsuit.
- **Injury beyond the scope of waiver.** A lawyer may try to prove that the activities causing the injury don't fit into the concept of a

Wellness Program Waiver and Release of Liability

I, _____[print name]_____ , an employee at __[Company Name]__ acknowledge and agree that my participation in the wellness program offered by _[Company Name]_ (hereafter the "Wellness Program") is voluntary and is not required as a condition of my employment.

Assumption of Risk. I AGREE THAT MY PARTICIPATION IN THE WELLNESS PROGRAM, WHETHER I TAKE PART IN ACTIVITIES ON A GROUP OR INDIVIDUAL BASIS, IS AT MY OWN RISK. I UNDERSTAND THAT TAKING PART IN PHYSICAL EXERCISE, SPORT, FITNESS, AND OTHER RECREATIONAL OR PHYSICAL ACTIVITIES COMES WITH AN INHERENT RISK OF INJURY, DAMAGE, ILLNESS, OR LOSS. I WAIVE MY RIGHT TO FILE A LAWSUIT AGAINST _[COMPANY NAME]_ FOR ANY INJURY OR LOSS RESULTING FROM WELLNESS PROGRAM ACTIVITY. I ALSO RELEASE AND HOLD HARMLESS _[COMPANY NAME]_ FROM ANY CLAIM OR LAWSUIT FOR PERSONAL INJURY, DAMAGE, OR WRONGFUL DEATH, BY ME, MY FAMILY, ESTATE, HEIRS, OR ASSIGNS, ARISING OUT OF PARTICIPATION IN THE WELLNESS PROGRAM, INCLUDING BOTH CLAIMS ARISING DURING THE WELLNESS PROGRAM ACTIVITY AND AFTER I COMPLETE THE WELLNESS PROGRAM ACTIVITY, AND INCLUDING CLAIMS BASED ON NEGLIGENCE OF OTHER PARTICIPANTS OR _[COMPANY NAME]_ , WHETHER PASSIVE OR ACTIVE.

No Warranties. I FURTHER UNDERSTAND AND AGREE THAT __[COMPANY NAME]__ MAKES NO WARRANTIES, EXPRESS OR IMPLIED, AS TO THE WELLNESS PROGRAM, THE PROPERTY ON WHICH THE WELLNESS PROGRAM WILL TAKE PLACE, ANY PERSONS IN ATTENDANCE AT WELLNESS PROGRAM ACTIVITIES, WHETHER I HAVE ANY HEALTH LIMITATIONS THAT WOULD PRECLUDE MY PARTICIPATION IN THE WELLNESS PROGRAM, OR ANY OTHER WARRANTY, CONDITION, GUARANTY, OR REPRESENTATION, WHETHER ORAL, WRITTEN, OR IN ELECTRONIC FORM, RELATING TO THE WELLNESS PROGRAM.

Personal Responsibility. _____[Company Name]_____ has advised me to consult a physician before I undertake any physical exercise program. To the best of my knowledge, I am in good health and sufficient physical condition to participate in the Wellness Program. I will read and follow the rules for any activities that I participate in, including reading the directions for any exercise or other equipment, and will follow the rules or instructions to the best of my ability. I understand that the Wellness Program does not provide medical advice or diagnosis and is not intended as a substitute for a licensed physician.

Emergency Care. In the event that I am physically injured or otherwise require emergency care, I give permission to _____[Company Name]_____ or any of its agents under the Wellness Program to secure from any licensed hospital, physician, or medical personnel any treatment considered necessary for my immediate care. I agree to be responsible for payment of any and all medical services rendered.

Miscellaneous. In the event any provision of this Wellness Program Waiver and Release of Liability form is found to be legally invalid or unenforceable for any reason, all remaining provisions will remain in full force and effect. This Wellness Program Waiver and Release of Liability is binding upon me as well as my heirs, children, personal representatives, or anyone else entitled to act on my behalf.

Signature: _____

Date: _____

wellness program—for example, arguing that herbal remedies do not belong in a smoking cessation program and therefore, any injuries caused by them are not covered by the waiver.

- **Ambiguous language.** Courts tend to view waivers with some suspicion. We have attempted to make our waiver clear, but in the event a court finds the language of the waiver to be ambiguous or difficult to understand, the court may refuse to enforce it.

- **Unforeseeable injuries.** A court may look past or "pierce" a waiver if a wellness program participant could not have reasonably foreseen a particular injury—for example, your employee would not expect that the floor would collapse from the weight of a spinning class.

- **The party being sued is not named in the waiver.** A waiver protects only your company—or whoever is named in the waiver. An injured employee can still try to sue third parties who may have contributed to the injury but are not named in the waiver. This means, for example, that if you hire wellness consultants, they should use their own waivers because they won't be covered by your company's waiver.

- **The waiver is not prominent.** Release language must be prominent and conspicuous. This is why we've capitalized the release language in our sample agreement.

- **The injured party didn't have the authority to sign the waiver.** In order to make an informed decision, the employee must be able to read and understand the language at the time of signing. Any employees under the age of 18 should provide a consent form, signed by a parent or legal guardian.

While we've tried to highlight some general issues concerning waivers, individual states often differ in their enforcement. Also, waivers will not protect you from other issues that may arise in the course of a wellness program—for example, if someone you hire to teach exercise classes makes "fat" jokes or discriminates against disabled workers, those activities may trigger other claims not covered by the waiver.

Ingredient #4: Individual Follow-Up and Treatment

Up to now, we've mostly been describing activities directed at health awareness and maintenance that apply to most or all of your employees. But now let's get back to the Bobs and Yolandas among your employees: those who have specific, immediate health risks or needs, not all of which will be shared by the rest of your employees.

If, for example, Yolanda is your only smoker, you probably don't want to bring in a lunchtime speaker on how to quit—but you do want to give Yolanda some follow-up options. This might include things like financial and other support for attending a smoking cessation program (perhaps through your HMO), access to telephone or other counselors, and more.

> **TIP**
>
> **Why personal coaching or counseling is effective.** You'll notice that throughout this book we often mention telephone or other personal coaching or counseling as a worthwhile program option. What's behind this, as explained by Dr. Metz , is that, "All programs that show good outcomes have some form of human interaction—it could be face-to-face coaching, telephone conversations, or even e-based coaching. It's not the technology that matters; it's about one human being building a healing relationship and supporting another around a health improvement goal."

If, on the other hand, a number of your employees are affected by a certain condition or habit, there's nothing wrong with holding on-site classes or other group activities especially for them. Such classes and information typically focus on:

- how to manage an illness or problem, including advice on the importance of taking prescribed medications, and
- how to live a healthy lifestyle—focusing on fitness, nutrition, and stress management—while managing the illness.

Ingredient #5: Incentives and Rewards

After years of experience administering a wellness program, Rae Lee Olson agrees with many other wellness experts: "Your incentives are a critically important ingredient in the success of your program."

By incentives, we mean positive rewards, like money or prizes, given to employees who participate in or reach certain goals within your program. Such incentives have been shown to raise worker participation by as much as 23% and are, says Rae Lee Olson, "an integral part of tipping the balance toward new, healthier behavior."

Legal Limits on Incentives

Before we delve into the types of incentives that work best, it's important to know the limits of what you can do. As a provider of a wellness program, your company must, if it offers financial incentives tied to its health plan (such as rebates or discounts on employee contributions), abide by certain terms of the federal Health Insurance Portability and Accountability Act (HIPAA). Most notably, HIPAA prohibits your incentive program from discriminating against any participants based on any "health factor." An example of such discrimination would be if you offered health insurance discounts to everyone who reaches a normal cholesterol level within the next year, but one of your employees has high cholesterol due to genetics and allergies to cholesterol reduction medication. Fortunately, it's not hard to design your program to either avoid HIPAA's reach or comply with its directives, and the law contains some special exceptions for wellness program incentives.

Easy exceptions to the legal rules. For starters, you're on solid ground—and can avoid HIPAA's restrictions—if you make sure any rewards you offer depend solely on participation, not on satisfying a health-related standard. In other words, you could offer incentives for participating in a class or reaching a behavioral goal (such as walking every day or completing a treatment program), but not for changing a health factor such as weight or cholesterol level. (Even so, you need to make sure that no one is unable to participate in your program because of a disability, and make accommodations to allow their participation or provide an alternate activity.)

A second simple way to sidestep HIPAA is to make sure your rewards are not directly linked to your health plan. If you don't offer your employees, for example, discounted, rebated, or surcharged premiums, increases or decreases in the amount of copays, or any other kind of cost-sharing mechanism, such as adjusting part of a deductible based on their achieving certain health results, HIPAA won't apply to your program. You can offer plenty of meaningful rewards in the form of cash, gift cards, or T-shirts and not have to worry about HIPAA.

Rules for more complex rewards. There may be situations in which you want to offer a reward that both depends on satisfying a health-related standard and is tied to your health plan. For example, says Kelly Kuglitsch, "Many of my clients want to set up programs where employees must stop smoking in order to either qualify for a discount or avoid paying extra on their health insurance." Or you might want to reimburse copayments for various programs—for example, if your wellness program will include a weight loss initiative, but the weight loss program at your health plan comes with a high copayment, offering to pay this for medically eligible employees will make the program more accessible.

One benefit of creating such financial incentives within the health insurance plan is that you typically avoid the income tax that employers otherwise have to pay on a straight cash incentive. (See "Paying Taxes on Incentives," below). Another benefit is the potential easing of your administrative burden. If, for example, you offer employees points for meeting various health goals, with each point redeemable for a monetary contribution toward their health insurance payments, you save yourself from creating lots of different prizes along the way. The catch is that, in order to offer an incentive that is both related to a health standard and tied to your health plan, your wellness program must meet the following five requirements (Source: www.dol.gov/ebsa/faqs/faq_hipaa_ND.html):

- The total possible reward an employee can earn under the wellness program can't exceed 20% of what the employee (and dependents, if any) and employer collectively pay for health coverage. For example, if you pay $2,000 per year and the employee pays $800, for a total of $2,800, the potential rebate the employee can earn under the wellness program can't exceed $560. (Note: At the time this book went to print, Congress was considering increasing the dollar amount of incentives allowable under HIPAA.)

- The wellness program must be reasonably designed to promote health and prevent disease. Attorney Kelly Kuglitsch notes, "As long as your program is not overly burdensome, not a subterfuge for discriminating, and not using suspect methods, you should be okay on this one."

- The program must give employees the opportunity to qualify for the reward at least once per year. For example, if qualifying depends on taking a class, that class must be available a minimum of once a year.

- The reward must be available to all similarly situated individuals—another way of saying it must not discriminate. In practice, this means that if an employee can't satisfy the standard due to a medical condition or restriction, you must provide a reasonable alternative standard or waive the initial standard altogether. If, for example, someone claims they can't stop smoking because they're too addicted (you'd be within your rights asking for a doctor's letter to prove this), you'd need to offer an alternative, such as completion of a smoking cessation class.

- You must disclose in all materials describing the terms of the wellness program the availability of a reasonable alternative standard or the possibility of a waiver of the initial standard. For example, if you create a handbook outlining your program and you say something like, "Everyone who brings their weight within normal limits will receive a $25 rebate on their health insurance," you would also need to add something like, "If you are medically unable to reach this standard, you may qualify for the rebate by walking a total of 90 minutes each week."

Practical Strategies for Offering Incentives

Offering incentives—such as cash, movie tickets, discounts on medical care, or gifts—definitely works, but not all incentives work equally well. Here's what employers who've gone before you have learned about when to offer incentives and what kind of rewards work best.

You'll likely need to use incentives at different stages during your program. Many employers use a small incentive right at the start, to get people to register or to take an initial health screening.

After that, you might offer incentives for meeting short-term goals—for example, you might give something to everyone who walks ten miles or more within a two-week period. And, you might offer more for longer-term achievements—for example, to whoever walks the most miles or accrues the most fitness points (based on different activities) within a six-month period. (See "Using a Points and Rewards System," below.) One industry expert, Aaron Hardy, suggests creating a series of four-week miniprograms—about six per year, with breaks in between—each with its own incentive, to keep people interested. (For details, see "The Power of Utilizing Incentive Campaigns," a publication available from The Wellness Council of America at www.welcoa.org.)

What's important, says Rae Lee Olson, is that you:

> Don't get trapped into thinking of incentives as mere immediate rewards for behavior or achievements. Rather, design your incentives to create self-sustaining habits that will endure for the long term. We've found in our program that the wellness goals that people were working on a year ago have now become part of the fabric of their lives, and now they've moved on to new goals.

We asked Dr. Metz what types of incentives work best:

> The first three are cash, cash, and cash. We've done everything from T-shirts to gift cards, to vouchers on our website for free products, discounts on products, donations to HSAs. The results? Even before the economy got tight, providing an American Express or Visa gift card for $50 got people's attention like nothing else. The higher the amount, the greater the participation—up to a threshold. Once you hit a point

between $100 and $300 (depending on the population) it sort of levels off, and you won't see big changes in participation levels.

Here's the on-the-ground reality: A 2008 survey by the ERISA Industry Committee (ERIC) found that, among large employers with wellness programs, the incentives paid out per employee per year ranged from $100 to $300, with an overall average of $192. Dr. Metz continues:

You can get away with noncash rewards like T-shirts and things of that nature for what I would call high-touch, on-site programs. Say, for example, you're having a biometric screening done on-site, and giving out company T-shirts to people who take it. That will work, as will giving out T-shirts at a lunch-and-learn. But a T-shirt won't get people to take an HRA on their own time.

Paying Taxes on Incentives

Many employers forget that anything of value you give to your employees has tax implications. Unfortunately, straight cash incentives are always subject to tax, meaning you'll have to make the appropriate deductions through payroll during the same pay period that you hand out the money, so that it's counted as taxable income. Even gift certificates or coupons that can be redeemed for a variety of items (as opposed to only one type of item) are considered a taxable cash equivalent, no matter their amount. So, for example, a $25 gift certificate to a department store offering a wide variety of items would be taxable, while a coupon for the employee's size and color choice of a specified item (such as a company logo shirt) or a voucher redeemable for a Thanksgiving turkey, would not.

TIP

Watch the news for tax changes. At the time this book went to print, Congress was discussing ways of making it easier for employers to implement wellness programs, including exempting wellness program cash incentives from taxation. Check for updates at www.nolo.com.

Contributions to health benefits or health savings accounts (HSAs) and other payments for medical expenses are *not* taxable income. Nor, in many cases, are payments for classes. But get a tax pro's advice for the details. For example, the IRS has said that employer payment for a smoking cessation class isn't considered taxable income; but in the case of payments for a weight loss class, the person must have been diagnosed as obese by a physician, and only certain types of classes or treatments are nontaxable.

Whether other small, occasional, noncash gifts, such as mugs, T-shirts, cookbooks, or water bottles are taxable depends on their value. They're considered "de minimis," and therefore not taxable, if the value is so low that dealing with the accounting would be comparatively burdensome. It would have been nice if the IRS had set a specific dollar limit, but it hasn't—though adviser Kelly Kuglitsch notes, "It did rule in a 2004 case that a $35 gift coupon redeemable for groceries was taxable." For more information, see the IRS website at www.irs.gov; search for "de minimis fringe benefits."

How to Rein in Spending on Incentives

The cost of incentives can add up fast. But as a businessperson, you know that time has its own value. Without incentives, you might spend so many hours trying to convince people to participate in your program that simply paying them starts to look like a pretty good deal. Also, there are ways to limit your spending.

Ask employees to pitch in. One way is to have employees front some of the cash. For example, if everyone in the walking club puts in $5, and whoever walks the most steps or miles within a certain time period takes the pot, you'll have both created healthy competition and provided a cash incentive.

Mix it up to save cash. As your program gets underway, you can also combine straight cash incentives with less-expensive variations on that theme. For example, you might mix in intangible gifts, like an extra day's vacation, participation in a fun employee field trip, or free access to the boss's lakeside cabin for a weekend. Or offer only one actual gift

Using a Points and Rewards System

At Rae Lee Olson's workplace, Vita Benefits Group, employees and their spouses earn points for a wide variety of wellness activities, which are then converted into employer contributions toward their HSAs.

"Our motto," says Olson, "is 'Every Choice Matters.'" Points are offered for everything from participating in fitness activities (100 to 400 points) to cutting out soda for a week (30 points), eating fruits and vegetables (40 points), flossing one's teeth (30 points), getting at least seven hours of sleep for five nights out of the week (50 points), or volunteering for a charity (20 to 60 points).

Employees can earn additional points by taking part in that week's bonus-points activity, which might be something like walking two miles, doing 100 sit-ups, or performing a random act of kindness. (Vita takes a broad, holistic view of wellness, to include community and "green" activities, spiritual health, and financial wellness.)

Olson says:

> It takes about ten minutes each week to log the points, which might not be worth it if the total reward were only $200 or so. But we'd tried other approaches, such as rewards for meeting short-term goals, or creating competition between employees, and they eventually fizzled. Plus, the points are high value: We've set aside enough in our budget so that each point is worth two cents, for a potential total of up to $3,000 per year, deposited into the employee's HSA account.
>
> Still, there are so many different options that there's no way anyone could earn all the possible points. Most of our employees earn in the range of $1,500 to $3,000 in HSA contributions per year. (How they earn them is confidential, and all recording is based on the honor system.) Ultimately, this creates an easy way for an employer to do a lot of different things within the wellness program, tie it all together, and keep people interested.

card, either as a door prize or in a drawing. Eligibility for the drawing could be based on simple participation or attendance, on meeting a goal, or on sustained activity, such as six months without smoking. Just make sure the chances of winning aren't so low as to turn away participation. If possible, also make sure everyone who participates in wellness activities gets a little something, even if it's just a water bottle or an energy bar.

Kudos are cheap. You can augment the value of a gift by giving the winners lots of in-house publicity, perhaps an employee recognition award. That makes the winner feel good, and reminds everyone else that it could have been them on the medal podium. While you're at it, try writing up employees who've made impressive life changes in your employee newsletter or an office email. (Get their permission first, of course, and don't ask for or include sensitive personal information that would normally be kept confidential. We'll discuss privacy concerns later in this chapter.)

Make penalties pay. Another, less-surefire strategy involves basically turning a penalty into a reward. For example, flat-out insisting that employees who refuse to participate in the program pay a higher contribution to their health insurance coverage may not go over well. But you can achieve a similar result by announcing that you can no longer afford to pay as much for health care coverage and that employee contributions will rise; then, offer to pay a higher amount for employees who participate in your wellness program. (The new year is a logical time to do this, when your insurance rates may be increasing anyway.) While these premium discounts have been successfully used by a number of employers, and legal experts say they are acceptable under HIPAA rules if properly structured, some employees will probably view them as punitive.

TIP

Offer more than material incentives. You don't want to create a situation where your employees are participating only for the goodies. If that happens, you'll end up needing to increase the value of the rewards as the years

Incentives Others Have Used

To get you thinking about the variety of possible incentives, here are some used by other employers:

- a $50 bonus for filling out an HRA
- a drawings for shopping mall gift cards during the holiday season for those who fill out an HRA
- a $10 monthly bonus for not smoking
- a $225 contribution to the health savings account of an employee who participates in the wellness program
- $15 added to the employer contribution to health insurance for participating in each program component, such as health screening and smoking cessation classes
- a $100 reimbursement for membership to a health club, weight loss program, or smoking cessation program
- monthly, quarterly, semiannual, and annual drawings for prizes based on logs where employees track minutes exercised each month
- a $500 cash bonus to any employee who loses 25 pounds or quits smoking
- reimbursement of monthly gym dues, based on documenting at least three trips to the gym each week
- reimbursement of out-of-pocket costs for annual physical screenings, such as mammograms and colonoscopies
- reimbursement of deductibles or copayments for participating in a disease management program, and
- $200 health insurance rebates for employees who can maintain healthy levels of blood pressure, cholesterol, and other risk factors, or demonstrate efforts to improve them (note that this would need to comply with HIPAA requirements).

go by. Remind everyone that the goal, both yours and theirs, is to improve their health now and for years to come. For example, adviser Janet Greenhut of HealthMedia says, "We help people find internal motivations for maintaining healthy behaviors, such as 'I want to be around so I can see my grandchildren grow up,' or 'I want to live a full and active life.'"

Reevaluate your budget. Another way to pay for incentives is to shift some costs around. Rae Lee Olson suggests moving future allocations for salary increases into your wellness budget:

> *If your company was slated to have a 2½% salary increase across the board next year, then you could instead make the increases two percent, while shifting the remaining ½% into wellness incentives. Then you can start putting some real money into your wellness program and make a strong statement about your commitment to your employees' health and wellness. And I'm talking about upping the average incentive from, say, $200 to $2,000 or more. The compensation remains available to your employees; they simply have to do certain health-promoting things in order to get it.*

Ingredient #6: Supportive Workplace Environment

It's crucial that you gear your workplace environment toward respecting and actively supporting your wellness program. If your company says one thing in its wellness materials but fails to follow through, or conveys another message in everyday practice, your employees will assume the wellness program is just talk. If, for example, you're encouraging people to bike to work, you'll need to have bike racks in place.

This respect and attention to detail must extend from top management down. If the CEO looks suspiciously at everyone who comes in late—despite the fact that they were at the gym and your policies now allow flex time for this—your program will die on the vine. Conversely, a CEO who stops smoking and invites people to go jogging during the lunch hour can motivate more people than any pamphlet or statistic ever will. Dr. Metz has found that:

> *Communications directly from senior management are exceptionally powerful motivation tools about the importance of healthy living.*

Rae Lee Olson adds:

> *Without support from the top, any wellness program is a nonstarter. Management must believe in the program in order to bridge the time gap between the investment and the return—it's going to be longer than is considered standard for most business investments, not to mention the fact that many of the results will arrive in soft- rather than hard-data form. If you're an HR person, and your upper management is saying "Bah, humbug" to the prospect of the wellness program, now may not be the right time to invest in one.*

Before launching your program, consider your company's starting point—that is, its current culture. A wellness program will work best when people feel comfortable admitting to imperfections or—horrors—having interests outside the office! If you're in a competitive corporate office where no one even takes breaks, much less admits to being sick for fear they'll be seen as the weakest link, you'll need to work on changing that. (See Chapter 7 for tips on reducing stress within the workplace.) Such changes can't happen overnight. Your top management will most likely need to evaluate its own behavior, admit to a little weakness in the health arena, and lead the charge for change.

You may need to loosen up related office policies—for example, rules about flex-time or working at home, so your employees can create the schedule they need to get and stay healthy. (Workplace policies will be discussed in Chapter 13.)

It goes without saying that your workplace also needs to do its part by attending to basic safety issues concerning machinery, equipment, materials, ergonomic desk setups, security, and more. There's little point in your employees guarding their health if they're going to get injured on the job.

> **TIP**
>
> **Pace yourself.** Don't try to offer a complete array of wellness program activities the first month! In fact, starting slowly, with events every few weeks or once a month, is a good idea. It gives you time to figure out what works for your employees and team leaders as you build up your program. After that, two events a month is said to be a good pace—not counting ongoing classes such as yoga.

Avoiding Legal Troubles

A well-run program shouldn't add to your worries about legal liability. And we've already discussed the importance of making sure any incentive offerings tied to your health insurance benefits don't run afoul of HIPAA's nondiscrimination rules. But there are other murky waters to avoid. You're safest if you:

- Don't make your wellness program mandatory, but keep employee participation voluntary.
- Carefully protect your employees' private, health-related information.
- Treat your employees in a consistent and fair manner.

More topic-specific issues, like what's legal when trying to get employees to stop smoking, will be discussed in the relevant chapters of this book.

> **SEE AN EXPERT**
>
> **The law on wellness programs is still developing.** Various open questions still exist, which we haven't covered here. It's worth keeping an eye on the business news and consulting an experienced attorney before launching your program. A good attorney can also tell you about relevant laws in your state.

Make It Voluntary

As you work out the details of your wellness program, keep in mind what a good program should *not* include, namely top-down force or

Summary of Laws Covering Wellness Programs

In this chapter and throughout the book, we refer to various federal laws governing important aspects of wellness programs, such as privacy and non-discrimination. Here's a quick review of the main laws potentially affecting your program and sources for additional information online:

What the Law Is Called	Where to Find it in the Codes	How it May Affect Wellness Programs	Where to Get More Information Online
The Health Insurance Portability and Accountability Act (HIPAA)	42 U.S.C. §§ 201 and following	Protects people with health insurance from health-related discrimination and violations of privacy	Department of Labor website at www.dol.gov/ebsa/ (under "Compliance Assistance," click "For Health Plans")
Americans with Disabilities Act (ADA)	42 U.S.C. §§ 1201 and following	Protects people with disabilities from discrimination in the workplace (and elsewhere)	www.ada.gov
Age Discrimination in Employment Act (ADEA)	29 U.S.C. §§ 621–634	Prevents employers from discriminating against job applicants and employees age 40 and older	Equal Employment Opportunity Commission (EEOC) website at www.eeoc.gov (under "Discrimination by Type," click "Age")
Genetic Information Non-discrimination Act (GINA)	42 U.S.C. §§ 200 and following	Prevents employers from making hiring, firing, or other employment decisions based on genetic information, and requires employers to keep employee genetic information confidential; also prohibits health insurers from using genetic information to deny insurance coverage or determine premiums	Human Genome Research Institute, at www.genome.gov (click "Privacy & Discrimination")

coercion. For both practical and legal reasons, people who opt out of your program shouldn't have their pay docked or be punished in other ways that could be interpreted as discrimination.

Not every employer has followed this advice. Some employers, frustrated or uncertain about their employees' willingness to change, have tried measures such as the state of Alabama's pending plan to place a $25 monthly surcharge on insurance for state employees who are clinically obese—quickly dubbed a "fat tax." Other employers have fired anyone who doesn't quit smoking within a certain time. While such measures might work in the short term, they can backfire in many ways, both practical and legal.

Pressure from on high creates a negative atmosphere and angers some employees. It could even lead to lawsuits claiming that your program is discriminatory or unfair. Even if matters don't reach such a boiling point, anger can lead to situations where people comply with program requirements only when they think you're watching, or find ways to game the system—such as signing into an event and then slipping out the back door. And angry employees may talk with each other, ultimately reducing company morale and working against your hopes that employees will spur each other on and have fun in their health attainment efforts. Dr. Metz adds:

> *Even disincentives, such as higher premiums for those who use tobacco versus those who don't, can backfire. Why not just use positive incentives, which have been demonstrated to be helpful?*

By making your program voluntary, you sidestep most issues of legal liability under federal, state, or other laws. (You can, however, carve out an exception for companywide introductory activities like a mandatory orientation.) In fact, by making your program not only voluntary, but a draw for employees, you'll increase the likelihood that they'll participate enthusiastically and take initiative to enhance its success. Rae Lee Olson adds:

> *Disincentives are a downer. Ultimately it should be the job of well-designed incentives to drive participation, not a heavy hand from above.*

TIP

An exception for employers requiring HRAs? Many employers make taking an HRA a condition of receiving health insurance and, so far, the federal enforcement agencies haven't tried to say that this violates any law. However, attorney Kelly Kuglitsch warns, "There are some indications that the Equal Employment Opportunity Commission (EEOC) may disallow that in the future." Check for updates at www.nolo.com.

Maintain Employee Confidentiality and Privacy

Both federal and, in some cases, state laws protect the confidentiality of employees' medical information and their right to privacy. HIPAA and the ADA are the main federal laws affecting you as an employer, essentially saying that:

- You and any outside vendors must safeguard the confidentiality of health and medical information gleaned from your wellness program.
- You cannot use that information for any other employee benefit program or for any employment-related decision—such as whether to promote or terminate someone.

The new federal Genetic Information Nondiscrimination Act of 2008 (GINA) additionally protects your employees from unfair treatment because of differences in their DNA that may affect their health. And some states' laws prohibit employers from taking disciplinary action against employees who take part in lawful activities during nonworking hours and away from your premises, such as smoking, drinking, or eating unhealthy foods.

What does this privacy protection mean in practice? For one thing, it means that the less personal medical information you have, the better, since you can't leak information you don't know. If your employees choose to reveal things to you, however, that's fine—but it doesn't give you the right to pass it on. Take steps to ensure that, even within the company, any medical information that comes into your hands doesn't get shared beyond the employee's supervisor and safety and first aid personnel, if they need to know it in order to accommodate the person's disability or assist in an emergency.

This gives you a good reason to hire outside vendors for things like HRAs, so that there's a barrier between you and the medical information being collected or passed back and forth. You'll need to ask for a general summary of the HRA data, with no names or other potentially identifying information included. You'll also need to give each participant a statement explaining your confidentiality policy. (We'll talk more about conducting these assessments in Chapter 3.)

Outside vendors can also be a helpful shield as your program gets underway. For example, if you'd like to reimburse all employees for their screening exam copayments or coinsurance amounts, you could potentially be accused of invading employee privacy by requiring them to present you with proof of their mammogram, prostate exam, or the like. But a third party can, with employee permission, act as intermediary. (The same principle applies when paying for employees to attend treatment programs, such as for drug or alcohol addiction.)

TIP

A HIPAA authorization form may help. If you don't want to use a third-party vendor as a privacy shield, there's another option to consider—so long as it fits your workplace culture and privacy practices. You can ask employees to sign what's called a HIPAA authorization form as a condition of accepting payments or reimbursements. This form authorizes you to receive certain medical information—such as proof of attendance—from an employee's health care provider. Unfortunately, no single government form has been created for such purposes, although the U.S. Department of Health and Human Services website provides information on what the form should contain, at www.hhs.gov/hipaafaq. Your best bet is to see whether the health provider has an appropriate form that you can use or adapt, or to ask a lawyer to help you craft one.

Another thing to know is that you shouldn't add health information about individual employees to their personnel files. So, for example, if certain employees agree to take an HRA or to participate in biometric screening, their results and responses should be kept only by the professional staff who administer the screening or tally the results, not by you, the employer. (How likely do you think an employee will be to admit to an alcohol or drug habit or consent to genetic screening if that information will go straight to a supervisor?)

Finally, try not to stumble into privacy violations as your program gets underway. For example, you'll no doubt want to announce the successes of program participants, but you'll need to consider how to do it. If Bob wins a prize drawing, that's worth a congratulatory email or an announcement at a company meeting, but sending an email saying, "Bob lost 25 pounds!" may not make Bob so happy, nor inspire others to compete. Even an email saying "Our five employees lost an average of five pounds each" is problematic if everyone knows that Bob was the only one trying to lose weight.

Be Consistent and Fair

Outline your program's health goals at the beginning, including what types of health-related programs or treatments you will help employees pay for, and then do your best to stick with these. You want to avoid situations where employees are coming to you with their own ideas like, "Will you pay for hypnosis for my anxiety disorder?" Trying to handle such situations case by case could lead to morale problems and even claims of bias if employees think you're treating some people more favorably than others.

After your program is up and running, you may learn that particular issues are especially important to your employees. For example, you may have a number of employees who care about healthier eating or alternative health treatments (like acupuncture) that you didn't think to include in your program. It's fine to add elements to the program as you go along, in response to employee needs. But once you decide to offer a benefit like hypnosis or acupuncture to one employee, make sure it's available to everyone.

Should You Invite the Employee's Family to Join?

Although your employees may spend most of their waking hours at your worksite, eventually they will go home. And the environment that awaits them may not be as health savvy as your workplace is becoming. In fact, they may face frustrations such as families that refuse to eat new, healthier recipes and complain about the time spent away from home exercising or children who throw tantrums if they're not taken out for fast food.

What's more, the number of family members (spouses and children) seeking care under your health insurance plan may actually outnumber your employees. That means that if these family members are in poor health, your health premiums are likely to feel the effects no matter how healthy your employees themselves become.

What can you do? One option is to expand your wellness program to include family members of employees in selected activities. Yes, this will increase your expenses, but it will also improve your outcomes. Adviser Rae Lee Olson says, "I think it's great to include family members in wellness events. I believe it makes a big difference to program outcomes."

And adviser Dr. Janet Greenhut points out:

> In some companies, most of the employees are male. But it's women who tend to make most health decisions for the family. So if you really want some changes to happen in employees' health behavior, it would probably be beneficial to include spouses. It might cost more on the front end, but you might get better results down the line.

To keep costs down, you can require family members to contribute slightly more for certain benefits or services, such as classes held at your worksite. This could be particularly helpful if the instructor requires a minimum number of participants to justify a regular class.

If you decide to hold events or classes that welcome family members, be sure to schedule events with that in mind—for example, during the lunch hour or after work. Weekend hikes or charity activities can also be a good time to include family, thus increasing the likelihood that the employees themselves will attend. Also be clear in both planning and communicating about the event that the main goal is wellness, not just social time. (If you're designing an event whose main goal is truly employee bonding, don't invite family.)

Checklist for a Successful Wellness Program

As you design and implement your workplace program, make sure it incorporates all the features and characteristics we've discussed—and think about making these offerings available to employees' family members, too.

☐ An initial HRA and possibly a biometric screening

☐ Health education, information, and self-help tools

☐ Organized group wellness and fitness activities or incentives toward making individual health and fitness changes

☐ Individual treatment and follow-up options

☐ A supportive workplace environment, in which a wellness program becomes part of the workplace's core culture at every level of management

☐ A marketing strategy, to get employees informed and enthusiastic about the new opportunities

☐ An element of fun, with incentives, prizes, and opportunities for recognition

☐ A focus on voluntary, not mandatory, participation

☐ Opportunities for employee-driven efforts

☐ Activities to draw in a large segment of your employees, but also some to address particular needs

☐ Privacy and confidentiality for all who participate—or choose not to

Making It Real: Worksite Evaluation and Program Launch

Meet Your Adviser

 **Dr. Douglas Metz,** a licensed chiropractic physician who serves as Chief Health Services Officer and Executive Vice President at American Specialty Health (ASH) and its subsidiary Healthyroads, an Internet-based, personal health improvement program. Dr. Metz is also the chairman of the Health Standards Committee and Wellness Standards Development Committee for URAC, a national organization that accredits health and disease management organizations. Previously, Dr. Metz served as medical director in the Health Services Operations department for Aetna Health Plans and was in private practice.

What he does: Dr. Metz oversees policy, research, product design, and health quality for ASH products, including wellness programs. He has also published a number of articles in national scientific journals including a recent coauthored article, "Emerging Trends in Health and Productivity Management" in the *American Journal of Health Promotion.*

Favorite healthy food: "Homemade gluten-free waffles."

Top tip for staying fit and healthy: "Eat well. Remain active. Be at peace. For me, finding time to exercise at least 60 minutes a day makes a big difference in my energy levels."

U p to now, we've been talking primarily about why and how to start a workplace wellness program. Now we'll turn to how your business, with its unique characteristics and concerns, can begin to implement such a program.

To start a workplace wellness program, you'll need to take five basic steps:

1. Assess your employees' health-related interests.
2. Pull together a team to manage and implement your wellness measures.
3. Announce your program and market it internally.
4. Administer individual health-screening assessments.
5. Track and evaluate the success of your program once it's underway.

This chapter walks you through each step, helping you focus on the needs of your workplace. We'll ask you to collect some data, but nothing too complicated. The important thing is to gather information that's both meaningful to you and aligned with your goals as you decide how to invest in the health of your workforce. If you bring in outside vendors to help administer your wellness program, you'll be able to delegate some tasks (including data collection) to them.

Step 1: Assess Your Employees' Interests

By now, you may have sold yourself and your top managers or HR staff on the benefits of instituting a wellness program—but what will your employees think? Learn from other employers' mistakes and don't roll out a program full of activities that don't match your employees' interests. Some early conversations with your workers—or a representative group of them—will help you meet two worthy goals:

- refining the list of what your program will include, and
- helping employees feel like they've been heard during the planning process.

In a small shop, the best way to check in is informally, either by asking around or posing some questions during a meeting. (You can draw these questions from the sample survey below.) Before you start, however, you'll want to conduct some focused discussion among your management and team leaders about what program elements are realistic for your company.

If this sort of informal conversation doesn't work in your company, another option is to ask your employees to fill out a survey designed to help you plan your wellness program. Interest surveys work well for many businesses, though it's wise to consider the warning offered by Adviser Rae Lee Olson:

> Be careful about overloading your employees with too many surveys, especially if the HRA—which will ultimately give you more valuable information—is yet to come. On an interest survey, employees are far less likely to come forward with their need for things like an antidepression or smoking cessation program, while a good HRA will capture this information. At least keep any interest survey short and simple.

Remember, however, that the smallest businesses—those with fewer than 50 employees—won't receive summary HRA results. If you're among them, doing an interest survey makes good sense. Such was the case, for example, at Frett Barrington Ltd., an independent, ten-person insurance brokerage firm in Pewaukee, Wisconsin. Account Executive Patty Frett explains:

> The interest survey was especially important for us, because of our size. We didn't receive any negative feedback about people having to fill out yet another survey. (We distributed it after the HRAs.) In fact, we now reissue the interest survey once a year and include questions that help us measure our program's progress, such as "Has your activity level increased this past year based on the offerings of our wellness program?" The answers help us determine whether our program is hitting the goals we have set forth—and they help us plan the coming year's activities.

If your workforce is small or if you feel that your employees won't mind filling out a few forms—or if for some reason you won't be doing HRAs—you can adapt the short interest survey, below, for your use. (You'll also find a copy on the CD-ROM at the back of the book.)

Wellness Program Interest Survey

We're thinking about starting an employee wellness program to help you feel better and stay healthy. Would you help us by telling us (anonymously) about your interests in the following health promotion and health-related activities?

Although some of the possible activities listed below could be based at our workplace, be assured that your participation, performance, or health results would never be recorded in your personnel file or made a part of your performance evaluation.

Thanks for taking a few minutes to fill out this survey. As you make your choices, please be realistic about what you're likely to take part in—in other words, don't check a box unless you're really prepared to attend the activity or event. We need to make program choices within a limited budget, so it's important for us to know both what you *would* and *would not* want to do.

1. Which of the following activities would you be likely to join in if they were offered, and how many times per week would you go? (Make sure your totals are physically possible!)

   ☐ yoga classes: _____ times per week

   ☐ Pilates classes: _____ times per week

   ☐ tai chi classes: _____ times per week

   ☐ meditation or other stress reduction classes: _____ times per week

   ☐ aerobics classes: _____ times per week

   ☐ walking event or club: _____ times per week

   ☐ biking event or club: _____ times per week

   ☐ sports team, such as baseball, basketball, or soccer: _____ times per week

   ☐ (Please state the types of teams in which you are interested: _____)

   ☐ other regular activities (please specify): _____ _____

2. Which of the following classes, seminars, or events would you join in if offered, and how many times per year would you participate?

☐ nutrition or cooking classes: _____ times per year

☐ healthy foods potluck: _____ times per year

☐ other health or wellness seminar: _____ times per year

(Please state the types of health and wellness seminars in which you are interested: _____)

3. Which of the following health-related programs would you be interested or willing to participate in? (Some of these might be off-site or offered on an individual basis.) Check as many as apply:

☐ smoking cessation program

☐ weight-loss program

☐ cholesterol screening

☐ blood pressure screening

☐ chronic disease management program

☐ other (please describe): _____

4. The best time of the day or week for you to participate in classes or group activities is: _____

5. Would you eat fruit at meetings if it were available?   ☐ yes ☐ no

6. Would you buy healthy snacks at work (such as granola, yogurt, or fresh or dried fruit) if they were available in vending machines or elsewhere?   ☐ yes ☐ no

7. Would you be interested in taking breaks during the day to stretch, meditate, or take a short walk—or in doing so with other people as a group?   ☐ yes ☐ no

8. Would you be willing to take part in a meeting held during a walk (rather than sitting down)?   ☐ yes ☐ no

9. Indicate any topics about which you'd like to learn more:

☐ healthy eating

☐ appropriate amounts of exercise

☐ weight management

☐ stress management

☐ keeping blood pressure down

☐ keeping cholesterol down

☐ other _____

10. Have you seriously considered making some health-related lifestyle changes recently (such as becoming more physically active, losing weight, eating more healthy foods, reducing alcohol consumption, or stopping smoking)? ☐ yes ☐ no

11. Would you find it easier to get motivated about making lifestyle changes if you worked with a buddy or with a group of people from work? ☐ yes ☐ no

12. Are you interested in helping develop our office's workplace wellness program? ☐ yes ☐ no

If yes, do you have any health-related expertise? Please describe:

_____

13. To receive information from our wellness program, which of these are you most likely to look at or listen to?

☐ emails

☐ printed fliers or letters

☐ a website

☐ a dedicated bulletin board

☐ presentations at staff meetings

14. Is there some other workplace-based health benefit or activity that you're particularly interested in? Please describe: _____

_____

15. Would you be sufficiently interested that if the cost of your desired benefit is too high for the office budget, you'd be willing to partially pay your own way? ☐ yes ☐ no

> ⓘ CAUTION
> **This inquiry isn't about employees' health status or needs.**
> For now, you just want to find out things like their levels of enthusiasm for
> workplace wellness efforts and what kinds of activities and classes they might
> sign up for. Now isn't the time to ask about things like whether they know their
> cholesterol levels or are struggling with depression.

If you plan to distribute a survey, be organized and thorough. Be sure to tell your employees where to return it—and give them a deadline. Incentive points or another little gift would help boost participation levels, too.

Once you've tallied the results, use the information to tailor your program plans. Be sure to share the survey results with your employees, and refer back to the results in later announcements of program activities. This serves as a gentle reminder that you're not ordering your employees to participate, you're responding to their own stated interests. For example, if you're sending an email announcing your first healthy foods potluck, you can remind employees that, in the survey, almost everyone expressed interest in participating.

Step 2: Assemble Your Team

No question, instituting a wellness program will require some time and effort on the part of top management, both now and as your program develops. Here's how to bring different voices and skill sets to the process.

Choose the Right Leader

If you're reading this, we assume you're in a position to recommend or decide on the priorities and scope of your workplace wellness program. If you're an owner or manager, your enthusiasm and participation will no doubt make a huge difference to the program's adoption and effectiveness. But are you also the best person to organize and follow through on program implementation and activities? Not necessarily. Instituting a workplace wellness program requires a leader who has:

- the time and interest to focus on the program's design and implementation
- knowledge about health issues and solutions or a willingness to learn about them quickly
- a natural desire to help others, and
- if possible, a certain charisma, to inspire others to follow.

You might find someone who fits the bill on your own staff. Many employers turn to the person who handles health benefits and other personnel matters, but you might think twice before doing the same. That person may already be seen as the "bad guy" who deals with layoffs and delivers other news that no one wants to hear, like reductions in benefits. (Remember Toby from the TV show *The Office*?) You don't want your wellness program to look like just another set of bureaucratic personnel rules.

Of course, everyone on your staff is probably plenty busy already. But, as our adviser Dr. Preston Maring (whom you'll meet in Chapter 5) suggests:

> *Look for someone who's got what I call 'discretionary energy'—the one who's always trying to organize the team to have some fun. Sometimes they are happy just to create something that's appreciated by other employees, without needing any specific bonus to participate.*

It's best to choose a program leader with some independent credibility, for example, someone with a medical or fitness background. A person who's good at planning parties or events is also an asset. These qualities can also be brought to the table by putting together a team to manage your program.

Round Up a Team of Helpers

No matter who leads your program, that person may want to enlist the help of a small team of people to share the workload and bring their own strengths and energy to particular initiatives. Four to seven people is usually enough for a small business. If your company is big enough to have departments, you might choose people to represent those departments.

Your wellness team members should be formally appointed and their new responsibilities should be written into their job descriptions. Those responsibilities may include designing and implementing the program, or you could create separate committees for each function. (Don't let just one person do all the program design; it's important that a mix of people study the options and make recommendations to senior management.) Once your wellness program is up and running, the committee should plan to meet at least once a month, if not more often, to both plan future activities and evaluate ongoing activities, making enhancements or changes as necessary.

Rae Lee Olson notes:

> *Be careful to carve out appropriate time for people to get their new tasks done. Throwing responsibility for a wellness program onto the plate of someone who doesn't have the time to execute it well gives conflicting messages about high-level support for the program and will—as has happened in many cases—inhibit the program's ultimate success.*

Consider Bringing in Outside Professionals

Time is valuable at every workplace. When it comes to setting up your wellness program, as in many areas of business, it's worth exploring some tradeoffs: Do you have the energy and skills to run a program in house, or would it be worthwhile to bring in outside consultants or vendors? A growing field of professionals focuses on workplace wellness—and a growing number of small businesses find it efficient to use them. Many outside providers offer comprehensive services; they'll analyze your workplace's needs, design a program to meet those needs, and set you up with the following:

- newsletters and other educational materials—fun ones, that people actually want to read
- lifestyle coaches
- Web-based health improvement tools, and
- speakers and other specialized professionals.

Some also offer irresistible high-tech goodies. For example, Dr. Metz explains:

> *Some companies include wireless devices that send health activity information, like number of steps walked, to a secure website with a private page for each employee who participates. The tracking devices include pedometers, scales, and blood pressure devices. After the employee takes a walk, steps on the scales, or takes a blood pressure reading, the data wirelessly loads to the employee's personal page on a health improvement website, and the employee can see how he or she is progressing. A lot of business owners like this because you don't need to rely on people's word for what the scale says and so forth; you collect objective data. Of course, it's protected information just like any medical information, so the employer sees only a summary for the entire group. Other than the employee, the only person with direct access to individual medical information is his or her coach.*

To look for a consulting firm that meets your needs and budget, get recommendations from other companies in your area—or nationwide (this can be done long distance). Lists of quality vendors can be obtained from organizations such as:

- WELCOA (Wellness Council of America): www.welcoa.org (WELCOA can also help employers that pay annual membership dues—$365 when this book went to print—run a wellness program in house, by providing prepackaged materials such as monthly health bulletins, downloadable programs with which to run health-based campaigns, *PowerPoint* presentations, and more.)
- URAC (formerly called the Utilization Review Accreditation Commission): www.urac.org
- NCQA (National Committee for Quality Assurance): www.ncqa.org

Interview at least three vendors to make sure their experience is proven and documented. When it comes to prepackaged programs, Dr. Metz cautions, "Watch out for anyone that tries to sell you a ready-made program, without offering an industry-standard, comprehensive employee health assessment first." Ready-made programs can lead to disappointment if the program doesn't match your workforce's culture and needs, or if it feels so hard to access that no one takes it seriously.

If you don't find a provider that meets your budget, don't panic. As Theresa Islo, Director of Operations for the Wellness Council of Wisconsin explains, "Small businesses, particularly those with fewer than 50 employees, can't always afford to bring in outside vendors. They can, however, take advantage of many resources to help them implement a program internally, such as WELCOA" (described above).

You can also create a hybrid program by bringing in outside experts or vendors for some parts of it, such as HRAs, biometrics, health coaching, Web-based tools, or professionally led worksite health seminars. Then it will be up to you to plan other program elements.

At Frett Barrington (the ten-person firm described above), they brought in vendors to do HRAs, but formed a four-person wellness committee to design and implement their actual (and ultimately award-winning) program. Patty Frett notes that, between the company's health insurance carrier and its health risk assessment (HAS) vendor, a number of things are available at no charge, like speakers for lunch-and-learns. Their HRA vendor, for example, provides four free sessions each year, and the Frett Barrington wellness committee has a lot of flexibility to determine what those offerings will be. Here's a favorite, described by Patty Frett:

> *We developed a lunchtime session with our HRA vendor where each person brought in their own brown bag lunch—something that they realistically would eat. We then had a nutritionist analyze the group's lunch choices. It was very informative and well received.*

Theresa Islo adds:

> *Sometimes you can find good resources right at your fingertips. Consider, for example, what your employees do for hobbies. If there's someone who's interested in healthy cooking, that person might share some of their knowledge with the worksite at a lunch-and-learn.*

Encourage Employees to Get Involved

Some of the most effective programs are those created or requested by employees. Your office may already have some informal employee-initiated activities, such as an ultimate Frisbee team, a group that regularly jogs together, or a weight-loss competition within a department. If so, such efforts should be fostered—so long as you don't sanction risky behavior, such as extreme efforts to lose weight.

Even if your employees aren't this organized, it's worth giving them some control over the process where possible. One good way to do this is to provide a variety of activity choices within your program—at least more than one. If joining a softball league is the only option, people will inevitably feel left out. Or if using a pedometer to count one's steps is the only offering, you might have the same experience as one employer, in which the same employees always won the prizes, leaving the rest discouraged.

Offer as wide a range of choices as you can, keeping in mind that this doesn't have to mean planning a lot of formal activities. Even in a small workplace, you can add depth to your program by recognizing (with points or rewards) employees who participate in and keep track of healthy activities like walking the dog or taking a morning swim in the local pool.

Step 3: Market the Program to Your Employees

Let's go back to Bob, our example (from the last chapter) of a 56-year-old worker in poor shape. If your program can support Bob in changing his health behavior, you'll have done both your office and him a huge favor. It's possible that your program will be just the nudge and opportunity he was waiting for. But it's equally possible that he'll grumble at your very efforts and flat out refuse to take part. Experts say that first-year participation in a wellness program typically goes no higher than 20% to 30% and is sometimes less than 10%. The nonparticipants may be, among other things:

- feeling too short on time to invest in new health improvement activities
- set in their ways
- in denial about their existing or impending health problems
- critical of your program as authoritarian, intrusive, or patronizing (despite the efforts we know you'll make to prove otherwise)
- stuck in the belief that a simple pill should cure their ills, or
- afraid to try new things and face difficult changes.

You'll need to accept that you can't get every last employee enthused about your program, even as you keep looking for ways to do so. As Rae Lee Olson says:

It's easy for the healthy population to jump on the bandwagon, because it validates their good health and behaviors they already value. The real challenge for your wellness program is to motivate the unmotivated, the disinterested, and the discouraged.

Small-business owners do have an advantage here. A multicompany survey (by McMahan, et. al., published in the Summer, 2001 *American Journal of Health Studies*), found higher-than-average participation rates in smaller companies (two to 500 employees) when it came to six program areas:

- weight management
- violence prevention
- immunization
- mental health programs
- ergonomics training, and
- first-aid training.

The study authors theorized that this was primarily due to three factors particular to small businesses: greater social and family interactions among employees, closer interaction between employees and top management, and less employee diversity. All of these factors may make it easier for small employers to design programs that match the needs of most of their staff.

Here are some ways to make the most of your unique access to employees and inspire them to join in the wellness program.

Start With a Bang

Although your employees should probably be grateful that you're rolling out a wellness program, not all of them will see it as a good thing—or even notice what's going on—unless you put focused effort into marketing and creating a "grand opening" feel. Consider creating a kickoff event, such as a health fair with screenings or a healthy breakfast and program introduction.

This doesn't have to be a huge deal. For example, Theresa Islo, of the Wellness Council of Wisconsin, says:

> We opened our program with a potluck lunch and encouraged people to bring in something that was healthy according to at least one of three criteria: low fat, low sodium, or whole grain. A few people raised their eyebrows; they didn't know where to start. It was the beginning of an education process.

Attorney Kelly Kuglitsch (an adviser you'll meet in Chapter 13) says:

> The way a wellness program is announced, described, or presented has everything to do with its success. I've had friends come to me because they were given a health risk assessment, but were concerned because the cover letter from the employer just wasn't clear. Rumors were already flying, like "If we smoke, or if this or that, we won't get health insurance, and we'll be fired." When already nervous employees receive a letter saying only that health information will be collected, and when the letter doesn't carefully explain the purpose of, or the limits on, how that information will be used, employee anxiety will rise. So it's key to be transparent about the purpose of any policy, and especially any test.

An introductory announcement from your CEO or company owner is a good idea—in fact, says Dr. Metz, "it's essential to success." (See the "Sample Wellness Program Announcement Letter," below and on the CD-ROM at the back of the book.) The letter might announce your special kick-off event. If you have an employee newsletter, that's also a good place to make an announcement. (Again, there's a sample below and on the CD-ROM.) If you don't have a newsletter, you can recraft this as an email message.

Sample Wellness Program Announcement Letter

Dear Employee:

As one of our valued employees, much of our company's strength and success depends on you. We spend many hours of the day together. That's why I want to make sure that our workplace helps you maintain or even improve your health. Good health is a resource that helps us all meet our goals.

I strongly believe that the everyday choices we make can help us live healthier and happier lives, both at work and at home. Therefore, beginning [*date*], [*your company name*] will offer a new wellness program that will help all of us increase our knowledge about health matters, explore fun ways to eat healthier, improve our level of physical fitness, and more.

The program is completely voluntary, but I hope you'll find activities that inspire you to participate. For example, you will have access to:

[*Adjust these to fit your program*]
- a $50 bonus when you complete a health risk assessment, which will help you understand your current health and your best options for making improvements
- affordable discounts at local fitness clubs
- regular meetings during lunch breaks where experts on topics like fitness, nutrition, and stress management will provide information and tips on how to make changes and feel better
- potlucks and contests featuring healthy food with lots of fruits and vegetables
- a qualified health coach to talk over the practical aspects of setting and meeting your new health improvement goals

I'll be working toward various health goals of my own, as part of this effort to build a healthy company here at [*company name*]. If you see me looking tired after a workout or grumpy after a week without cigarettes, I hope you'll give me a wave of encouragement!

Sample Wellness Program Announcement Letter (continued)

Please encourage your coworkers to join in the fun. After all, what better teamwork and support network could you have than the people you see every day?

Soon, you'll see posters and fliers throughout the company promoting this new initiative, including more information about the special kickoff party in the employee lunchroom on [*date*]! In the meantime, if you have questions about the program, feel free to contact [*human resources*]. I look forward to sharing this program with you.

In good health,

[*Your name*]

[*Your title*]

Sample Wellness Program Newsletter Announcement

Imagine Yourself Working for a "Healthy" Company

Are we a "healthy" company? As coworkers, do we eat right, exercise regularly, and manage our stress well? If not, how do we make changes for the better?

Fitness is more than just working out at a gym every day. It's maintaining a comfortable balance between our work and home lives. It's working in a healthy way while on the job. It's keeping our blood pressure in check and making sure we get enough good sleep each night. It's eating plenty of fruits and vegetables and low-calorie foods.

Beginning [*date*], [*company name*] is launching a new wellness program, which will allow each of us to identify and pursue health improvement goals that are right for us. This program will be offered to you at no charge, as part of your overall benefits package.

An important part of the new program is to help you understand your current health by filling out a short health risk assessment form. After you complete the assessment, you'll receive a detailed report about your health and opportunities for improvement, plus a $50 cash card that you can spend toward your new health goals—or on whatever else you want.

An important note: This program will include optional activities for everyone in the company, including those with a health challenge or disability.

What are you waiting for? Keep your eye on your inbox for more information, or contact [*human resources*] if you have specific questions. Soon, you'll be on your way to helping us build the healthiest company in the county.

Some companies also create a notebook or booklet describing what's available from the wellness program, including activities, incentives, coaching, individual treatments, and other benefits. (For reasons described in Chapter 13—mostly to do with the fact that your program may evolve very quickly—it's best if you don't put this information directly into your employee handbook.) And along with distributing the notebook or booklet, some employers ask workers to sign a "Commit to Fit" pledge card, vowing to track and measurably increase their exercise or other health improvement activities within a certain time period, such as 90 days.

Ongoing written communications should be handled by a skilled team member who can clearly explain the program's events and offerings—without forgetting to include details like the time of day or location—and the health benefits to be gained. It will be even better if that person can use attractive layouts, illustrations, and more to promote a festive atmosphere and draw people's attention to the hard information.

Make It Easy and Accessible

Employees may not take any initiative when it comes to your wellness program. In fact, some will ignore the emails and stuff any newsletters into a growing pile in their inbox. That's why it's important to make the program offerings easy to understand and to sign up for.

Get the word out in multiple ways. Use repeated invitations to events, frequent reminder emails, posters around the office, announcements during meetings, an easy-to-find calendar listing all wellness events, and any other good strategies you can think of. For example, in a small office, there's nothing like one-on-one conversations or phone calls saying, "I hope you can make it!" (Of course, one of your communication methods should be the one you usually use for sending important information, whether that's an email, formal letter, or a paycheck envelope stuffer.)

TIP

How about a custom calendar? That's what Frett Barrington Ltd. created for its employees, starting with the third year of its wellness program, when it was known in advance all the events to be held that year. Patty Frett says, "It's one of the parts of our program I'm most proud of. It's fun, with photos of past wellness activities and a 'Penguins on the Move' theme, in which each coworker's face is shown in a penguin costume next to his or her favorite wellness tip. Everybody posts the calendar on their office wall, so we all know what we can look forward to—including not only activities put on by our wellness committee, but some suggestions and national health observances from the American Institute for Preventive Medicine."

Also, make events such as seminars easy to remember and attend. Hold them at a regular time and place, such as every other Tuesday at noon. At the event itself, make sure any information you present is so clear that it can be easily absorbed by people who secretly wish they could either get back to work or go home.

Making participation easy is doubly important if anyone in your office has a disability that might require reasonable accommodations (which, under the ADA, you're required to provide). You might already know about individual disabilities if, for example, you've made workplace accommodations. But not all disabilities affect someone's ability to do a particular job. Ask your employees to let you know if a particular accommodation would help them take part in wellness program activities. And remember that, under HIPAA, any rewards, incentives, or penalties tied to your health plan must be equally accessible to everyone on the plan.

Create a Fun Atmosphere

Getting fit and healthy doesn't have to be drudgery—in fact, eating healthy food and exercising can become as addictive as any habit. Still, your employees may be up against some old, tough-to-break habits.

Before bemoaning your employees' lack of will power, let's reflect on the barriers that can arise to changing daily habits. Most people are already putting plenty of time and energy into work, family, and other commitments. On top of that, any existing health troubles can create a downward spiral. A person on antidepressants, for example, may experience drowsiness as a side effect, which makes going to the gym after work even more of a chore—despite the fact that exercise might combat the very roots of that depression. Being overweight can make someone embarrassed to get into a swimming pool or suffer chafing on the inner thighs when walking (really, it's painful). And it's no secret that smoking is more than just a habit: It's an addiction, with withdrawal symptoms that include dizziness, lack of concentration, and more.

To counterbalance these forces, your wellness program should be made fun wherever or however possible, even if it's only in the "fun" way you communicate a message. Your educational materials should contain cool facts that people will want to repeat to their friends—for example, that exercise has been found to be as effective as Prozac in reducing depression. If you have onsite lunch-and-learn wellness presentations, your speakers should be lively. If you offer classes or team exercise activities, they should make people forget that what they're doing is "good for them."

Here's an example from Rae Lee Olson of how Vita Benefits Group worked some fun into its wellness program:

> In addition to our individual points and rewards program, we offer corporate, team prizes. So if everyone on the team gets a certain minimum number of points during a month, then everyone gets a gift card that month, for around $25. But it's not just $25 straight cash—that's kind of boring. We discovered that people get more excited if there's a grab bag of gift cards from different places, like a movie theater, Home Depot, Macy's, Nordstrom's, and so forth. Then when people pull them from the bag, you hear, "Ooh, I'm going to Home Depot" or "I'm going to the movies," and some trading starts up—it gets some energy going.

Step 4: Health Screenings

Now it's time for the truly revealing—and highest priority—surveys and tests. The first is the HRA questionnaire, in which your workers provide information about their health, including their lifestyles, habits, known health conditions, goals, and readiness to make changes. The second is the biometric screening, in which medical professionals administer various tests (such as a blood test for cholesterol and glucose levels), perform simple weigh-ins for body mass index (BMI), and more.

As discussed earlier, evaluating your employees' health needs is important for both further program planning and for their own health awareness, care, and maintenance.

Getting Help With This Step

For both HRAs and biometric screenings, it's best to bring in the pros. Even if you have a medical degree in your back pocket, directly surveying your own employees on their personal health issues—much less telling them to stand on a scales—is not going to go over well and is likely to violate privacy laws. You could ask employees to go online and fill out HRA-type surveys on their own—such as the one offered at www.realage.com (with follow-up wellness advice and plans). But this approach has a downside: You won't receive any summary results or information about what your employees learned. When looking for help, the best place to start might be your health insurance provider, who may provide HRAs or biometric screenings at low or no cost.

If your insurer can't help with screenings, and you haven't already lined up a provider that offers comprehensive wellness services, you'll need to shop around for a private company that administers HRAs and biometrics. For example, these services may be available from local hospitals and medical groups like Kaiser Permanente, national clinical laboratories like Quest Diagnostics, or biometrics companies like Kronos Health. Not all health assessments are created alike, so ask fellow employers for recommendations and compare information about issues like these:

- **Cost.** But keep in mind that the lowest price doesn't always mean the best services. Basic HRAs typically cost between $5 and $25 per person, depending on factors like the sophistication of the report and whether you buy other services from the HRA provider. The cost of biometrics varies much more, depending on the type of testing, the size of your workforce, and other factors—and is often between $45 and $150 per person.
- **HRA survey scope and philosophy.** For example, adviser Rae Lee Olson says, "The HRA shouldn't feel like a warning message from the Grim Reaper. A well-designed HRA will highlight areas where each employee is taking good care of himself or herself. No one wants to get a report saying only what they're doing wrong—which, unfortunately, describes some HRAs

I've seen. There should be a feel-good element in the reports to employees. Otherwise, the well-intended data collection process may demotivate and discourage employees before your program even starts."

- **Look and feel.** Get a sample of several different HRAs from the companies that you're considering and have several different people try them out. In particular, they should comment on whether each HRA is easy to read and understand. But keep in mind that, as Rae Lee Olson explains, "There's no one perfect HRA. Your employees' reactions may reflect your office's culture more than anything else. Sometimes one HRA just won't feel right, while another one will."
- **Services included.** For example, exactly what biometric tests will the provider conduct?
- **Follow-up reporting.** Ask to see samples of the summary information that you'll receive and of the individual reports your employees will get.
- **Follow-up services.** With certain wellness companies, HRAs and biometrics lead to direct follow-up by the service provider, including services like personal coaching or treatment recommendations.

Encouraging Employees to Participate

It's important in most cases to encourage widespread participation in your initial HRA and biometric screenings. Not only is the big-picture information helpful for planning the rest of your program, but studies show you aren't likely to get data from many of your highest-risk employees unless at least 50% of them do an HRA. Also, if you're using a service that ties follow-up activities (such as personal coaching) to needs revealed in the surveys, early nonparticipation could leave people entirely out of the loop.

Offering incentives, such as cash or a gift card, will help drive participation. In fact, HRAs are so important that you might want to

Should You Survey Employees About Their Productivity?

As a small business, you probably already have a good idea about the degree to which health problems affect productivity levels in your workplace. However, larger employers, being more removed from this information, often turn to written surveys asking employees to report (anonymously, of course) on their health and productivity levels. These employers use the survey results to make decisions about their workplace wellness efforts. The catch, and the reason we don't recommend this approach for most small employers, is that filling out a series of surveys eventually lowers employee goodwill—and you'll want that goodwill when you ask employees to fill out the most important survey of all: the HRA.

That said, if you know your employees are happy to fill out surveys— for example, because there are incentives involved—and you're not hiring a separate wellness provider to take care of such things, here are three highly rated productivity surveys that you can find online, for free:

- the Stanford Presenteeism Scale (SPS-6), available from LifeSolutions (part of the University of Pittsburgh Medical Center), at www.eapsolutions.com. (Click "For Providers," then "Forms," then "SPS-6.") Our adviser Dr. Kenneth R. Pelletier helped to develop this survey.
- the Health and Labour Questionnaire (HLQ), available from the institute for Medical Technology Assessment (iMTA) in the Netherlands at www.imta.nl. (Click "publications," then "Manuals & Questionnaires," then "Health and Labour Questionnaire (HLQ).")
- the Work Limitations Questionnaire (WLQ), available from Tufts-New England Medical Center at http://160.109.101.132/icrhps/ resprog/thi/wlq.asp.
- the Health and Performance Questionnaire (HPQ), available from the World Health Organization and Harvard University at www. hcp.med.harvard.edu/hpq.

Before distributing any survey, however, we recommend that you check with your attorney to make sure the one you've chosen won't violate employee confidentiality.

make an exception and create a mild penalty for nonparticipation. Rae Lee Olson says:

> *More and more employers are conditioning health insurance coverage, or at least the deluxe version of the coverage, on taking the HRA. It might tick some people off, but it's legal.*

As an employer, you won't receive copies of all the individual HRA forms or biometrics reports, for confidentiality reasons. However, if you have 50 or more employees, you will receive summary information. The summary will give you a broad picture of the health issues and risks within your workforce and help you further plan your program. If you have fewer than 50 employees, normal industry practice is that you *not* be given a summary report, because it would too easily breach individual confidentiality. But it will still be useful for the employees to receive individual feedback from the HRA provider, along with any follow-up services that you build into your program. Note that if the service provider will follow up with your employees, then each employee must sign a statement agreeing to this.

Step 5: Chart Your Program's Progress

Your company's long-term commitment to wellness should not depend on instant or obvious health improvement results. The very best programs take time to become ingrained in the organization and develop momentum. Nevertheless, it's worth charting, to the extent possible, the degree to which your program is having the effects you want. This is particularly true if you still have doubters on your management team.

If you're using an outside service provider, it should take the lead role in performing evaluations and creating regular outcome reports. Adviser Dr. Metz underscores that you should "demand quantitative reporting" that covers the following:

- HRA completion rates
- program participation and engagement (how many of your employees are aware of the program and how many are actually using it)
- employee satisfaction with the program
- changes in health-related behaviors and how (particularly over the long term) those changes impact health status and health risks
- biometric changes, either self-reported or through wireless monitors or other screening tools, and
- projections of the financial return that you'll get for each dollar spent on your wellness program (most readily predicted in large employee populations).

If you're running a wellness program on your own, however, you don't need a Ph.D. in mathematics to do some monitoring, just an interest in seeing whether your wellness program is doing a good job of addressing the issues that concerned you. Keep reading for some helpful tips.

Know Your Starting Point

Three years from now, you don't want to say, "Gee, I think our wellness program has made people healthier, but I don't really remember where we started and I'm not sure what worked." To avoid that scenario, gather some baseline data on the health of your workplace.

You can do this using data already in your files. (An outside vendor would probably gather more sophisticated data, but we're trying to keep it simple here.) Remember: Never sneak illegal peeks into your employees' medical histories—just take a look at your personnel records to find answers to the questions below. (You can find a printable version of this questionnaire on the CD-ROM at the back of the book.)

Your Wellness Program's Baseline Data

1. What was your workplace's rate of absenteeism or use of sick leave in each of the last three years? (You may even want to chart this out month by month, to notice seasonal variations.)

   Year: _____ _____ _____

   Percentage: _____% _____% _____%

2. What percentage of your employees accounts for the majority of the absenteeism or use of sick leave? _____%

3. How many of your employees have taken advantage of preventive health screening covered by your medical plan during each of the last three years? (Note: You can ask your health insurance provider for the number, without obtaining individual names.)

   Year: _____ _____ _____

   Number of employees: _____ _____ _____

4. How many of your employees have gone on temporary or permanent disability during the last three years?

   Year: _____ _____ _____

   Number of employees: _____ _____ _____

5. How much have you been charged for workers' compensation insurance in each of the last three years?

   Year: _____ _____ _____

   Amount charged: _____ _____ _____

6. How much have you been charged for group medical insurance in each of the last three years?

   Year: _____ _____ _____

   Amount charged: _____ _____ _____

7. What is your workplace's rate of employee turnover in each of the last three years?

   Year: _____ _____ _____

   Percentage: _____% _____% _____%

8. Have your employees been acting disinterested or showing signs of work-related stress within the last year, such as filing complaints, having issues requiring management intervention, producing less work, or the like? ☐ yes ☐ no (or not a major concern)

9. Have your employees complained within the last year about health or safety-related aspects of your workplace, such as lighting, noise level, long work hours, workstation ergonomics, temperature, or ventilation? ☐ yes ☐ no

10. Are productivity levels declining, or less than you believe they could be? ☐ yes ☐ no

11. Have you noticed some employees drinking to excess at office functions where alcohol is served? ☐ yes ☐ no

When you look at your answers to the questions above, you may notice trends that point to your workplace's need for a health tune-up. If, for example, your workers are using more sick leave and your medical insurance costs have been rising at a faster rate than is normal industry wide, you've already got a good argument for starting a wellness program.

Of course, you may already have an explanation for certain trends. For example, some spikes in your employees' use of sick leave may be due to seasonal variations (such as allergies) or by an unusual circumstance such as a flu epidemic. Even a change in office culture might make a difference—for example, if you're doing a better job of encouraging employees to stay home when they're sick. Or perhaps your rising workers' compensation insurance rates can be tied to the increased risk posed by a new piece of machinery in your office.

Try to avoid getting too caught up in examining causes, however. In the beginning, the primary purpose of gathering this information is to set a baseline. Then, in the coming years, you'll be able to compare your data to see what differences your wellness program has made.

Besides, even if your answers don't show any alarming trends, you can't necessarily conclude that your workers are in perfect health. A wellness program remains useful for boosting productivity and morale and for helping your long-time employees stay healthy as the years go by. If your baseline looks good, your program can probably focus on basic health maintenance strategies like nutrition, fitness, and stress reduction.

Keep Track as You Go

Now let's fast forward into the future, to when your program is under-way. Having gathered your baseline data, you're now in a good position to monitor changes in your employees' lifestyles and health, and the overall success of your program. Although you can't expect changes to happen overnight, it's worth tracking your program's success and effectiveness early on, with an eye to making immediate adjustments if appropriate. Also, plan to do a broad review of program results at intervals such as every year or two. (This is especially important if any members of your top management doubt the program's worth.) Here's how to keep an eye on your wellness program from the beginning:

- **Track participation.** Collect names of program participants—for example, by using a sign-in sheet at all events, classes, and seminars. If the numbers are low, don't just tuck this information into a file—take measures to address the problem. If the numbers are high, congratulations! That's an important indication of program success.

- **Create a feedback channel for employees.** Your employees will probably be the first to tell you if something is going wrong—but assure them that you welcome this, and ask for more general feedback. For example, you might place a suggestion box in an obvious place or designate a special email inbox. Be sure to respond to each suggestion, at least with a "Thanks, we'll consider that"—and then do so! Rewarding employees for the best suggestion of the month or year also helps keep your program vital and responsive to employees' needs.

- **Distribute evaluation forms after classes or seminars.** Create a standard form, so that you can compare answers for all activities. Ask how participants would rate the class—for example, on a scale of one to ten—and whether they learned something new, felt that it was appropriate for the audience and their schedule, and would sign up for something similar in the future. If a regular class isn't working, don't wait until your annual review to drop it.

TIP

It helps to have thick skin. Like movie critics, people put far more effort and eloquence into complaints than compliments. Take the best of the advice, and comfort yourself about any negative feedback by realizing that participation and results are the best indicators of program success.

Review the Big Picture

As mentioned above, you'll want to get an overview of your wellness program at regular intervals. Here's what you should do after the first year—or after two years, if that's the earliest you can manage—and every year or two after that:

- **Gather follow-up internal data.** Collect updated answers to the questions you answered in "Know Your Starting Point," above (concerning issues like absenteeism and office stress) as well as participation data (as described under "Keep Track as You Go"). Observe any increases or declines.

- **Gather data on program costs.** Add up the amounts your company spent on the wellness program, including staff time, fees for outside service providers, spending on prizes and incentives, facilities costs, and so forth. Is the final tally what you'd originally budgeted, or did costs get out of hand?

- **Survey your employees regarding overall program satisfaction.** This can be done either in writing or by convening focus groups. Find out what's working for people, and what you could change or drop. Also ask to what extent your employees (and their families, if they're included) are aware of what the program has to offer; if you have less-than-effective communications efforts, your plans may have simply dropped off some of their radar screens.

> **TIP**
>
> **It's okay to talk to people one on one.** Surveys and groups can be impersonal, and some people just won't participate—often the very people who refused to take part in the program in the first place. If you have employees who are resistant to the program—especially if they exhibit obvious high-risk factors, such as smoking or obesity—a member of your wellness team can do a one-on-one interview, requesting feedback and constructive suggestions on the program. Difficult though this sounds, experience shows that some employees appreciate the expression of concern.

- **Readminister HRAs.** Depending on what questions were in your original HRA, a retake should tell you about changes in health behavior, attitudes, knowledge, and in some cases, results. For purposes of gathering health data, it's good to do this once a year. However, more frequent HRAs are appropriate in some situations, as Dr. Doug Metz explains: "If your HRA is designed to motivate the person taking it, you'd want to make it available very frequently. We sometimes arrange to let employees take an HRA every 30 days, to see whether their scores are improving."

- **Readminister biometric tests.** Signs of change can be very exciting —for example, if you're able to report back to your employees that as a group, they've achieved overall drops in blood pressure, cholesterol, or other health indicators. But don't expect miracles. Dr. Metz advises:

  A lot of these health changes are slow to take effect—you'd hardly see the needle move at all if you readministered the biometrics tests more than once a year. Every two years is fine from a scientific perspective, but from a business management perspective, two years can feel like a long time to wait to see whether your investment has paid off. That's why many employers settle on one year.

- **Gather vending machine data.** If you have vending machines and have stocked them with healthier-than-average food options, check on what's selling and which way the trends are going.

- **Take a look around!** If you're seeing happier, healthier faces, new friendships forming around healthy activities, and even dramatic changes in the health of a few employees, you don't need any fancy statistics to tell you that your program is working.

All of these measurements should help you decide whether your program is changing employees' behavior, and hopefully improving their health, at a cost you can afford. Putting it all together, try to answer these four questions:

- Is the wellness program going forward as planned, with program activities and a good amount of employee participation?

- Has the program had a positive impact on participants' health and wellness?
- Were the costs within the anticipated budget?
- What should we change going forward?

If you're seeing positive changes, you can all but assume your program is helping your bottom line. If the results are discouraging, hang in there: Some wellness programs don't find their legs until after three or four years.

You may be wondering whether you can figure out your actual ROI on your own. In truth, after just one year, it's probably not worth trying—people haven't had long enough to either change their behavior or see corresponding results. Even after that, calculating ROI is a bit tricky to do on your own, because you'd have to know how to put a dollar value on your employees' changes in productivity, including any reduction in absenteeism, and weave in other factors such as changed medical costs and benefit plans. For this and other more sophisticated types of evaluation, such as a comparison of your medical claims costs year by year, it's best to enlist the help of outside professionals.

Again, however, you don't want to get overly obsessed with measurable returns. Theresa Islo, of the Wellness Council of Wisconsin, explains:

> I'm concerned that businesses can place too much focus on ROI rather than looking at how wellness programs impact quality of life—or even save lives. There was an employer here in Milwaukee that did a campaign to promote seatbelt use. One of its employees had never worn a seatbelt in his life. But one morning, getting into his car, he remembered the message of the campaign and decided to buckle up for the first time. He was involved in a serious car accident that very day—without the seatbelt, he would not have survived. How do you put a dollar figure on something like that—or on a heart attack that your program prevented, or a health problem that you helped turn around?

TIP

Celebrate your program's successes. Don't hide those positive statistics—your employees may be more interested in them than anyone, given that their lives, health, and hard work are at issue. Regular wellness award ceremonies, an annual wellness anniversary party, or whatever else you can think of are all good ways to keep the energy high. Even if you can't point to measurable health changes yet, celebrate participation, winning teams, and so forth. Remind your employees that your company is on its way toward being the healthiest, happiest, most productive organization it can be.

Take Your Success Stories to the Media

If your workplace wellness program is leading to healthier, happier employees, that's a story you might want to share. In particular, the business or health pages of local newspapers—and even money-related magazines—often highlight workplace wellness programs. Publicizing your program offers a chance to both celebrate the employees who participate and build the reputation of your business.

But don't expect to call the media and have them do all the work. It's best to draft a press release, using a snappy opening paragraph that a journalist could cut and paste if necessary. You might consider highlighting one employee's success story, providing a few engaging facts and details about your program, and describing who to contact for more information or to arrange interviews.

You'll find lots of press release samples and more detailed advice online, by searching in your favorite browser for "how to write a press release."

Prevention and Early Detection

Meet Your Adviser

 **Charles P. Gerba, Ph.D.,** professor at the University of Arizona and author of many books, including *The Germ Freak's Guide to Outwitting Colds and Flu: Guerilla Tactics to Keep Yourself Healthy at Home, at Work and in the World,* cowritten with Allison Janse.

What he does: Dr. Gerba researches how diseases are spread through the environment, from one person to the next. Lately, he's been researching how long swine flu survives on surfaces in offices. (The answer is that it survives fairly well, maybe several hours to a couple days depending on the surface.) Dr. Gerba's office also tests and researches new consumer products. Right now, his office is working on an antimicrobial face mask that you can use over and over again, since there was a shortage there for awhile.

Favorite healthy food: "Dried figs"

Top tip for staying fit and healthy: "Keep containers of disinfecting wipes and hand sanitizer in your desk. That's what I do."

S ome people actually look forward to coming to work, as a place to see colleagues and friends, get a break from family responsibilities, and demonstrate their skills or settle into a comfortable routine. However, with many people spending most of their waking hours on the job, the workplace inevitably becomes a place where people share germs, spread illness, and sometimes ignore their own developing health troubles.

This chapter discusses how your workplace can be a place that actively promotes basic disease prevention and early detection—within your wellness program and in general.

How Early Detection Measures Keep Workers Healthy

In later chapters, we'll discuss how your wellness program can help workers deal with chronic diseases, such as cancer and heart disease. But an even more important goal of your program is to help them avoid such diseases altogether, through better nutrition, exercise, and the other lifestyle changes discussed throughout this book. If that goal seems overly optimistic, realize that your efforts may at least help your workers arrive at a happy middle ground: The earlier they are screened or examined for certain diseases—ideally before any symptoms appear— the better the odds that the disease can be prevented, cured, or at least successfully managed.

Colorectal cancer provides an excellent example. It's one of the most curable forms of cancer if detected early. In fact, colonoscopies and certain other screening tests can detect precancerous polyps, which can be removed before they have a chance to turn into cancer. Such polyp removal could head off an estimated 75% to 90% of colorectal cancer cases. Yet the unfortunate truth is that an estimated 40% of adults who've reached age 50—the age at which doctors recommend that people begin getting regular colorectal cancer screenings—have not been screened. And given that colon cancer often presents no symptoms at all in its early stages, they aren't likely to consult a doctor about this issue until the cancer has advanced to a point where treatment is much more challenging.

Similarly, screening for breast cancer is an important early detection tool. Although the studies of mammography's effectiveness are ongoing, the U.S. Preventive Services Task Force (USPSTF) has found evidence that having a mammogram every 12 to 33 months significantly reduces women's deaths from breast cancer, particularly for women ages 50–69.

We'll discuss exactly which screening exams are recommended for people at different ages below, under "Education: You Really Can Prevent Disease."

Colds and Flu: How Common Illnesses Impact the Workplace

Although everyone worries about major chronic diseases like cancer, the truth is that the cold is the most common infectious disease in the United States, affecting approximately 23% of the U.S. population each year and responsible for the majority of workplace absences. The flu isn't far behind, affecting about 20% of the U.S. population each year. It can also lead to relatively long work absences, up to five days per person.

You probably didn't need statistics to convince you of the impact of colds and flu on your workplace. During cold and flu season, it's not uncommon to see people at the office sneeze, cough, or use elaborate hand gestures to indicate "I lost my voice!" People who haven't yet caught the bug may look at them suspiciously, wondering how contagious they are and why they didn't just stay home. And yes, they should have stayed home.

For one thing, the most important and effective treatment for both colds and the flu is bed rest. Equally important for the sake of other employees, those with a bug should realize that, according to the Centers for Disease Control (CDC), both the cold and flu viruses usually spread from person to person when an infected person coughs or sneezes. To be more graphic, nasal mucus is the primary culprit in transmitting these viruses. Since the hands are often involved in covering up a cough or blowing one's nose, these too become means of passing viruses. And the cold and certain other viruses and bacteria can survive up to three hours on surfaces such as door handles or shared office equipment.

But for one reason or another, many people feel they can't miss work. As we'll discuss in Chapter 13, that's a good reason to have written policies in your employee handbook saying not only that people should stay home while sick, but that you as the employer may send sick people home, especially in the event of a health crisis like a flu pandemic.

CAUTION

Cold sufferers are contagious for longer than they think. Research shows that cold germs are at their highest levels in the body during the 18 to 24 hours before symptoms appear and in the first three to five days of the illness— but can hang around for as long as two weeks after the person has started feeling better.

No matter how careful everyone is, however, you can't block every germ at the door to your workplace. Next, we'll talk about wellness education and activities to combat or prevent common viruses and more serious illnesses. Later in the chapter, we'll give some tips on what you, as an employer, can do about the germ-sharing problem outside the context of your wellness program.

How to Help Employees Stay Well

Since we can't look inside our own bodies, it's sometimes hard to tell how eating right, staying fit, and other such measures not only help us stay healthy, but also help us avoid any of a number of illnesses, both major and minor. After all, if you never develop the illness, you never know how close you came to getting it.

But your workplace wellness program can drive the point home and reaffirm for people that their newfound healthy behaviors really are making a difference, even if they can't see it. And if there are particular diseases that they're worried about or that run in their family, you can provide information and activities to help them address their risks head-on.

As part of this commitment to staying well, it helps to get your employees attuned to having regular screenings for cancer and other illnesses. Studies show that only about half of insured adults receive these screenings according to guidelines for their age and gender. You can't directly track your individual employees' record of going for regular screenings, for privacy reasons. But we'll suggest some other ways to help make sure they get them done.

Education: You Really Can Prevent Disease

For many people, fear of illness or disease blocks their interest in reading about or researching it on their own—until the day they get a frightening test result or diagnosis. But your wellness program can combat the tendency toward denial by providing positive messages about the truly great impact that good health behaviors and early detection can have on disease avoidance—or at least on its after-the-fact treatment. Here are some ways to convey those messages:

- **Educate employees about the importance of screenings.** Few people are sure about which medical tests they need and when. The most important tests, at different ages, are shown on the chart below. (Note that the ages shown assume average risk; people at higher risk should, in most cases, undergo the tests earlier and more often, according to a doctor's advice.) In addition, the industry standard is to have an annual physical, at which the doctor performs certain tests and screenings such as measuring weight and blood pressure. While few people will come to a seminar to hear this information, you can transmit it in newsletters, fact sheets (perhaps on bulletin boards), emails, other mailings, at a health fair, and using posters, including gender-specific notices in the restrooms. The CDC (www.cdc.gov—click "Diseases & Conditions") offers fact sheets about various illnesses and screenings, including posters about the importance of screening for colorectal cancer (hopefully, it will make posters about other disease topics someday).

Colorectal Cancer
Screening Saves Lives

"*Now THAT I understand.*"

If you're over 50, get tested for colorectal cancer.

Polyps and colorectal cancer don't always cause symptoms. That's why screening is so important… screening helps find precancerous polyps, so they can be removed before they turn into cancer.

See your doctor and get screened.

- **Explain what your health insurance plan offers.** Your employees may not realize how many screenings are offered for free, or how easy they are to arrange. You won't be able to track whether individuals have had their screenings done, but you can ask your health plan for a summary of how many of your employees are showing up.

- **Educate employees about cold and flu symptoms and treatment.** Because of the lack of definitive cures for the cold or flu, rumors and home remedies abound. Many of these are fine—chicken soup never hurt anyone (except the chicken). But it's worth conveying information, whether in a health newsletter, workshop, or elsewhere, about often-misunderstood basics like how to tell a cold from the flu, why antibiotics won't help (unless a separate bacterial infection has also taken hold), which decongestants work (and which are risky for people with high blood pressure or heart disease), and more.

- **Remind people about proper hand hygiene.** Washing for a full 15 to 20 seconds in hot, soapy water is recommended. Washing works by literally getting the germs off one's hands, even if it doesn't kill them. You can find posters to put up by kitchen and bathroom sinks at the CDC website at www.cdc.gov/germstopper.

- **Provide information about child immunizations.** This has been a hot topic in the news lately. If you have many employees with children, you can bet that they're struggling with the decision of whether to immunize their children despite the rumored risks of autism and other problems. You could address this in writing, or bring in a highly qualified expert to dispel rumors, give a straightforward analysis, and answer questions.

- **Hold seminars about disease prevention strategies.** For example, there's a lot to know about cholesterol: how it's created within the body and its effect on cardiovascular health. Employees could also make good use of information about prevention, detection, and risk factors of the many types of cancer. Speakers might include a health care provider, a cancer survivor who can talk about the benefits of having caught the disease early through screening, and a nutritionist to give positive suggestions about cancer-preventive or cholesterol-healthy foods. If you're doing biometrics, it's helpful to schedule such seminars soon after everyone's results come in, when interest levels are high.

Recommended Health Screenings		
Test	Starting Age (for those with no obvious symptoms)	Frequency
Blood pressure	(No age minimum)	Every one to two years—the goal is to remain below 120/80.
Colorectal cancer screening (fecal occult blood test (FOBT), sigmoidoscopy, or colonoscopy)	50	FOBT every one to two years; sigmoidoscopy or colonoscopy at least every ten years
Cervical cancer screening (Pap smear)	21, or three years after becoming sexually active (women only)	Every one to three years for most women; depends on age and individual health factors
Breast cancer screening (mammogram)	40 (women only)	Every one to two years
Prostate cancer screening (physical exam or PSA blood test)	50 (men only)	Discuss with doctor; this topic is subject to controversy because some believe that the slow growth of many types of prostate cancer militates against aggressive screening and treatment.
Cholesterol	40	At least every five years
Diabetes	50	Every five years
Osteoporosis bone density scan	65 for women, 70 for men	Every two years or as recommended by doctor

- **Distribute written materials specific to the latest threats or outbreaks.** For example, if a pandemic flu arises or an outbreak of another contagious illness, such as tuberculosis or meningitis, occurs, employees should be warned of exactly what to look for, how to prevent catching the disease, how to seek treatment, and what your company expects them to do during the outbreak.

Activities: Flu Shots, Massages, and Blood Tests, Oh My

Some of these won't be the most fun things your wellness program asks your employees to do, but you can make people feel good about taking positive steps to safeguard their health.

- **HRAs.** As discussed in Chapter 3, HRAs are a good way to start off your wellness program. The vendor will normally remind people about screenings in the follow-up reports, based on each person's age and other health needs. And if your vendor also provides coaching services, the coach should provide ongoing recommendations about preventive care.
- **Biometric exams.** These are also discussed in Chapter 3 and commonly include screenings for cholesterol levels, blood glucose levels, and more. A good biometric report will direct people toward medical follow-up as needed.
- **Make seasonal flu shots readily available.** The best weapon against the ever-changing flu virus is immunization—preferably about six to eight weeks before the December-to-March flu season hits (it takes the immune system that long to respond). Flu shots are particularly important for anyone with heart disease, diabetes, kidney disease, asthma, or a depressed immune system or who is pregnant. Although scientists always do some guessing about which flu strains will arrive that year, the vaccine is usually effective against the major strains and safe for most people. (It uses a killed virus raised in an egg, so people with egg allergies need to stay away.) Depending on the number of employees, you may be able to hire a nurse to administer shots at your workplace. The cost is usually between $8 and $30 per employee. Or your

health insurer may provide flu shots for free, in which case you'll need to get creative about persuading employees to go—perhaps by offering a half day off to those getting their shots, helping to arrange carpools, or rewarding proof of immunization with a small prize.

- **Reward employees for getting their screenings.** If your wellness program operates on a points system, be sure to offer a generous number of points to those who complete their screening exams. (As as practical matter, for privacy reasons, this works only if employees either track their points on an honor system or you have a third party administering your wellness program.)

Preventing Repetitive Strain Injuries

We're assuming you already keep your workers informed of proper safety practices and that you address workplace safety issues. However, a particularly appropriate topic for your workplace wellness program is the type of injury that creeps up on people through repetitive activities. Whether someone works in a factory or a corporate office, doing the same thing day after day can lead to sore muscles, pinched nerves, and ultimately disabling conditions like carpal tunnel or thoracic outlet syndrome. The following activities can help:

- **Repetitive-injury prevention classes.** Consider holding classes on stretching exercises and encouraging stretch breaks. Try taking meeting breaks where someone leads people in stretches.
- **Offer ergonomic analyses of workstations.** An ill-fitting chair can be enough to cause injury in someone who is otherwise healthy and has good posture. Workers may not realize, for example, how little back support a chair is giving them and how their altered posture presses on nerves and reduces circulation as a result. Bringing in an ergonomics expert to analyze everyone's work setup can be invaluable.

> **TIP**
> **Your employees will love you for on-site massages.** Massage is useful for preventing or dealing with repetitive strain issues and for relieving stress. Even a ten-minute massage can help tired muscles and ligaments. You can split the costs with your employees and perhaps arrange group discounts.

Support: Helping Workers Help Themselves

Here are some ways to create a workplace environment that's conducive to maintaining good health. There's so much good information about how to prevent the spread of germs in your workplace that we've devoted a special section to the topic. See "It's Not Nice to Share Germs: Behind-the-Scenes Measures," below. Other ways to help employees include:

- **Buying a blood pressure cuff.** This lets people who know they have high blood pressure monitor their condition and lets others keep an eye on on their own. Adviser Rae Lee Olson explains, "We bought one in our office, knowing that few people would pay the $80 or so to buy a cuff for home use and might not visit the doctor regularly enough to keep tabs on their blood pressure. It sits in our fitness room, where people can use it at any time." Another option is to bring someone in periodically for blood pressure screenings, but the cuff will probably be cheaper in the long run.

- **Making it easy for people to get their screening exams done.** While it makes sense for large employers to do this with on-site screenings (such as mammogram vans), you may need to get more creative. For example, you might offer extra paid time off or other incentives.

- **Offering telework options where appropriate.** Someone suffering from a contagious cold or flu is sometimes happy to get work done at home—and may be able to accomplish a fair amount. This can also help employees who are either determined to get their job done or can't afford to miss a day.

It's Not Nice to Share Germs: Behind-the-Scenes Measures

Since 2001, adviser Dr. Gerba has been doing an annual study of germs in the workplace, including where they collect and how long they last. He looks not only at cold and flu germs, but at common viruses and bacteria found in the digestive tract, such as salmonella and shigella, and other cleanliness issues like mold. The good news, says Dr. Gerba, is that:

> *Germ levels in offices have been declining quite a bit. When we started, it seemed like no one was doing anything in the office to disinfect the space. Disinfectant products and cleaning sanitizers have made a big difference.*

Now for the bad news. Some areas of the office tend to be seriously germ ridden—as Dr. Gerba calls it, a "bacteria cafeteria." Among the worst spots are:

- **Office desktops.** He explains, "There's usually about 400 times more bacteria on the desktop than on a toilet seat, mainly because most facilities use disinfectants in the restroom areas. And also because so many people eat at their desks—half the employees in some offices we've visited. We can actually track the bacteria levels as they rise during the day, most likely from all the food that falls down and doesn't get cleaned up. And janitors won't do anything to clean the desktop, because it's personal space."

 TIP

Men's desks are cleaner than women's! According to Dr. Gerba, "We've found bacteria levels at women's desks to be three times higher than at men's. It's probably because a little over 70% of all women store food in their desks—about double the number of men."

- **Telephones.** These are used over and over again and come in close contact with both the hands and the mouth, creating a ready vehicle for germ transmission.

- **The restroom sink and taps.** "These are areas where we find salmonella and shigella. The reason is that when people wash their hands, the first thing they do is turn the water on, which can contaminate the tap. Even after washing, some organisms stick to the sides of the sink. Because the area is wet, the bacteria tend to survive a long time."

- **Office kitchens.** "What's really happened is that office coffee rooms have become like unregulated restaurants. You've got conditions in there that wouldn't pass a health department inspection. There are typically cloths and dish rags with bacteria growing, and every time someone wipes something, the bacteria gets spread around. In our studies, we found that 50% of all office cups had fecal bacteria in them, and we traced that to people wiping the cups off with sponges and dish cloths in the coffee prep area. Plus, 10% of the sponges we've tested indicate salmonella."

Now that you're seriously grossed out, we'll look at what can be done to make the office environment cleaner and healthier.

- **Provide wipes for hands.** In the absence of a nearby sink, both sick employees and others worried about whose hand they just shook will be happy to see a box of wipes. And the wipes will be especially useful in certain situations—for example, where you've got a morning receptionist who has a cold, with a lunchtime relief receptionist taking over the phones and coming into close contact with the same surfaces. Dr. Gerba recommends, "Choose a product with the word 'disinfecting wipe' on it, which means it's regulated by the Environmental Protection Agency and kills stuff that you're concerned about to a level that's deemed safe."

> 💡 **TIP**
> **No need to buy antibacterial soap.** The common cold and the flu are viruses, not bacteria, so an antibacterial soap is worthless against them. Besides, studies show that these soaps aren't all that effective against bacteria, either.

- **Give everyone a bottle of hand sanitizing gel or spray.** Dr. Gerba says, "This is my number one tip for what an employer can do to reduce absenteeism from colds and flu. You want to look for the word 'sanitizer.' It's regulated by the Food and Drug Administration, and means the product is effective."

- **Buy a dishwasher.** Now that you know what's on the office sponge, do you really want to eat off dishware that it has touched?

- **Scrub down commonly touched and horizontal surfaces.** Ask your cleaning person to carefully wipe or scrub all commonly touched surfaces such as doorknobs and light switches using clean water and detergent. Horizontal surfaces are important to clean frequently, because that's where droplets land after someone sneezes or coughs. Also, ask your maintenance folks to put a little extra effort into kitchen and bathroom sinks.

- **Replace coffee room or kitchen sponges regularly.** You can alternatively disinfect the sponges in the microwave or using a bleach solution, but for most busy offices, throwing them out and getting a fresh one is the most practical approach. Dr. Gerba recommends replacing them at least once a week.

- **Take a closer look at your coffee room or kitchen cleanliness.** If regular cleanings don't occur often enough to keep surfaces crud free, consider taking extra measures. For example, at Nolo, a rotating team of two people is responsible for cleaning the main kitchen twice a day each week, with precise instructions on which surfaces must be attended to. Neither seniority nor high position gets anyone out of this duty!

- **During a major outbreak of illness, seat people three feet apart at meetings.** That reduces the chances that they will cough or sneeze on each other or inadvertently touch each other's possessions.

- **Consider hiring a sanitizing service.** Dr. Gerba explains, "If your office is like others we've seen, the regular cleaning service may not be doing enough. These sanitizing services come in once a week and specialize in eliminating harmful viruses and bacteria. Companies like Swisher and Coverall Health Based-Cleaning

System are examples. They use persistent disinfectants that work pretty well from what we've seen."

TIP

What Dr. Gerba does to avoid catching office germs. "I have a bottle of sanitizer on my desk and ask people who are sick to use it. Also, I don't shake their hand. If a sick person shares my desk, I wipe the area down when they're done. If my door was closed before a sick person came in, I use a wipe on that, as well. Particularly during the cold and flu seasons, I get a little paranoid. But I've learned that if I do those things, I can usually avoid a cold."

Healthy Eating and Nutrition

Meet Your Adviser

Dr. Preston Maring, a primary care physician at Kaiser Permanente in California.

What he does: With 38 years of experience in obstetrics and gynecology, Dr. Maring treats patients and promotes wellness through good nutrition. He's a vocal advocate in the health care industry, for using locally farmed, organic produce and he initiated the hugely successful Friday farmers' markets outside Kaiser Permanente medical facility locations. At home, Dr. Maring is a skilled cook with a passion for food and participates in a men's poetry group.

Favorite healthy food: "A Meyer lemon vinaigrette. I'm very fortunate to have generous good friends with an amazing Meyer lemon tree. I squeeze a lemon or two into a jar; mince then mash in a clove or two of garlic with some Kosher salt; let sit; add extra virgin olive oil to equal the amount of lemon juice; shake; and add a few grinds of black pepper. I often use this as a dressing for a one-dish meal of farro, diced tomatoes, baby arugula or spinach, and some kind of sauteed protein. It's also my "go to" vinaigrette for any kind of salad—arugula, sliced celery with shaved parmesan, or butter lettuce."

Top tip for staying fit and healthy: "Eat fruits and vegetables of many different colors and don't worry about the details."

Thanks to the paychecks you give out, your workers probably aren't going hungry. But what they're eating is another matter. The widespread availability of cheap but junky sweets, sodas, snacks, and fast food means that many Americans (whether underweight or overweight) are going without the important nutrients they need.

Your workplace may be contributing to the problem by providing unhealthy snacks at meetings or by tempting workers with vending machines full of enticing, but nutritionally empty, choices. Whether you're providing the food or not, the fact is that most workers eat at least one of their meals and snacks while at work, and often more. As an employer, you might not be able to tell people what to eat, but there are lots of things you can do to encourage and support better nutrition at work. Better yet, helping your employees to eat right may be good for your bottom line—in more ways than one.

In this chapter, we'll examine:

- how nutrition impacts health and wellness, and
- what your workplace can do to promote healthy eating.

The Connection: Poor Nutrition Equals Poor Health

In the words of adviser Dr. Preston Maring, "What's more important to good health than what we eat?" Food is literally the building block with which we create and maintain healthy muscles, organs, and tissues. Good nutrition bolsters the immune system and wards off diseases, all the while enabling our bodies to efficiently store and use energy; regulate hormones and mood; and much more.

Poor eating habits not only deprive the body of important benefits, but can lead directly to health problems. The most obvious one is obesity, which is widely considered one of the gravest public health problems currently facing the United States. According to the U.S. Centers for Disease Control and Prevention (CDC), obesity increases the risk of coronary heart disease, Type 2 diabetes, many cancers, hypertension, high cholesterol, stroke, liver and gallbladder disease, sleep apnea and respiratory problems, osteoarthritis, and gynecological problems (including abnormal menstrual cycles and infertility).

But even for people who don't become overweight or obese, poor nutrition leads directly to numerous health problems. For example, the American Institute for Cancer Research (AICR) says that diet (along with regular exercise and maintaining a healthy weight) is one of the three essential components of cancer prevention. The National Institutes of Health (NIH) says that, "eating well may reduce the risk of heart disease, stroke, Type 2 diabetes, bone loss, some kinds of cancer, and anemia."

Dr. Maring elaborates:

> *Having been a primary care physician for 38 years, and having cared for some patients for many years, it's clear to me that what people eat drives so many aspects of their health. A healthy, normal-weight person at age 65 is still going to be running all over the place, potentially productive, as opposed to someone whose body mass index is 35 or 40, who can hardly move. So many metabolic diseases, joint problems, pain problems, hormonal problems, and heart disease problems are related to what people eat. Obviously, some troubles come from genetics—and people can't really change that—but you can do something about what you eat every day.*

We could go on, but you get the point—in fact, you probably already knew, as most of your employees do, that eating well has many health benefits. But as anyone who's ever tried to change a habit will report, there's often a disconnect between what we know and what we do. That's why you, as an employer, can play an important role in bringing about employee awareness of both the importance and the pleasures of healthy eating.

Promoting Good Nutrition in Your Workplace

Your job may not be as hard as it looks. In fact, many employers, when asked about their workplace wellness program, are especially excited to talk about the successes of their nutrition program. Adviser Rae Lee Olsen, at Vita Benefits Group, for example, says:

> *Our office is sort of isolated, so getting healthy food at lunch was a hassle for people. We decided to start buying the ingredients for every employee to have a healthy breakfast and lunch, every day. Now we have a fully stocked refrigerator and kitchen, which we refill every Monday. It's like a salad bar refrigerator, full of fresh fruits (we have blenders with which to make smoothies), vegetables, fresh breads, sandwich meat, condiments, and more. It's become an important part of our culture and our wellness program, and costs us between $100 and $120 per employee per month. I probably wouldn't eat nearly as much salad otherwise, even though I love salads.*

For another success story, see "Candy Sold for Charity Is Still Candy," below.

To promote good nutrition in your workplace, there are three important things you can provide:

- nutrition education and skill building
- relevant activities or follow-up, and
- a workplace environment that supports, rather than detracts from, good nutritional habits.

In addition, your employees may have been given specific nutritional or weight loss recommendations after taking their HRAs upon entering your wellness program. Your job is not to make them comply with these, but to help make it easy and fun for them to do so. (We'll talk separately, in Chapter 10, about program elements to address obesity issues.)

CAUTION

Are your employees too busy for a lunch break? That's true of about 15% of workers, many of whom rely on vending machines to satisfy their hunger. You'll need to address such issues separately, either by reassigning work or assuring people that the company won't collapse—in fact, its output is likely to go up—if they take a lunch break.

Education: What's a Trans Fat?

Before you can help your employees eat better, you and they need to have some idea of what good nutrition is. As Dr. Maring notes, some experts look at nutrition "in a very scientific, food-as-medicine way, down to how much lycopenes or omega-3s or selenium you're getting." But keeping up with the latest studies can wear you out: One year, fats are supposedly the great evil, while the next year "good fats" are in favor and carbohydrates are vilified. One year, tofu is said to cure all manner of diseases, and the next year it's suspect.

Unless your business is nutrition science, there's no need to chase down all the details. Certain basic truths have long held steady. For example, no one has ever said fruits, vegetables, and fiber are bad for you. In fact, the current recommendation, which is worth repeating to your employees, is that everyone eat five servings of fruits and vegetables every day.

You can't get much simpler, more straightforward advice than that provided by noted journalist Michael Pollan, whose book *In Defense of Food: An Eater's Manifesto* answers the question of what we should eat as follows:

- **"Eat food."** As Pollan describes, this means real food, not that which is processed, refined, or laden with substances like high fructose corn syrup, trans fats, or chemicals our ancestors would not have recognized.
- **"Not too much."** We each bear responsibility for how much we eat, but Pollan also makes the interesting point that U.S. food marketers have put a great deal of energy into coaxing Americans to put many of the surplus calories that are being produced right into their stomachs.
- **"Mostly plants."** Pollan advocates doing your body and the farming system a favor by going heavy on organic fruits and vegetables, and light on meats—though, notably, he argues that certain fats—while still caloric—are not as inherently unhealthy as they've been made out to be. Better fats include those found in nuts and seeds, salmon and other cold-water fish (but

watch out for fish with high levels of mercury), and avocados. Unfortunately, there's no way around the truth that trans fats—included in processed foods to extend shelf life, and therefore most of the items in your average vending machine—are terrible for you.

If you haven't already read Pollan's book, we recommend that you do so, and then leave your copy in the employee lunch or break room, or health library, if you have one. You might even post his three main bits of advice on your office bulletin board.

In fact, we recommend focusing your educational efforts not on what's right or wrong with particular foods, but simply on helping your employees find easy ways to incorporate a wider variety of natural, unprocessed, plant-based foods into their daily diets. It doesn't have to be complicated. Relatively simple changes can make a big difference in most employees' diets.

What types of educational or skill-building programs should you choose? It depends partly on your workplace culture and people's starting points. As adviser Dr. Doug Metz explains:

> *If you're in a work environment where most people live on steak and potatoes, starting with posters about eating a healthy, plant-based diet will not make a dent in anyone's thinking or habits. However, posters about how to manage portions while eating steak and potatoes is a place to start, and then you can gradually add more information over time.*

Dr. Maring suggests that your educational efforts include a cooking class with recipes for healthy eating. He says:

> *It could be a way for people to get to know each other, celebrate the diversity of their workplace with international recipes, and learn practical tools for good health. Think of what a powerful message that would be for any company to say, 'We care about your health, we know that food is critically important to your health, and here's a fun way to think about getting started.' Plus, cooking at home is good for personal family economy. A family can easily cut 10% off their food budget by cooking at home.*

> **CAUTION**
> **Don't focus on weight loss.** Healthy eating will, for many people, naturally lead to weight loss. But you'll attract more participation in your nutrition program if you stick with a positive approach, emphasizing the joys of healthy eating, rather than a "you should eat less" message. If appropriate, your company can subsidize separate weight loss seminars or opportunities for any employees whose HRA report or doctor recommended weight loss as a priority, as discussed in Chapter 10.

Here are some other ways to provide information about good nutrition:

- **Provide tips and healthy recipes.** You can add these to your office health newsletter or emails.
- **Include a nutrition booth if you hold a health fair.** Here, you can pass out pamphlets on healthy eating, tasty samples, and more.
- **Show DVDs.** Good ones to include are *Dr. Andrew Weil's Guide to Eating Well* (80 minutes) or the popular feature-length films *Fast Food Nation* and *Supersize Me.*
- **Stock your library.** If you're developing a health library for employees' use, make sure it includes helpful cookbooks and nutrition books and videos.
- **Bring in speakers.** For example, you might invite a nutritionist to discuss how to eat healthy during a 12-hour workday.

Your educational efforts might also focus on helping people observe what's stopping them from eating right, even when they know what types of foods they should be eating. Common culprits include long work hours, lack of sleep, and stress, including work-based stress. "People tend to eat if they're stressed," says Dr. Maring, "and if you're running a small business right now, in this economy, there's going to be stress. I'm just thinking of what happens on my own floor when things are going nuts—somebody's got a jar full of those little Halloween candies, and they become hard to resist."

If employees have a better sense of why they choose unhealthy foods, they'll have a better chance of turning around their habits. This is especially true if the larger workplace community supports more mindful eating. The rest of this chapter focuses on providing the encouragement and support your employees will need to make changes.

> **TIP**
>
> **Can your employees buy healthy food where they live?** A number of studies have shown that in low-income neighborhoods, fast food restaurants are the norm, while grocery stores with fresh and affordable produce are nearly impossible to find. If you know that the majority of your employees live in neighborhoods where healthy food is scarce, you can help by identifying resources in their area, such as small groceries with good selections of fresh produce or farmers' markets. Or create a list of good grocery stores or farmers' markets near your office, and allow some flexibility to shop during the lunch hour. The more options you can turn up, the better, for purposes of selection as well as price comparison.

Activities: What's for Lunch?

You'll have no problem introducing the fun factor into program activities that feature food. Everyone loves food. (No, we don't have a statistic to back that up, but you've probably noticed how many more people attend a meeting if you promise a free lunch or snacks.) Although sugary or junky food might draw people faster than healthy food, participants will soon discover how delicious, even decadent, healthy food can taste.

Here are some possible activities to incorporate into your wellness program:

- **Healthy foods potlucks.** Arrange employee lunches or parties at which everyone is encouraged to contribute a homemade dish made from a health-focused cookbook.
- **Recipe contests.** Ask employees to bring in their favorite healthy dish, with a copy of the recipe. Winning is based on nutritional content and tastiness. Print up and distribute the recipes—at least the winning ones.

- **Seasonally themed food events.** For example, you could have cooking demonstrations on how to healthy up a Valentine's Day chocolate cake or a Thanksgiving dinner.
- **A "five servings" challenge.** Dr. Metz explains this activity, which is offered at his workplace and to its wellness program clients (as the "Fruit and Veggie Challenge®"): "Employees who sign up are given the challenge rules, a log book, as well as a booklet explaining the importance of the five daily servings of fruit and vegetables, with recommendations on how to choose among them, and definitions of 'serving size.' In addition, they're given five silicon, colored wrist bands. Each time they consume one serving they move a band from one wrist to the other. As they go through the day, seeing other employees with the wrist bands is a great conversation piece and motivator. At the end of the day, if all the bands have been moved, then they've met their goal for that day and record their success in their log book. Everyone who meets the total goal (a certain number of days of eating all five servings) by the completion date (both of which the employer sets) receives an incentive gift."
- **Personal food diaries.** Pass out forms for employees to record their fruit and vegetable intake at work and home. This is particularly important because it helps people notice whether there are certain times of the day that their will power dips, or when stress makes them reach for a candy bar.
- **A food-tasting exercise.** One of the most important ways to enjoy healthy food is, according to Dr. Pelletier, to "slow down and taste it—unlike so many people who wolf down food at their desks, often eating past the point of fullness because their mind literally hasn't caught up with their body." Someone on your own staff can lead workers, perhaps at a meeting, through the following exercise: Place small items of healthy food, such as fruit slices, berries, or raisins, in front of everyone. Ask them to eat a few while imagining that they're on a deadline. Then ask them

to imagine that they've got lots of time, and pick up another piece—but not eat it yet. First, ask them to balance it on their palm, look it over, and enjoy the aroma. Then they should place it in their mouth, feel the first hints of flavor on their tongue, bite down carefully, and finally chew slowly, paying attention to flavor. "This simple exercise," says Dr. Pelletier, "can surprise people with how much pleasure they've been missing, and lay a basis for a healthier approach to food."

- **Individual coaching.** If you're bringing in outside providers to provide comprehensive wellness services, these may well include helping your employees, particularly those with health or weight problems, to modify their eating habits. Adviser Dr. Janet Greenhut notes, "The best programs are personalized for the individual. For example, if somebody has a poor diet, there could be a variety of issues; the person may be eating a lot of fat or not many fruits and vegetables. A good coaching program will address those needs."

TIP

Celebrations can be fun without being decadent. As Jackie Grabin, co-president of Arrow Exterminating Company in Lynbrook, New York, explains, "We always have a kickoff lunch when our busy season starts. It used to be at an Italian place with lots of bread, fried zucchini, and clams—and those were just the appetizers! Now we've started going to a place with a great salad bar, and we still have a terrific time."

Once you've held a few enjoyable activities, ideas will no doubt emerge for future events. Who knows, maybe some of your employees will band together for a regular healthy potluck club or simply start exchanging recipes on a regular basis.

Candy Sold for Charity Is Still Candy

For years, the lunch table at Buffalo Supply, a wholesaler of hospital equipment based in Lafayette, Colorado, always offered candy for sale, with the proceeds going to a local charity. "But people started realizing—even without any formal wellness program in place—that this just wasn't healthy," says Kara Parker, their vice president of finance and human resources.

"Fortunately, we try to have an open environment here, so that when people have ideas, we bounce them around and look at the feasibility of making a change. What we ended up doing was stopping the charitable sales and replacing them with a free, daily supply of fresh fruits and vegetables. If people's kids are selling candy, we don't restrict that, but at least it's no longer a constant supply. We spend between $40 and $80 a week on the fruit and veggies. If things aren't eaten, we buy a little less."

Support: Where'd the Doughnuts Go?

Take a look around your workplace. Do you see big pink boxes that held doughnuts for a morning meeting, jars of candy for sharing, packaging from fast food lunches that your employees picked up, or a vending machine full of candy bars and chips? If so, don't be too embarrassed—yours is a typical workplace. But it may also be worsening your employees' health.

Temptation is always hard to resist, but if you can shift some of those temptations to healthy foods, you'll be taking an enormously powerful step toward workplace wellness. Here are some simple steps that will help you reorient your workplace environment:

- **Drop the doughnuts.** "The worst food in the world is high-trans fat doughnuts," says Dr. Maring. If you traditionally bring food to meetings, he suggests replacing junk food with whole grain bagels or other low-fat baked goods, yogurt, granola, and fresh or dried fruit.

- **Put out fresh fruit for snacks.** You can't tell everyone to put away their candy jars, but you can provide healthy alternatives. It doesn't cost much to fill a bowl with fruit. Dr. Maring notes, "The best salespeople for good nutrition are the fruits and vegetables themselves." Ask your local grocer what's in season, and have fun trying out items like kiwi fruit or pluots. Or, if you'd rather someone else do the shopping, see whether The Fruit Guys, or a similar outfit, operates in your area—they specialize in delivering farm-fresh produce to business offices (www. fruitguys.com). As Dr. Maring adds, "I really do think the idea of delivering fresh fruit, having it available in the back rooms and break rooms, courtesy of the boss, is the beginning of a message that we care about you, these are tasty and healthy. It also gives the boss a chance to put an imprimatur on what they think about the environment, going green, and supporting local farmers. It says volumes about the boss putting money where his or her mouth is." If ongoing fruit supplies are more than your company can afford or manage, do as ten-person Frett Barrington does, and schedule regular "Fruit Fests." Patty Frett explains, "We bring in fresh fruit for people to snack on every two weeks during the summer, and schedule it right on our wellness calendar."
- **Redistribute some holiday sweets.** Your office may be deluged by temptation during the holidays, particularly if you receive gifts of candy and cookies from customers and vendors. This is often the case at Frett Barrington where, Patty Frett says, "In response, we started a program called "Sweet Relief," where our wellness committee puts out healthy alternative snacks like hummus and pita, or vegetables and dip. That lets us leave some of the packages of sugary treats unopened. We encourage people to take these to family holiday gatherings where they can be shared among a greater number of people."
- **Fill vending machines with healthy food choices.** The average machine contains chips, chocolate bars, and soft drinks, which tend to be high in sugar, fat, and salt, and low in nutritional value and fiber. But vending machine companies offer more

and more options, particularly in refrigerated machines. And experience has shown that people will buy healthier snacks if they're available and comparable in price to other options. You may need to rotate different healthy snacks until you find which ones sell best in your office. Chocolate milk, fruit juices, string cheese and peanuts usually sell well. Dr. Maring describes Kaiser Permanente's experience with this:

> *We did a trial a couple of years ago, where in some vending machines we replaced the existing snacks with 25% healthy picks, replaced 50% in other machines, and 100% in the rest. We found that the revenues didn't really change, even when the machine was filled with 100% healthier choices.*

See "Choosing Healthy Vending Machine Snacks," below, for guidance.

TIP

Got a cafeteria? We're assuming your business isn't large enough to have an employee cafeteria, but if you do, that's obviously a great place to implement good nutrition principles. Try to offer a wide and attractive array of fruit, vegetable, whole grain, unprocessed, and other healthy food and drinks, prominently displayed, and accompanied by health information. French fries should never be the only starch option!

- **Make it easy for employees to bring their own lunch.** This helps people avoid local fast food joints or other restaurants with dubious offerings. A lunchroom outfitted with a refrigerator, microwave, toaster oven, and plates and silverware is ideal.
- **Create an outdoor seating area.** If your workplace has access to outdoor space, adding a table and chairs will encourage employees to eat together, bring their own lunch, and get a little fresh air.
- **Use healthy caterers for company events.** Don't be shy about asking your regular caterer for nutrition information and suggestions.

Choosing Healthy Vending Machine Snacks

The following items are commonly offered by vending machine companies. They provide reasonable nutritional benefits with reduced health risks—though many of them are still processed foods, which are less than ideal:

Beverages

- 2%, 1%, skim, and chocolate milk
- 100% fruit juice
- vegetable juice

Nonrefrigerated food

- whole grain crackers
- pretzels
- canned fruit
- baked chips, soy crisps
- cereal bars
- fruit bars
- nuts, sunflower seeds, peanuts
- dried fruit
- trail mix
- healthy soup or chili in a cup

Refrigerated food

- fresh fruit cups
- whole fruit
- vegetable sticks
- salads with low-fat dressing on the side
- low-fat cheese
- yogurt
- sandwiches made with whole grain bread and lean meat

If you decide to maintain a mix of healthy and other food in your vending machine, we suggest placing the healthy food at eye level, with a sticker next to it indicating that it's a healthy choice. You might also poll your employees about which healthy choices to include, and send out a memo explaining the change when it happens.

You can even switch caterers if necessary. The catering industry is well aware of people's interest in healthy, as well as organic, locally grown, and sustainable food, and many caterers are taking impressive steps to meet the demand. For help choosing menus, see "Catering a Healthy Meal," below.

- **Create a policy *limiting* fundraising candy sales in the office.** See "Candy Sold for Charity Is Still Candy," above. This depends on your company culture, but if you're seeing a constant stream of candy, this may need to be addressed. (The charities will soon get the message that it's not fair to promote the social good with temptations that may ultimately harm health.) But don't try banning candy jars on people's desks, or you'll breed resentment and resistance.

- **Offer healthy food items as incentives within your workplace wellness program.** For example, people who participate or meet goals within your program might be motivated by gift certificates to a healthy restaurant; free delivery of a box of fresh fruits and vegetables from a CSA (Community Supported Agriculture; see www.localharvest.org/csa/ or www.nal.usda.gov/afsic/pubs/csa/csa.shtml for more information and links to local CSAs) grower; or a healthy-recipe cookbook.

TIP

Freshness matters. While some processed foods are rumored to have a shelf life of 20 years or more, fresh fruits and vegetables start losing their nutritional value and good flavor as soon as they're picked. To maximize the flavor of your offerings, buy from local farmers whenever you can. Produce picked when it's ripe always tastes best. And keep an eye on the freshness of what you serve. At catered events, make sure the food doesn't sit around for more than half an hour before serving.

Catering a Healthy Meal

Here are some basic principles to follow when planning a catered meal or snack for a workplace event.

- **Breakfast.** Include one serving of whole fruit per person, plus whole grain, low-fat breads and muffins, yogurts, and cereal or muesli. Instead of the ubiquitous, year-round watermelon, pineapple, and cantaloupe, which is shipped from afar and never tastes good, look for fresh, local, seasonal fruits.

- **Lunch.** For sandwiches or wraps, avoid white bread and ask the caterer to go light on the mayo, butter, and other high-fat spreads. For interesting alternatives, consider sushi, frittatas, bean or vegetable soups, and mixed green salads, with chicken, turkey, or beans for protein (and dressing on the side).

- **Dinner or hot entrees.** Choose broiled, baked, grilled, stir-fried, or roasted options rather than fried or deep fried. Tomato sauces make a light alternative to butter or cheese. Avoid huge portions, and have meatless options available. Enchiladas, curries, and stews are often good for minimizing meat and incorporating lots of vegetables.

- **Beverages.** Have pitchers of water and drinking glasses readily available. (Bottled water leads to excessive waste, and in most cases is no healthier than tap water.) Offer pure fruit juice (or juice mixed with sparkling water) instead of sodas. Coffee and tea(s) are okay, but put out milk instead of cream or artificial substitutes.

- **Vegetarian and other alternatives.** Even if none of your staff are strictly vegetarian, some may appreciate a nonmeat alternative. You may also want to poll your staff about eating restrictions—some employees may be vegans, gluten-intolerant, or avoid certain other foods.

- **Snacks.** Good options include raw vegetables with hummus, salsa, or yogurt dips; dried fruit and nuts; and unbuttered/unsweetened popcorn, seasoned with herbs.

- **Dessert.** Go with fruit kebabs, angel food cake, baked apples, or recipes that have been specially adapted to minimize sugar and fats.

It's also wise to post or pass out the menus, so that people know what they're eating and recognize your efforts to provide healthy food.

Fitness and Exercise

Meet Your Adviser

 **Dr. Robert Sallis,** a board-certified family physician with Kaiser Permanente in Southern California, who holds a Certificate of Added Qualifications in sports medicine.

What he does: When he's not treating patients of all ages, Dr. Sallis enjoys serving as team physician for local college and high school sports programs, as well as teaching medical students, residents, and sports medicine fellows. He also chairs the Science Advisory Committee to the California Governor's Council on Physical Fitness and Sports. Dr. Sallis currently serves as immediate past president of the American College of Sports Medicine, the largest sports and exercise science organization in the word. In this role, he developed and continues to lead an international initiative called "Exercise Is Medicine," which strives to make exercise assessment and prescription a standard part of the disease prevention and treatment paradigm around the world.

Favorite healthy food: "Fresh sushi."

Top tip for staying fit and healthy: "Engaging in 30 minutes of moderate exercise (like a brisk walk) every day is the single best thing you can do for your health and longevity. Exercise *is* medicine!"

I f you'd been running a business in 1900, the most serious health concerns for your employees would probably have been tuberculosis, pneumonia, and infectious diarrhea—in other words, contagious diseases. That picture has completely changed. Today, the major U.S. health concerns are heart disease, cancer, and stroke. What do those have in common? They're all linked to physical inactivity and can be offset by regular, moderate exercise.

And those aren't the only medical conditions that are either exacerbated by inactivity, improved by regular exercise, or both. Across the board, adviser Dr. Robert Sallis says, "The lower people's activity levels, the higher their level of doctors' visits and health claims. We often call it the 'sedentary death syndrome,' because your chances of dying prematurely are dramatically enhanced if you're inactive, and your risk of developing chronic diseases, like diabetes, cancer, hypertension, osteoporosis, dementia, and cardiovascular disease, is dramatically worsened." No wonder he refers to physical fitness as "the fountain of youth" and has dedicated much of his career to helping the medical establishment and others come to see exercise as just another form of medicine—in fact, one of the cheapest, most easily accessible forms of medicine around.

As an employer running a workplace wellness program, there is perhaps no more important thing you can do than to include a fitness component. Even without surveying your employees, chances are good their level of fitness could be improved—unless you're in that rare workplace, such as a bike shop or health club, where everyone is already dedicated to fitness. And for the truly sedentary among your employees, it's no exaggeration to say that their health prospects get worse with every passing year.

This chapter will acquaint you with some of the latest information about how regular activity contributes to good health. (Even if you're already convinced, you'll be surprised by some of the statistics!) We'll then lay out affordable ways to include fitness elements in your workplace wellness program.

TIP

Understand the distinction between fitness and weight loss. True, one benefit of getting fit may be losing weight. But, as Dr. Sallis cautions, "If we focus solely on our weight we're missing the boat. Honestly, you're better off being moderately overweight and fit than being at normal weight and sedentary. It's a mistake to think that because the scale says you're not overweight that you're fit and not at increased risk for chronic diseases. The sedentary folks are more at risk than the mildly obese folks." Whether or not we need to lose weight, getting fit is key.

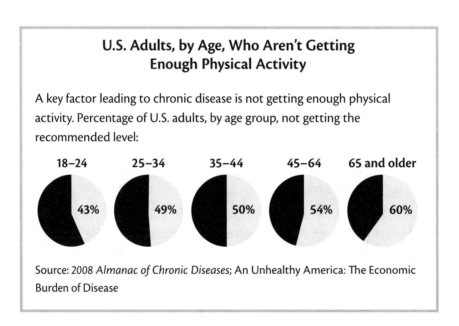

U.S. Adults, by Age, Who Aren't Getting Enough Physical Activity

A key factor leading to chronic disease is not getting enough physical activity. Percentage of U.S. adults, by age group, not getting the recommended level:

18–24	25–34	35–44	45–64	65 and older
43%	49%	50%	54%	60%

Source: *2008 Almanac of Chronic Diseases*; An Unhealthy America: The Economic Burden of Disease

The Connection: Inactivity and Poor Health

When it comes to the medical effects of inactivity, Dr. Robert Sallis doesn't pull any punches: He calls inactivity "the biggest public health problem of our time." And he's got the research to back it up. Here are a few of his favorite tidbits:

- It costs at least $1,500 more per year to provide health care for an inactive patient than for an active one.
- People who exercise report catching fewer common colds than those who are inactive.
- A study of people diagnosed with clinical depression found that those who did 180 minutes of exercise a week, either on a treadmill or a stationary bike, showed a 40% improvement. That's similar to the improvement level provided by anti-depressants like Prozac.
- Regular physical activity prevents or delays the development of high blood pressure and reduces blood pressure in people with hypertension.
- Regular physical activity also lowers the risk of developing noninsulin-dependent diabetes, colon cancer, breast cancer, and heart disease.
- People who exercise during the workday are notably more productive and less stressed out than those who don't.

Convinced yet? Now consider the everyday benefits of physical activity, including better sleep, clearer thinking, increased agility and flexibility, and the satisfaction of looking and feeling good. And we didn't even mention the studies on nonworking-age people—for example, children (who do better in school if they're physically fit) or the elderly (whose Alzheimer's rates are lowered by exercise).

As Dr. Sallis reiterates, "Studies show that people who are fit and active are more productive at work and have less absenteeism—and certainly their health care costs are significantly less." For example, one study showed that employees with a high participation rate in fitness activities missed 4.8 fewer work days per year than employees whose participation in fitness activities was low or nonexistent. (See Lechner, et. al., "Effects of an Employee Fitness Program on Reduced Absenteeism," *Journal of Occupational and Environmental Medicine,* (1997) Vol. 39, No. 9.)

Why Aren't They Working Out Already?

Blame modern life. Your employees are probably juggling competing demands as workers, spouses or partners, parents, caregivers, homeowners, and more. (Let's not forget book club members, gardeners, aspiring novelists, and hobbyists!) This leaves little time or energy for a workout routine—in fact, by late evening, many of your workers may be in a state of near collapse.

As the overseer of your employees' daytime hours, however, you're in a great position to carve out exercise time while people still have some energy. In fact, many workers report that it's a great relief to be able to dedicate time to themselves alone during the day, perhaps at the lunch hour, away from clamoring kids or hungry pets.

Promoting Fitness and Exercise in Your Workplace

As adviser Dr. Doug Metz says, "I believe that fitness, consisting of physical activity and consistent exercise, is the most important health improvement activity and an important cornerstone of your wellness program. If you can get a population of employees regularly active, it helps manage stress, increases calorie burn, helps those trying to stop using tobacco, and more. And there are a lot of inexpensive ways to do this."

Where do you start? The wide range of beneficial physical activities means that all employers should be able to find ways to engage their employees. The space and amenities available at your workplace will obviously play a role in your program planning. For example, if you want to host on-site classes, you'll need a large room. And if you'll be arranging activities where people sweat a lot, such as aerobics classes or a running club, it's helpful if you can offer showers afterward, or at least a place to change clothes. Your next best bet is to schedule these activities at the end of the day so that people can go home to shower.

Some workers may already be getting some exercise on the job—for example, food servers or childcare providers who are on their feet all day. This counts as moderate exercise, but even those with active jobs might appreciate a chance to work other muscles, or stretch out the overused ones with yoga or similar training.

Adding team sport activities to your slate of options might work for your employees and offer side benefits to your business, too. Team sports give people a chance to build camaraderie and learn to get along in a nonwork context.

> **TIP**
>
> **Is there anyone who shouldn't exercise?** No—unless they're in the middle of an acute illness like the flu. Disability, pregnancy, and chronic illness are no bar to exercise, though they may require adjustments to the person's exercise methods, movements, or intensity. In fact, cancer survivors, people with arthritis, stroke victims, and others have all been shown to benefit tremendously from exercise. Anyone who is unsure should consult his or her doctor.

Education: What's So Great About Fitness?

Although some of the health effects of inactivity are scary, you can deliver a positive message to your employees: No matter what disease or illness worries them most, there's a good chance that becoming more physically fit will either reduce their chances of getting it or help them survive it. Here are some ways to deliver that message:

- **Put up posters.** The Exercise Is Medicine website offers a nice one (for free) at www.exerciseismedicine.org. (Click "Public," then under "Additional Resources," click "Public Service Announcements" and choose the poster for "Consumers.") More are available from the Eat Smart Move More initiative in North Carolina. (Go to www.eatsmartmovemorenc.com, click "Programs and Tools for Change," then "Worksite," then "more tools and resources," then "Motivational Posters.")

- **Teach the FITT concept.** According to the latest guidelines, people can get the biggest bang for their exercise buck by paying attention to the frequency, intensity, type, and time of their exercise (FITT). The frequency should be at least five days a week, although seven is better. The intensity can be moderate, meaning that you couldn't sing while exercising, but can still talk. (More intense exercise, however, can reduce the amount of time you need to spend on it.) The type of exercise, according to Dr. Sallis, "can be just about anything: dancing, gardening, or walking the dog—so long as you're working out large muscle groups and getting a bit winded." And here's the most interesting—and perhaps encouraging—part: The ideal time should be 150 minutes a week total, but it's okay to break that down into sessions as short as ten minutes at a time!

- **Explain the importance of weight-bearing exercise.** It's crucial for healthy bones and the prevention of osteoporosis. "So," Dr. Sallis explains, "while swimming is great for the heart, you should also lift some weights and walk to exercise the bones of your upper and lower limbs."

- **Pass out walking maps or booklets.** Do your employees know what streets or paths are pleasant to walk on near your worksite, or what recreational areas are nearby? Even in urban areas, you may find that someone has developed handy walking guides. Do an online search, or check with your chamber of commerce or local bookstore.

- **Show educational DVDs.** The Exercise Is Medicine website offers a number of short ones about the benefits of fitness (and risks of inactivity) via YouTube.com, contain powerful ways to motivate your employees during a lunch hour.

- **Make sure fitness concepts are covered in your employee newsletter.** If you're subscribing to a newsletter from an outside source, it probably covers fitness. If you're writing it in house, look for inspirational material on www.exerciseismedicine.org or the President's Council on Physical Fitness website (www.fitness.gov), which includes a calculator to help people estimate their current fitness level and track improvements.

TIP

Do your employees travel for work? Keeping up with fitness goals can be a challenge on the road. Check out the tips offered by the Mayo Clinic at www.mayoclinic.com. (Search for "traveling for work," and you'll find the article "Traveling for business? Work in a workout.") For example, it suggests wearing walking shoes during travel and walking through airports or train stations; checking into hotel facilities in advance and packing swimsuits or workout gear accordingly; and packing a jump rope or an exercise DVD.

Activities: Groups, Games, Gyms? Yes!

The question isn't really what types of activities would promote fitness among your employees, but how to narrow down your options. Whether sports leagues, gym memberships, or in-house classes, you're sure to find activities that fit your workplace's culture and resources—preferably more than one. As Dr. Sallis notes, "What works for one person doesn't work for everyone; you need a menu plan."

Hopefully, you've already narrowed down the list to some extent, based on what you found out about your employees' personal interests (as described in Chapter 3). Below are some activity suggestions that have worked well at other businesses. Be sure to choose activities for people at different levels of fitness. For example, if you bring in a boot-camp style aerobics instructor one evening, bring in a beginning-level instructor on another. Also, give very precise instructions on what people should bring—such as comfortable sweat pants and a towel.

Our top suggestions include:

- **Form a walking group.** Walking is by far one of the most popular workplace wellness activities. It requires no special training, no equipment other than comfortable shoes, and it offers a chance to get outdoors and socialize with coworkers. The planned activity can be as simple as saying "The walking group meets at this time every day: Join in!" Or you might, for example, create competitions for who has walked the most during a month.

> **TIP**
>
> **Is it too hot or cold outside to walk?** If the climate where you work becomes prohibitively hot or cold during certain seasons, you might help organize carpools—or offer up the company van—to shuttle people to a better walking environment. (Realistically, your only choice may be the local mall; remind people to steer clear of the food court!) Joline Woodward of the Metropolitan Milwaukee Association of Commerce (MMAC) says that since their wellness program began, people in her office have gotten so committed to walking that even during cold Wisconsin winters, "they'll either bundle up and head outside or walk in the parking garage below our building."

- **Launch a stair-climbing challenge.** Create teams and see which can climb the most stairs in one month, for a prize. Or make it a competition between individuals. This is another simple one, because the only equipment you need is stairs. You might style it as a "skyscraper climbing challenge"—in which participants try to climb the same number of steps as in famous structures like the Empire State Building (approximately 2,000 steps). This idea comes from state of Texas; see their further suggestions at www.dshs.state.tx.us/wellness. (Click "Worksite Wellness," then "Worksite Wellness Resources," then "Skyscraper Climb.")
- **Hold outdoor scavenger hunts.** They're a favorite among the 35 employees at the MMAC. Joline Woodward explains: "The idea is that people walk around downtown Milwaukee looking for answers to questions like, 'What type of symbol is on this building?' or 'What color flag do you see?' We regularly hold these scavenger hunts, usually once a week for around seven weeks. If you successfully complete six of the seven hunts, you get an extra vacation day."
- **Organize sports leagues.** If your company is large enough, you might field your own softball, soccer, or other team. (Some communities sponsor more unusual team activities, like kick ball—something uncommon or purely playful might encourage employees to turn out.) If your workforce is very small, you

might join up with other employers. Team sports might require an investment in team T-shirts or registration fees. But hey, the T-shirts will be walking advertisements for your company. And there's nothing like some healthy competition to get people motivated.

- **Sign up for charity events.** Encouraging employees to participate in a charity event that requires physical activity can build community at the same time it enhances your business's local reputation and improves employee health. This doesn't have to be your standard walk-a-thon or golfing day; building homes for Habitat for Humanity or doing a beach cleanup or environmental restoration project will get people moving, too.

- **Offer discounted gym memberships.** The nice thing about gyms is that they can offer your employees a whole slate of activities in one place, from weight machines to swimming to yoga and spin classes. (Plus, your employees' water and energy bills might go down if they stop showering at home.) If your workforce is small, a gym membership is also an easy way to make up for the lack of enough warm bodies to field a sports team or justify an in-house class. If you pay all or part of the gym fees, you can condition your payment on proof that the employees are actually using the facility. If you can't afford to cover the fees, you might at least negotiate a discounted group rate for those employees who'd like to sign up on their own.

> **TIP**
>
> **Gyms can be intimidating for first-timers.** Some folks imagine that everyone else at the gym will be young and fit. Start by choosing a gym that caters to a more mixed crowd. You might even want to arrange a group visit to the gym before asking people to sign up, allowing them to get a sense of the environment.

- **Create an on-site gym.** As described in Chapter 2, this isn't necessary, and it's often cost prohibitive for small employers. But it's not impossible. For example, at Vita Benefits Group (which has around 30 employees in its main office), adviser Rae Lee Olson says, "When we moved into our new building, we set aside space for a small gym, which contains an elliptical trainer, a treadmill, a bike, weights, and so forth. We also bring in a personal trainer. People pay for the trainer individually, but it's convenient for them. And we've totally changed the culture, so that now it's fine for people to head over and exercise in the middle of the day. People are given kudos by their peers when they're heading to the gym in workout clothes."

- **Offer on-site fitness classes.** Possibilities include yoga, Pilates, aerobic and other dance classes, and more. If you're willing to buy equipment, you could add step classes (which require plastic steps) or body sculpting (which may require hand weights, elastic bands, balls, or other fitness tools). Costs may vary depending on the number of participants. If you can't afford to cover or subsidize the cost of an instructor, your employees may be willing to pay. Make sure the instructors have the appropriate certifications (if any) in their subjects and are CPR trained.

- **Show exercise DVDs.** If you've got a large room and a DVD player, this is one of the lowest-cost ways to get your employees involved in group exercise. Set a regular schedule, and don't feel bad about repeating the same DVD many times, so long as people like it. In fact, you may not even have to buy the DVDs—ask people to bring in ones that are sitting around their house, probably unused!

- **Find out what your HMO offers.** It may have affordable fitness classes available to members as part of its dedication to keeping patients well—and preventing expensive illnesses.

- **Let people set individual fitness goals.** Some employees may want to get fitter, but not through the activities offered at or through your workplace. If you're operating on a point system as described in Chapter 2, it makes sense to be inclusive and reward points for a variety of fitness activities, including some that the employees choose themselves.

> ⓘ **CAUTION**
>
> **Will these activities lead to injuries?** Certainly, there's a risk of injury with any sport or activity, which is why we recommended (in Chapter 2) getting participants to sign general waivers before starting your workplace wellness program. But keep your concerns in perspective: People who are physically unfit can as easily injure themselves getting in or out of their chairs as taking a healthy walk. Dr. Sallis recommends: "People should start low, go slow, then advance. I just think the benefits so outweigh the risks of injuries that it's not something to get bogged down worrying about."

Options for Individuals: Fitness Coaching

Although group exercise is often the core of a workplace wellness program, you may also want to offer some one-on-one options. For example, if you sign up with a wellness service provider that assigns each employee a personal coach, or at least sends email information and reminders, then fitness goals will no doubt be worked into their plan.

This coaching can be valuable because, as adviser Dr. Janet Greenhut explains:

> *Most people find that they're able to stick with behavior change better when they have to answer to someone about their short-term goals—for instance, walking every day for 30 minutes. After a habit is established (the time for this varies from person to person and activity to activity), a person may not need to be accountable to someone else.*

Dr. Doug Metz adds that coaching can help not only the employee, but his or her family as well:

> *The coach can educate the employee about how to connect with a spouse or significant other about reaching important, shared life goals, with the idea that, 'If we want to accomplish X, then we need to get healthy together.' Maybe they're planning to travel the world when they retire, for example, which is difficult if you don't stay physically fit."*

Support: Creating a High-Energy Workplace

Deep down, many workplace managers believe that the ideal workday scenario is one where employees are parked quietly at their desks or workstations, pounding out product. There's just one problem: Uninterrupted work puts people to sleep, reduces their fitness levels, raises their stress levels, and ultimately lowers productivity. So even if you're paying people to go to a gym after hours, a little flexibility about the standard working day will go a long way toward the health of both your employees and your business.

Here are some ways to raise energy levels at your workplace:

- **Encourage use of breaks or lunchtime for fitness activities.** Offer suggestions like a short walking route that can be covered during the break period. If you have access to outdoor space, make Frisbees, balls, and other "toys" available. (Note: If your breaks are only ten minutes long, you may need to extend them.)

- **Make the stairwells more inviting.** If you're in a multistory building, and the stairwells look like settings for cheap TV thrillers, it's no wonder people will take the elevator. Start by addressing cleanliness or security concerns—for example, by improving the lighting and reminding everyone of entry codes for doors that remain locked all day. To avoid confusion, make sure the floor numbers are clearly marked. Ask your cleaning staff to include the stairwells among its regular tasks. Other improvements (which you may need to negotiate with your building owner or fellow tenants) might include fresh paint, piped in music, colorful artwork along the walls, and carpeting or stair treads. Also put encouraging signs next to the stairwell doors, like those found at the Eat Smart Move More website mentioned above. Dr. Sallis says, "We've done this at Kaiser Permanente, and it's made a big difference among the staff— many now consider the stairs to be the default and would be embarrassed if people saw them taking the elevator!"

- **Allow flex time for fitness activities.** We've said it before, but we firmly believe that allowing employees to come in late (and make up the time later), take a long lunch hour, or otherwise rearrange their working day is one of the best ways to guarantee that they do their exercise—instead of putting it off until nighttime, by which time they may be exhausted—and give you their greatest productivity during the workday. You'll probably start noticing that employees who've just come from a workout are the most energized and productive of anyone.

- **Take away parking privileges.** Just kidding. But you can pass on Dr. Sallis's clever suggestion for doing the recommended minutes of activity each week: "Park farther away from the office, so it's a ten-minute walk to get to your workstation; at lunch, walk out five minutes, eat your lunch, then walk back five minutes; then at the end of the day, walk ten minutes back to your car. That adds up to your goal of 30 minutes for that day."

- **Don't reward employees who put in long hours.** If a 70- or 80-hour workweek is expected or applauded at your workplace, you're giving the worst sort of message. No one can stay healthy and fit on that kind of schedule.

- **Remind managers to encourage employee fitness initiatives.** An employee who, for example, wants to email coworkers about a triathlon and print out the brochures using company machinery shouldn't have to act in secret, but should have managerial support, with a mutual understanding about separately meeting work obligations.

- **Have stretch breaks during meetings.** It helps if a leader guides people through some simple movements like reaching one's arms high in the air or bending at the waist toward the floor. Stretch breaks are a great way to remind people that sitting too long, particularly in one position, is never a good idea. The break doesn't have to be very long. As Dr. Sallis assures us, "Any amount of activity is better than nothing. Even people who tend to fidget or move around a lot in their chair are often healthier."

> **TIP**
>
> **Nothing like a 7 a.m. bowling match.** At Frett Barrington Ltd., Patty Frett says, "We have a meeting every Monday morning at 7 a.m., which can be a bit of a challenge. But then we started asking everyone to take turns planning some sort of physical activity to start the meeting off. Half the fun has just been seeing what people come up with: hula hoops, miniature bowling, and even a lights-out round of catch with stress balls that lit up. It sure has made those meetings more engaging."

- **Provide equipment.** If you can afford to buy running shoes, pedometers (which count the number of steps someone takes), or other snazzy exercise equipment—perhaps as an incentive for participation—you'll increase the chances that your employees follow through on their fitness goals.
- **Set up bike racks.** This will make it easier for employees to use an aerobic—not to mention gas-saving and green—method of commuting to work.

> **TIP**
>
> **Making pedometers the incentive.** Health Media, where adviser Dr. Janet Greenhut works, is a small company. They decided to try a walking program as a way to get the highest number of people involved. Dr. Greenhut explains: "Every employee was invited to buy a pedometer; if they used it for 90 days, they were reimbursed. We have an ongoing competition, with people divided into teams. Everyone uploads the number of steps they take monthly, and the team results are reported to the whole company. Even without any incentive other than reimbursement for the pedometer, people really got into the spirit of it. Some of the teams printed their own T-shirts and had their picture taken—and they all came up with names, like the 'Holy Walkamolies.' The photos, along with the step totals, are displayed on a bulletin board in the main break room. Teammates help keep each other committed and involved."

Walk While You Work?

Here's one to put on your wishlist: Dr. James Levine. and colleagues at the Mayo Clinic's Non-exercise Activity Thermogenesis lab (or "NEAT," at mayoresearch.mayo.edu/mayo/research/levine_lab) have created an "Office of the Future," where people work out while they work.

It features treadmills connected to desks and computer platforms and a two-lane walking track that replaces the conventional meeting room. Dr. Levine himself regularly works using the treadmill, reportedly keeping up a one-mile-per-hour pace (100 calories an hour) while checking email or holding conversations.

Various versions of the treadmill workstation are now commercially available (and found in office supply stores)—for example from Steelcase (www.steelcase.com/na/) and AFC Industries, Inc. (www.afcindustries.com). Alternatively, some enterprising people have built their own.

Lowering Stress Levels

Meet Your Adviser

 **Dr. Albert Ray,** Physician Director for Patient Education and Health Promotion with Kaiser Permanente in Southern California, as well as Regional Assistant Medical Director of Business Management and Physician Director at Positive Choice Wellness Center in San Diego.

What he does: Dr. Ray's energetic involvement with people's health and welfare includes spending one or two days a week seeing patients, and then dividing the rest of his time among his other professional responsibilities.

Favorite healthy food: "If there's one food that I try to incorporate into my diet, it's more fish. I like sushi, especially the California roll, with cucumber, avocado, and artificial crab. It's healthy, filling, and doesn't have a lot of calories."

Top tip for staying fit and healthy: "I still wear a pedometer every day. You can buy one for about $10 at any sporting goods store. It's a very simple way, in addition to eating right, to fulfill your fitness and exercise requirement. And I walk my dog twice a day, mornings and afternoons."

S tress—variously defined as a form of anxiety, a state of mind, a way of interpreting the world, a pattern of behavior, or a type of fear—is simply a physical and mental response to real or perceived demands or threats. Everyone experiences some degree of stress; it even has its own day: November 5, which is dubbed National Stress Awareness Day.

Daily demands on time, attention, and finances commonly create stress, but the pressure to perform and deliver at work often tops people's lists of what's most stressful in their lives. In fact, numerous studies, articles, and books address how to deal with the stress in specific work-places, from prisons to corporations to libraries.

The Connection: How Stress Impacts Worker Health and Productivity

There's probably not an employee in your company who isn't facing some sort of stress, whether it comes from work or home. And while people might have once said that it's "all in their head," society and medical professionals are increasingly recognizing that the impact of stress on the body is not only real, but significantly detrimental to worker health and productivity.

According to the American Institute of Stress, employers lose an estimated $300 billion annually to absenteeism, job turnover, mistakes on the job, low productivity, and poor motivation stemming from unchecked stress. And that's even before the impact on health insurance and similar premiums. Workplace experts estimate that health care expenses are nearly 50% greater for workers who report high levels of stress.

Stress and the Body

Not all stress is bad. As you may have experienced, getting butterflies in your stomach before a public presentation can force you to prepare well in advance, and save your speech from sounding staged and soulless.

And some stress is lifesaving—for example, it could supply the energy you need to focus and flee from a burning building.

While the body's reactions to a stressful situation have benefits, they are not particularly discriminating. Physiological stress reactions, such as a burst of adrenalin and heightened reactivity, may kick into gear over a perceived slight from a coworker as fast as they do at the smell of smoke and sight of flames. And excessive or prolonged stress, such as many people experience on the job (in combination with whatever stress they're carrying from their home life), can have a wearing effect on the body and mind.

The body's stress response includes more than 1,400 physical and chemical reactions. Left unchecked, these can produce physical symptoms, such as headaches, stomach problems, muscle tension, ulcers, hypertension, weight gain or loss, fatigue, headaches, immune system disturbances, diabetes, strokes, and heart attacks. Experts say that as much as 80% to 90% of all disease may be stress related.

Although scientific understanding of stress is increasing, our coping abilities don't seem to be. According to a poll, more people reported physical and emotional symptoms due to stress in 2008 than they did the previous year. Specifically, as a result of stress:

- 60% reported feelings of anger or irritability, compared to 50% in 2007
- 53% reported feeling fatigued compared to 51% in 2007, and
- 52% reported sleeplessness, up from 48% the year before.

(Source: American Psychological Association, "Stress in America" poll (2008).)

Stress may also give rise to mental and emotional symptoms, such as depression, and behavioral symptoms like inability to focus. All of these combine to increase the original culprit: Stress leads to more stress.

The Workplace as a Common Stressor

Even interesting and energizing workplace challenges can turn into harmful stressors when an employee feels overwhelmed, defeated, or exhausted by job- or home-related demands.

American workers are known for putting in long hours and hard work during any economy. During good times, they often feel they must work harder just to keep up. During downturns, they put in longer or harder hours because there are fewer employees with whom to share the load. But that's not all good news for employers. When stress levels rise too high, and workers take time off because of stress, anxiety, or a related disorder, they tend to be off the job for about three weeks, according to the Bureau of Labor Statistics.

And yes, the workplace itself is often a major culprit. Recent studies from various sources (cited by the National Institute for Occupational Safety and Health or NIOSH, an agency responsible for preventing work-related illness and injury) show that:

- 25% of all employees view their jobs as the most stressful thing in their lives
- 40% report their jobs are "very stressful" or "extremely stressful," and
- 20% have quit a job because of workplace stress.

It's impossible to know whether today's workplaces are more laden with stress than ever, but many workers feel that way. A poll by NIOSH found that about 75% of workers believe they're confronting more stress than workers of the previous generation.

Whether or not they're right, it seems safe to point to outsourcing, downsizing, ailing pension plans, increasing competition in the workforce, and technological advances that give both the ability and expectation of being able to work all hours of the day and night as sources for the tensions many workers feel. Dr. Ray points out:

We're now so used to dealing with machines and computers that we sometimes forget how to deal with other humans. Plus, with electronic technology and voicemail, everything has timestamps, so people can see when a message arrived, when you opened it, whether you responded, and more. It's a pressure cooker environment.

Indicators of Job-Related Stress

Here's a peek at the indicators of job stress for many workers, adapted from a survey by the American Institute of Stress (www.stress.org). Try answering the ten questions on your own behalf. We don't recommend passing it out to your workers if you're having HRAs done—the HRAs should capture the same sort of information.

Using a sliding scale from 1 (strongly disagree) to 10 (strongly agree), enter the number that best describes you.

_____ I can't honestly say what I really think or get things off my chest at work.

_____ My job has a lot of responsibility, but I don't have very much authority.

_____ I could usually do a much better job if I were given more time.

_____ I seldom receive adequate acknowledgment or appreciation when my work is really good.

_____ I'm not particularly proud of or satisfied with my job.

_____ I have the impression that I am repeatedly picked on or discriminated against at work.

_____ My workplace environment is not very pleasant or particularly safe.

_____ My job often interferes with my family and social obligations or personal needs.

_____ I tend to have frequent arguments with superiors, coworkers, or customers.

_____ Most of the time, I feel that I have very little control over my life at work.

_____ Total Job Stress Score (add the replies to each question)

A score between 10 and 30 indicates you handle job stress well; between 40 and 60, moderately well; at 70 to 100, you're encountering problems that need to be addressed and resolved.

Reducing Stress in Your Workplace

Here, we'll consider how you can help your employees build skills to deal with some of the work and life tasks that cause them stress in the first place. And we'll suggest lots of things you can do to make your workplace both more playful and more productive.

Bringing Pets to Work

Animals are a proven stress reliever—dogs and cats have been shown to reduce depression, lower blood pressure and heart rates, and boost immune system functioning. (The latter study was careful to note that petting a stuffed dog did not have the same immune-boosting effect!)

Animals also help people network, because stopping to pet a cute animal is a natural conversation starter. And they give very persuasive demonstrations of how to flop down and relax.

It's no wonder that one in five U.S. companies—Nolo among them—allows pets in the office. Could your office be the next one? Here are some things to think about first:

- Is anyone in your office allergic to dogs, cats, or other pets? If so, better limit your new policy to goldfish and geckos.
- Is anyone in your office afraid of dogs? That might not ruin the deal entirely, if that person is willing to meet with the prospective new office members or sits far from where the animal will be. (We recommend allowing dogs in through only one entrance, to keep things predictable.)
- Can the office be cleared of materials that are either dangerous to animals or easily damaged by them?
- Do you have sufficient offices with closed doors that the animals can be contained easily?

If you can deal with the above issues, you might want to give pets a chance—perhaps a test run on National Take Your Pet to Work Day, which happens every year in late June. (See www.takeyourdog.

com/About.) Make clear to your employees that their dogs must be continually well behaved and nonaggressive, and that they must take care to clean up after the animal and find a backup caretaker if stepping out of the office. Once you've settled on your basic office procedures, include a description in your employee handbook or policies (general principles for which are described in Chapter 13).

To look further into the research about pets and health, see the website of the Delta Society at www.deltasociety.org. (Click "Education and Research," then "For Adults.")

Education: Getting at the Roots of Stress

There are many ways to deliver the message about stress. Some of this advice can be given informally, as supervisors train new employees or check in with those at work. In other cases, you'll want to arrange short classes or lunch-and-learns.

- **Offer help with time management.** Time—or usually the lack of it—contributes to feeling stressed. While it's important to give employees as much autonomy as possible over decisions about how to use their time on the job, time management advice can be invaluable for those who consistently feel that there aren't enough hours in the workday. Simple tips will often do the trick, such as suggesting to an employee who perpetually forgets meetings and wellness activities that he or she write them on a big wall calendar. We offer a list of suggestions just below. If you prefer to hand the teaching over to someone with outside credibility, you can bring in time management consultants for seminars. Or consider calling in an expert to coach a particular worker or department about how to manage time well.

CAUTION
Beware of technology's stranglehold. Workers are quickly finding that technological "improvements," such as computers, cell phones, PDAs, and pagers, can morph from timesavers into time drains.

Counsel employees to streamline such communications when possible. For example, not every email message and phone call requires an immediate answer.

Tips for Time Management

Here are some tried and true time management techniques:
- Keep a time diary for a week to track how your time is being spent and wasted.
- Set priorities. Keep a daily to-do list, and segment it into tasks that must be completed before leaving for the day—and those that can be accomplished later. Attend to the most essential tasks on time and during the point in the workday when energy is highest.
- Clear the decks by delegating less important tasks to others, if possible.
- Tidy up the work area—a task that has the added result of helping the mind feel ordered. Workplace experts estimate that the average person wastes more than 20 minutes a day looking for misplaced items. Clear the clutter from email boxes, too, by deleting nonessential messages and storing others in labeled files.
- Be realistic about how much work can be accomplished—even if that means saying no to proposed projects or increased duties.
- Be flexible enough to accommodate emergencies or changed work requirements that might disrupt even the most carefully crafted time management plan.
- Take charge of time-draining communication habits, perhaps by consciously limiting the time spent sending and reading email messages, the hours available for group meetings, and when office doors are open to coworkers and visitors.

- **Arrange classes on communication skills.** It's not uncommon for coworkers to have difficulty sharing their thoughts and concerns in constructive, appropriate ways. The natural result is that tempers, and therefore stress levels, can go nuclear pretty quickly. You'll find no lack of coaches, trainers, or teachers at local business schools or colleges available to help your employees develop business communication and related skills. The exact topics can be specialized as is appropriate to your workplace, for example, addressing primarily your middle managers or customer service staff. Email etiquette alone could be—in fact, already is—the sole topic of workplace seminars. (It also might make for some worthwhile printed tips, perhaps in your wellness newsletter.) Ask fellow business owners or industry associations for recommendations on coaches or classes—for example, through local university extension programs.

- **Arrange classes on financial wellness.** Money is a top source of stress for approximately eight out of ten Americans. As with other types of stress, there are constructive, proactive ways to deal with financial worries. You might bring in an expert to lay these out, such as a financial planner or credit counselor willing to do a free lecture in hopes of referrals. Make sure the speaker emphasizes themes like recognizing one's relationship to money, identifying financial stressors, taking stock of one's current financial situation, and making a plan for going forward. People who are having trouble paying bills or staying on top of debt should be encouraged to reach out to their banks, utilities, or credit card companies for help. Another worthwhile theme is turning challenging times into opportunities. A good group discussion could be built around thinking of creative ways to deal with the stress of economic challenges. For example, some people realize that having dinner at home with the family may not only save money, but help bring them closer together.

Activities: Let the Fun Begin

If you're worried (and stressed) that you'll have to remove all the stress from your employees' lives in order to reverse its damaging effects, there's good news. The newest buzzword among workplace experts is resilience—helping employees build their own strengths so that they're better able to deal with the stress that will inevitably bombard them both at work and home. Many of the ways to develop and maintain this resilience require only a few minutes of time a day. Here's how to help your employees learn and practice this:

- **Offer stress-reduction classes or DVD screenings.** Researchers have developed a number of effective—and often surprisingly quick—ways that workers can counteract the stress they feel. Once learned, these techniques can and should be practiced regularly, so that the person will have an effective tool at the ready in times of stress. We'll give a brief rundown of various types of stress reduction methods below, but don't feel limited by our list. Ask other employers in your area for leads on effective, affordable, and culturally appropriate stress management speakers and programs. The goal, says Dr. Kenneth R. Pelletier, is that employees learn to "not just break even, but actively manage their stress." To keep costs down, you might even find a trusted person on your staff to lead people through simple exercises that others have developed. Alternatively, look for DVDs that you can show in your conference room.

- **Show comedies over the lunch hour.** Frett Barrington in Wisconsin holds regular "Lunch and Laughs." Patty Frett explains, "We'll watch, for example, an episode of *The Office*. These events are nearly free, because we'll either access a show through the Internet or someone will bring in a DVD."

TIP

One class won't be enough. Studies have shown that, although workers might be initially enthusiastic about implementing newly learned stress reduction techniques, the attrition rate is high. They soon start skipping classes or forgetting to practice what they've learned. What's worse is that their reasons sometimes include feeling pressure from a supervisor to complete work assignments. Do what you can to hold repeat classes, and impress on supervisors the importance of people attending these.

Five Ways to Beat Stress

Here are a few proven ways to lower stress. Any or all of these, along with some of the more active methods discussed in "Keep it moving," below, would make fine additions to your wellness offerings:

- **Meditation.** In this practice, a person learns to achieve stillness and calm his or her mind through one of various methods, such as focusing on the flow of breath, silently repeating a relaxing word or phrase, or watching one's thoughts without judgment, in order to become more mindful and in tune with the present moment. Though many spiritual disciplines incorporate meditation techniques, that's not what you're going for here. A simple, practical meditation class, with instructions like sitting in a comfortable position, focusing on the breath, and clearing the mind is all you need for effective stress reduction.

- **Self-hypnosis or guided imagery.** Dr. Ray particularly recommends this method because, he says, "The topic can be easily taught in one or two classes, which is good for people who are short on time. It works like this: When you're in a stressful situation, you close your eyes, take a deep breath, and imagine you're visiting your favorite island or fishing spot or in your hammock with a book—then take another breath." It may sound corny, but taking oneself to a different place for 30 seconds or a minute, whether you're in a stressful situation or having a stressful day, can take the edge off. If a problem is serious, it can create some ease until there's time to address the issue in a balanced way.

- **Positive thinking.** This technique emphasizes changing one's thought patterns, so that instead of responding to stress with negative and self-defeating thoughts, such as "I'll never get caught up," "I hate being here," or "My boss is forcing me to do a job I can't handle," the person learns to replace these with more positive thoughts, like "If I take one step at a time, I can get the job done," "Once I complete this task, it will help make the customer's life easier," or "This project is similar to the one I did last month that got such good results."

Five Ways to Beat Stress (continued)

- **Progressive muscle relaxation.** Learning how to tighten and then relax various muscle groups in succession, a person can quiet the body; the mind follows suit.
- **Breathing exercises.** When people are stressed, their breath usually becomes shallow as the muscles of the stomach and diaphragm tense. But simple breathing exercises help replenish the body with needed oxygen—and instantly reduce stress. Teach some simple techniques and suggest that employees take a breathing break whenever they're feeling stressed, have been working concentratedly for more than an hour, or notice that their breathing has become shallow.

Meditation in Motion

Sometimes, the best way to settle down is to combine mindfulness with movement. Here are three popular techniques:

- **Tai chi.** This gentle Chinese martial art involves a series of postures or movements practiced in a slow, graceful manner accompanied by deep breathing.
- **Qi gong.** Not unlike tai chi, this is a movement practice drawn from traditional Chinese medicine, meant to restore and maintain balance and a relaxed state through repeated movements or a series of postures.
- **Yoga.** Most forms of yoga involve slow stretches and poses, in some cases accompanied by controlled breathing exercises. A practitioner can develop a stronger, more flexible body and a calmer mind.

RESOURCE

A relaxing read: Dr. Pelletier's book, *Stress Free for Good*, would make a good addition to your workplace wellness library. (It's coauthored with Dr.

Fred Luskin and available from HarperCollins books.) The book sets out simple stress management techniques that people can do in as little as ten minutes a day, with methods such as deep abdominal breathing, taking stock of what they appreciate in their lives, visualizing success, smiling, and accepting what cannot be changed.

- **Keep it moving.** It's been proven time and again that regular exercise is one of the very best ways to combat stress. The fitness components of your wellness program will do double duty when it comes to helping employees stay relaxed and focused. And some physical activities are particularly known for their power to calm the mind and help the body relax. We list those below, but remember that they aren't the only options. Some employers invent their own solutions—for example, bringing in local theatre professionals to teach stress-reducing movements like those used by actors before a performance. ("Swagger like a cowboy! Slither like a snake!")

- **Create mutual support pairings.** Peer support, where coworkers are paired up to offer one another assistance, can be a safe and effective—not to mention low-cost—way to help them cope with work-related stress. At the most basic level, peer support allows workers to share stressful incidents and to experience empathy from a trusted colleague. You can, for example, assign people buddies when they first start work at your company. Paying for their first lunch out together is a good way to start the bonding process.

- **Create some silliness.** It's important to encourage employees to reduce stress by blowing off steam and enjoying themselves in or out of the office. Providing some mandatory silliness on the job can be revolutionary. (You may not want to go as far as some companies have, with water fights in the hall. Too much forced fun can actually seem burdensome—just another task to cross off the List of Things to Do.) Try starting simply, perhaps with a costume day, talent show, or celebrations of events like staff birthdays. Stocking your wellness library with some cartoon or joke books wouldn't hurt, either. Eventually, you might ramp up to more unusual activities. (See "From Soap Bubbles to the Smithsonian," below.) Keep in mind that it helps to allow employees to pick and choose what feels like fun. If you're not feeling up to the planning task, you shouldn't be surprised to find that a bevy of "fun experts" are waiting and ready for you to enlist them.

From Soap Bubbles to the Smithsonian

You have endless options when it comes to workplace play. Fingerpainting is a favorite way to help solve on-the-job problems for Ohio-based workplace stress expert Todd Packer, who says the messy act not only helps relieve stress, but can also help employees break through mental logjams and reach creative solutions to workplace problems. Packer frequently sets out a palette of fingerpaints—or sometimes, soap bubbles or origami—to encourage employees to illustrate what's wrong rather than do traditional brainstorming.

Other offbeat workplace stress relievers include drumming circles—or other music making with easy-to-use instruments like tambourines—and laughter sessions. In the latter, employees are urged to laugh out loud—an exercise that is sometimes strained at first, but quickly gives in to group contagion. Laughter is a scientifically proven stress buster, releasing natural tranquilizers and oxygen into the brain.

Office field trips to local museums and sporting events can also help relieve workplace stress, while building camaraderie and relieving tedium. Some workplaces incorporate a volunteer project that employees can work on together, which has the added benefit of helping people in need and demonstrating management's goodwill. (It may help your company's brand awareness and image, too.)

- **Award wellness points for stress reduction activities.** Just as stress affects every individual differently, people find different ways to combat it effectively. If your wellness program is designed to reward people for earning a certain number of points over time, you're in an ideal position to encourage employees to seek forms of stress relief that don't necessarily happen at work. You might give points for things like enrolling in a music or pottery class, joining a knitting group, or taking part in any other hobby or activity that feels calming and fulfilling.

- **Help create personal connections.** The growth of technology, with its promise of increasing efficiency, also encourages more impersonal communication: an email rather than a face-to-face conversation, an instant message rather than a phone call. And that makes for more isolation, which is also stressful. Your workplace wellness activities, such as fitness competitions or cooking classes, will help people spend more face-to-face time with coworkers. Organizing activities that involve focusing on others, such as a volunteer day at a nursing home, childcare center, or animal shelter, or walking or running as a team in a fundraiser can also be helpful.

TIP

When being makes it so. At UPS, the package delivery company where smooth-running operations and efficiency are paramount, drivers are trained to walk briskly and to smile often. Why? It commands attention and respect from customers and coworkers, reflecting confidence and competence. And it's good for business. Wouldn't you rather receive your packages from someone who's cheerful than from a delivery person who's stressed and overworked?

TIP

Set out reminders of the half-full glass. San Francisco marketing firm MacKenzie Communications, Inc., equips its lunchroom with glasses etched with a horizontal stripe—the top labeled Optimista, the bottom, Pessimista. "In our business especially, so many people see the glass as half empty; it's important to be reminded that that same glass is half-full. That helps us all navigate the knocks we might get from the outside," says firm founder Janis MacKenzie.

In fact, it may help to remember that everything you do to reduce stress in your workplace lends itself to more optimistic workers. Consider one of the benefits of enjoyable seminars and classes, described by Dr. Ray:

> *There was a famous movie ad that said, "Try answering yes to everything!" But I think people who are stressed generally say "No" to anything, and are reluctant to participate in any new activities; their time is already so consumed with other things. But by starting this in the workplace, they wind up connecting with other people who are facing the same stresses. Talking it out and sharing with others helps them take another, more positive look at their situation.*

Individual Treatment: When Fingerpainting Isn't Enough

If particular workers are obviously so stressed as to need an immediate solution, they might benefit from more individualized stress reduction options. Ideally, your EAP or health insurance plans will cover some therapy—and you should make sure your employees understand what's available to them. In addition to therapy, your EAP might help with any number of things causing an employee stress. Theresa Islo, Director of Operations at the Wellness Council of Wisconsin, says:

> *EAPs can even help with things like guiding an employee who's advising his or her child on selecting courses to take in college. Any such issues can be stressful in an employee's life and thus distracting at work.*

However, your health plan may not be geared to help people until their situation rises to the level of a medical problem. Even in that case, it may cover only a few sessions with a trained counselor. That's why you might want to make more individual options available.

Many counselors specialize in coping with workplace stress. You can make it easier for your employees to get help by making referrals to, and perhaps helping to pay for, local therapists who have good track records.

To reduce costs, you might look for therapists that offer brief phone counseling (also helpful for employees who are on the road a lot). Also try to locate low-cost community resources. For example, local schools or training programs may offer free or reduced rates to meet with students who are about to graduate or doing required practice time.

Support: Cleaning Up Stress On-Site

Helping your employees deal with stress by offering activities and options within your workplace wellness program is good and will serve them well in all aspects of their life. But your program activities could be butting up against a high wall if your workplace atmosphere is infested with stress.

If you've observed low morale, health and job complaints, performance problems, and employee turnover—and if you administered HRAs that reported high levels of workplace stress—take these as cues that your workplace could use some stress cleanup operations. You may also see some indirect signs: people trying to relieve stress by turning to unhealthy activities such as smoking, drinking, gambling, or emotional eating.

CAUTION

Some clues may be well hidden. For example, during economic downturns when employees are especially likely to fear losing their jobs—a stressor in itself—they tend to hide their stress-related symptoms. Because stress is so ubiquitous and sometimes subtle, you can't always spot a stressed employee at a glance. So, if a handful of employees look stressed, you can probably assume that others are as well. Use the steps in this section to improve the environment for everyone.

The goal is to stop unhealthy workplace stress before it starts. You certainly want your workplace to be busy, and you can't eliminate every challenge—but there are many factors under your control. Stressed employees complain most often about things like poor communication between managers and workers, a lack of resources to do the job, and poor managers who tolerate workers who consistently deliver subpar

Mandatory Time Off for Stressed Behavior

Some laws may require that you give time off or other accommodations to workers who are unable to do their jobs because of the effects of stress.

Especially where stress on the job results in a serious or long-term depression or other disability, employers may be required to comply with various legal mandates, including:

- The federal Family and Medical Leave Act (FMLA), which entitles employees in workplaces with 50 or more employees to take time to deal with a serious health problem. Under the Act, an employee who requires inpatient treatment, has a chronic serious health problem, or is unable to perform normal activities for three days while under the care of a doctor has a serious health condition— and employees who are stricken by complications from stress may qualify.

- The federal Americans with Disabilities Act (ADA), which requires employers with 15 or more employees to make "reasonable accommodations" for those who are considered legally disabled by their conditions. Accommodations may include, for example, altered schedules and reduced hours.

- State discrimination statutes, many of which apply to workplaces as small as one employee. Most of these laws prohibit discriminating against those with physical and mental disabilities.

- Workers' compensation laws, which in about a half of the states recognize stress as a valid basis for a claim that a job has increased the chances of suffering from a related disease, such as a heart attack.

See Chapter 13 for more information on crafting legally compliant time-off policies.

performances or who fail to make work roles and responsibilities clear. These are all things you can do something about; this section of the book shows you how.

Don't expect to revamp your workplace culture in a day, or even a week. Where possible, incorporate changes one at a time and evaluate the true difference each makes.

- **Hire and assign workers appropriately.** Workers who feel incompetent or ill-equipped to do their jobs are stressed workers. During the hiring process, you should be very specific about what a job entails. Follow up with deeper questions than "Can you do this?" It's better to ask exactly what tasks a person has done before that were similar. Later, if someone you've already hired is proving to be ill suited to a job, providing additional training or a transfer to another position may help. If that's not practical, the kindest thing to do may be to fire the person. Remember, too, that coworkers teamed with someone who is consistently flailing or failing will feel the stress and strain of it—not to mention having to take on more work to pick up the slack.

> **TIP**
>
> **Look for the ones who can laugh.** It may be wise to favor job candidates who demonstrate a sense of humor. According to a survey by staffing firm Robert Half International (www.rhi.com), 84% of executives and human resource directors believe that a person with a sense of humor does better than others on the job. Plus, these people help reduce free-floating office stress.

- **Ask managers to set a positive example.** Most employees take their cues about workplace style and values from management—and here, actions speak more loudly than words. If supervisors habitually burn the midnight oil, for example, most workers will assume that working long hours is the best and only way to get ahead. Encourage management to demonstrate that having time and interests outside of work is valued, too. Having managers take the lead in other parts of your wellness program can be helpful—for example, a manager might invite others to walk outdoors at lunchtime, organize a team for a competitive event, or show up for a weekend charitable activity.

> **TIP**
> **Concern from others can help, too.** Dr. Ray discovered this after noticing that a coworker was calling in sick more, asking for more work excuses, smoking more, and asking for more smoking medication: "I sat the person down, told him what I'd observed, and said, 'I really recommend the stress program run by our health education department.' He was reluctant, saying he didn't have time. But I showed him how other, similarly busy members and coworkers have benefited. Based on my coaxing, he agreed to go, and enjoyed it so much he's now recommending the program to others. I think the fact that I took a personal interest and approached him face to face made a big difference."

- **Allow employees greater independence.** A prime component of stress is that it makes a person feel powerless and out of control. In a work setting, employees who have some say over the setting and substance of their work tend to be less stressed. It's important to allow employees to make choices and to encourage them to take responsibility for themselves rather than to issue dictates from on high. No, you don't have to let your employees run the company. But giving them a voice in matters such as scheduling, work hours, and even office décor can help them feel more in control and less stressed.
- **Encourage employees to take breaks.** Encourage regular short breaks that involve standing, moving, and stretching. Even getting up for a drink of water, checking for mail, or watering the plants can reduce pent-up stress. It's surprising that some employees won't take breaks even when you encourage them. Realize, however, that it can feel counterintuitive to step away

from work when feeling overwhelmed by the sheer volume of it. Unfortunately, you can't just ring a recess bell and shove everyone out the door. As adviser Dr. Kenneth R. Pelletier says, "It has to be totally noncoercive, not mandated." Here again, good examples set by managers and supervisors can make the difference. Or, supervisors might stop by workstations and say something gentle like, "Wow, you've been at it all morning— going to take a break soon?"

What's Wrong With Workers Looking Busy?

We asked Dr. Kenneth R. Pelletier why an employer shouldn't be happy to see workers who look busy all the time. His answer:

One reason is that the definition, if you will, of Type A behavior really characterizes an individual who is addicted to the process of being busy, not the output. So a person can act really busy—sending memos, making phone calls, and getting up and down from the desk. But what you need to look at is not the activity, but the output. Someone who is perpetually scurrying may not be productive at all.

The second reason is a Type A person may have a detrimental effect on coworkers. The person may be so annoying, or so hyper-kinetic, constantly bothering people or deluging them with emails, that the output of the workplace as a whole decreases.

Finally, recognize that in some cases looking busy is not what matters. If you go to Google or Apple or one of the other major computer companies, it looks like a playpen. Yet you realize that these are incredibly productive companies, with very bright people. So do you want to follow an unsuccessful 20th-century model? Or a successful 21st-century company model? Everyone will say the latter, but they need to get used to what that looks like.

TIP

Create a break-friendly space. If your workplace has a break room or lunch room, make sure it's an attractive place to spend time. Rae Lee Olson says: "When we bought our new building, we set up a room we call the 'bistro,' as a nice place for people to eat their lunch or take a break. The room is light and airy—in fact, it has more windows than any other room in our office. We put in three little tables with tablecloths on them, and one person is in charge of putting potted flowers on the tables—for example, during the winter holidays there will be poinsettias, things like that."

TIP

Create a space for quiet time. In addition to offering employees a good place to take breaks—which may include social activities from conversation to lunchtime games—it can help to create a quieter place at work. This is especially important if your wellness program has been teaching your employees valuable mental and physical skills like relaxation, meditation, guided imagery, yoga, tai chi, or mindful breathing. Those things can be hard to do in a busy workplace. If possible, set aside a small room or garden space so that employees can take quiet breaks and decompress on-site.

More Benefits of Breaks

There are physical benefits to taking breaks, too. A while back, when tense workers began to report injuries related to repetitive motions on the job, ergonomic experts began to pound on the importance of stepping away from the desk or workstation for breaks. Staying in the same, often unnatural position for too long can lead to serious injuries and potentially raise your workers' compensation insurance premiums. All of this is further evidence that it's good for both you and your employees to take regular short rests.

- **Be attuned to employee needs.** Individuals have unique ways of expressing feelings of stress. Some become withdrawn and introspective. Others act short-tempered, melodramatic, or even violent. Still others devise stress strategies that only a close coworker would recognize, such as dressing more and more fashionably as stress levels rise. Encourage supervisors to be attentive to employees under their charge. Suggest that they regularly ask open-ended questions such as, "How's your workload?" or "How's life been treating you lately?" and sincerely listen to the response. Employees should feel that it's permissible, even essential, to let management know when they feel buried by work. Of course, some employees may already be following the advice given in your workplace wellness program, and saying "No" to tasks that won't fit on their plate. Remind supervisors that this is exactly the behavior you've been suggesting, and that it shouldn't be followed with an automatic order to, "Do it anyway!" Supervisors will, however, need to keep careful track of employee assignments to be sure that the work is being evenly distributed.

How Much Is Enough?

The extent to which your employees should be encouraged to share personal problems, in addition to work concerns, depends on your workplace culture and on your managers' as well as your employees' personal inclinations. Many employers find that having an EAP helps deflect excessive discussion of personal problems in the workplace. Nevertheless, it can be helpful for the employer to have some insights into an employee's personal situation, given that stress at home so often affects how people respond to others at work. Studies have shown that even a small negative encounter before getting to work, such as receiving a speeding ticket, can make a person less trusting of people, such as coworkers, who weren't even involved.

- **Act quickly to solve problems.** As in other aspects of life, uncertainty is a great cause of stress in the workplace. Once a problem is identified—from a budget shortfall to a personal disagreement over a workplace policy—take decisive action to address it. While not all employees will like every solution, they'll be saved the stress of uncertainty.
- **Keep up your nutrition program.** There's a truism that stress and snacking go hand to mouth. Stress on the job prompts many people to mindlessly reach for unhealthy sugary or fatty foods and caffeinated drinks, to overeat, or to go for long periods without eating at all. During deadline-ridden or otherwise stressful times, it's especially important to make healthy snacks available instead of candy. The benefits of healthy eating are underscored in Chapter 5.

If You Need More Help

If your workplace is clearly corroded by stress, consider fashioning a program to change the culture, workers' habits, or both. People to invite to the planning table may include managers, labor representatives—and importantly—stressed employees.

Your first order of business is to diagnose problems, such as work overload or unclear expectations. This may involve gathering data or surveying employees about their job satisfaction and perceived levels of stress on the job.

Then get to work designing possible solutions and making a specific plan for putting them in place. Going forward, reevaluate the program periodically to make sure it meets the changing needs of your workplace.

Here's how adviser Dr. Kenneth R. Pelletier explains this process:

> *What we have found, in both large and small companies, is that whoever is going to be affected by decisions needs to be involved in those decisions. So whether it's a formal union or just a group of five people, what you want is to collectively sit down after work, or in some off-hours, and say, "Look, we know that stress is a problem, we've got*

If You Need More Help (continued)

a job to do, there's always too much to do with too few people, what can we do about it, how can we help each other. For example, how can we really take breaks? How does that become part of what we do, to honor the fact that if you have zero blood sugar at 2:00 in the afternoon, you can't concentrate?"

You have to work at it, make a commitment, get people involved, and have a timetable in which this becomes the worksite culture. And you have to understand that worksite cultures don't change very quickly; we normally say ten to 12 weeks. So that's about three months in which you're going to be working at this until the new style becomes the dominant style. Up until that time, it will be back and forth, with backsliding and not taking the changes seriously. But at about ten to 12 weeks, employees, and the company as a whole, will see that this is real and good, they'll start to feel it and experience it. That's where you want to get to.

You might also consider getting help from outside experts. Those known as "stress management consultants" may have tangible suggestions for changing working conditions. The irony is that solutions invariably involve changes in the workplace—new schedules, different work duties, a changed chain of command—and these changes themselves can be stressful. The best consultants and most savvy managers will be aware of this and factor in ways to ease the transitions.

Working Without Tobacco

Meet Your Adviser

Jonathan Foulds, M.A., M.App.Sci., Ph.D., professor and Director, University of Medicine & Dentistry of New Jersey School of Public Health, Tobacco Dependence Program.

What he does: Dr. Foulds directs a university program that aims to reduce the harm to health from tobacco use. This involves training health professionals, providing a specialist clinical service for smokers, and conducting research on smoking cessation.

Favorite healthy food: Greek salad.

Top tip for staying fit and healthy: "I like to play soccer and do 30 push-ups and 50 sit-ups every morning."

t's strange to remember that there was a time when smoking was considered not only glamorous, but healthy. Cigarette ads claimed that smoking would relieve asthma, hay fever, the common cold, "foul breath," and more.

Now, of course, we know better. Tobacco use (from cigarettes and, to a lesser extent, cigars or pipes) is the leading preventable cause of disease, disability, and death in the United States, causing one in every five deaths. Most cigarette smokers can subtract at least ten years from their life expectancy. In the meantime, smoking leads to debilitating diseases, including cancer, diabetes, emphysema, heart disease, and certain vascular types of dementia. We'll talk more about the health effects of smoking in this chapter.

Unfortunately, of all health behaviors, smoking is not only one of the most dangerous for everyday fitness and long-term survival, but one of the hardest habits to quit. So if some of your employees are smokers—and some probably are, given that around 20% of Americans smoke—you've got your work cut out for you. The stakes are high: The U.S. Centers for Disease Control (CDC) estimates that employees who smoke cost their employers an extra $1,300 to $4,000 per year, due to both direct health care costs and indirect costs such as lost productivity, absenteeism, and recruitment and retraining costs resulting from death and disability.

We'll spend the majority of this chapter discussing how to address the issue of smoking within your workplace wellness program. Also, see Chapter 13, concerning workplace policies, in which we recommend that your office or worksite go smoke free.

CAUTION

Do you or other top managers smoke? Get ready to give it up. Your wellness program will lose credibility if you aren't making the same efforts to quit that you're asking of others.

The Connection: Smoking Equals Worse Health and Lower Productivity

Tobacco smoke contains a potent mix of over 4,000 chemicals, such as carbon monoxide, tar, formaldehyde, cyanide, lead, arsenic, and ammonia, many of which are cancer causing, not to mention poisonous. These chemicals destroy the cleansing layer in the lungs, which causes mucus to build up, creating a place where cancer-causing particles get stuck.

Even smokeless tobacco (such as chewing tobacco or snuff) creates nicotine addiction and can lead to cancer, especially oral cancers. It may also contribute to high blood pressure and cardiovascular disease.

The chemicals in a cigarette become even more dangerous when combined with other toxins, such as asbestos. (If the air quality at your workplace is questionable, perhaps because the work involves using chemical solvents, that could be double trouble.) And people exposed to secondhand smoke are also at risk.

Why Haven't They Quit Already?

Seven out of ten smokers say they'd like to quit—so what's stopping them? Plenty. Nicotine is approximately as difficult to withdraw from as heroin—and the first three or four days are the hardest.

Willpower alone is rarely enough, and relapses after attempts to quit are common. Five to seven relapses is the average before a smoker quits for real. That's why nicotine addiction is medically considered a "chronic disease."

On top of that, smoking becomes an important ritual for many, who like to relax with a cigarette on their breaks, after a meal, or at other times. (Perhaps they don't realize that part of the "relaxation" is relief from withdrawal symptoms, which can start up a mere 30 minutes after their last inhalation.)

As with all bad habits, many smokers hope they won't feel the effects until some far-off day in the future. Unfortunately, smoking has a direct impact on day-to-day wellness. It tends to weaken bones, reduce memory and possibly reasoning abilities (especially if four or more hours have passed since the last cigarette), foster insomnia, increase susceptibility to bacterial infections, bring on early menopause among women and a need for Viagra among men, and increase the odds of developing macular degeneration (which can lead to blindness). It even causes wrinkles! Smokers also tend to take longer than others to recover from illness and injury.

And these everyday health issues are just the start of bigger stuff. Smoking has been linked to an overwhelming array of diseases including:

- cancer (not just lung, but others, including pancreatic, laryngeal, esophageal, renal, gastric, and bladder)
- heart disease (stroke, heart attack, vascular disease, and aneurysm)
- leukemia
- cataracts
- bronchitis, and
- pneumonia.

Pregnant women who smoke face an increased risk of miscarrying, giving birth prematurely, or having a low-birthweight infant. Even after a baby is born to a mother who smokes, it continues to ingest some of the toxins from smoking through breast milk.

As an employer, you can see how all of this—except perhaps the wrinkles—will directly correlate with absenteeism and reduced productivity. A number of studies in the United States and abroad have found that smokers are absent from work far more than nonsmokers (missing around six days per year as compared to the normal three or four for nonsmokers) and they are far less productive. One study estimated that smokers lose twice as many hours per week to nonproductive time as nonsmokers, putting smoking high on the list of health conditions that impact productivity. (Source: W.F. Stewart, et. al., "Lost Productivity Work Time Costs From Health Conditions in the United States: Results

From the American Productivity Audit," *Journal of Occupational and Environmental Medicine*, Vol. 45, No. 12 (2003).)

Your break-time policy may even suffer at the hands of nicotine addiction. According to a survey by the National Business Group on Health (NGBH, www.businessgrouphealth.org), smokers take between three and six smoking breaks per day, in most cases lasting between five and 15 minutes.

$\bigcirc$ CAUTION

Does your workplace inadvertently promote smoking? Some employees report feeling that the need for a cigarette is the only recognized reason to take a true break. You can combat this syndrome by providing other things for employees to do on their breaks, like play games—and by not giving them funny looks when they do so. How about a basketball hoop in the parking lot? (At Nolo, we have a ping pong table.) Or, suggests Dr. Foulds, "What about a popcorn break?"

Fortunately, the long-term prognosis for smokers has a bright side. The human body can make a comeback after quitting smoking, particularly if the smoker is relatively young and hasn't already developed cancer or another debilitating disease. For example, a 35-year-old man who quits smoking will, on the average, add five to ten years to his life expectancy. (See "Reversing the Damage," below.) Counselors who work with smokers trying to quit find that getting them to focus on the rewards of quitting can be quite effective; they're motivated by goals like feeling and looking better; having clean lungs, clean breath, brighter teeth, and greater stamina; and enjoying the taste of food more.

Is That Ash in My Coffee? Smoking and Customer Relations

At many workplaces, the first thing members of the public see when parking or approaching the front door is a group of smokers. That can create an unprofessional image, especially among people who are highly sensitive or allergic to cigarette smoke. (Just watch as they cover their noses and hurry inside.)

Even if customers and clients don't see your staff smoking, they'll be able to smell the cigarette smoke on them. This is especially problematic if you work in a food- or health-related industry. Food customers may not appreciate the competing smells or they may view smoking as a dirty habit. And it can be harder to listen to or trust a health care worker who doesn't follow the world's most obvious health advice and stop smoking.

A Small Company Tackles a Big Habit

With a workforce that rarely tops 25 people, Buffalo Supply, a wholesaler of hospital equipment based in Lafayette, Colorado, never felt the need to institute a formal wellness program. But with nearly 25% of its employees addicted to cigarettes, the company's CEO, Harold L. Jackson, became worried about the health impacts. He instituted a policy under which the company will pay for nicotine patches or gum to people trying to stop smoking, and give them $2,500 if they can quit for 30 days and sign a statement saying they're committed to giving up cigarettes permanently.

So far, six people have completed the 30 days and gotten the bonus. "Some of them chose to wait 60 days or more before actually signing their statement and collecting," says Kara Parker, their vice president of finance and human resources. She explains: "They wanted to first make sure they could really make that promise to us and to themselves."

Asked whether the company has seen a direct return in terms of health costs and productivity, Ms. Parker says, "We haven't crunched the numbers—we're doing this more out of principle. As a family-owned business, what we really want is for everyone to be healthy and live long."

How a Workplace Wellness Program Can Help

Many aspects of your workplace wellness program may contribute to a shift in lifestyle for smokers. Exercise and fitness activities in particular can help smokers change their routines and keep off the weight they may be afraid they'll gain by stopping smoking (nicotine boosts the metabolism so quitting sometimes invites extra pounds). In trying to get fit, they'll feel the benefits of developing good lung capacity. Yoga or stretching classes will help them relieve stress while improving flexibility. Your nutrition program will also help, teaching smokers to enjoy healthy snacks at times when they might otherwise reach for a cigarette. Any other stress-relief parts of your program will be right on target.

But as you might suspect, these measures probably won't be enough by themselves. Not only is quitting a challenge, but smokers aren't all created alike. They may have different reasons for smoking, face different barriers to quitting (including complicating factors like mental illness or another addiction to drugs or alcohol), and be at different stages in their readiness to quit.

But don't give up. Below are some additional ways your wellness program can help. And with the economy down, your timing may be particularly good. Nationwide, the average cost for a pack of cigarettes runs from around $5 to $10 a pack, with tax. For people with a pack-a-day habit, that could add up to well over $2,000 per year. As Dr. Foulds points out:

> *While many smokers already have a vague sense that they'd rather not smoke than smoke, that has been strengthened recently by the increase in tobacco taxes and reductions in household income. The result is that many smokers are getting serious about trying to quit.*

TIP

Make these activities and benefits available to the employees' immediate family, too. Of course, if you're requiring smokers to contribute higher amounts for your company-sponsored health plan, you want to give dependents the same opportunity to get a lower rate as others. And even if you're not, remember that dependents who smoke and are covered under your company's health insurance will raise your rates. Plus, family members' secondhand smoke may be adversely affecting your employee.

How Hard Can You Push?

Although we've recommended making your wellness program voluntary, smoking is one area where employers increasingly seek to mandate behavior change.

If you're thinking along those lines, here's what attorney and adviser Kelly Kuglitsch recommends as the safest legal and practical course:

The best practice is to announce, several months to a year in advance, that on a certain date, employees who do not smoke will pay $X for health insurance, and those who do smoke will pay an even higher $X. Tie the deadline to your health insurance open-enrollment period.

Then, distribute a tobacco-use certification form, which all employees covered under the health plan sign, stating whether or not they use tobacco.

To satisfy HIPAA—because the default is that you can't discriminate on the basis of a health factor, and this design does discriminate, with nonsmokers getting a different rate—you have to jump through the five hoops described in Chapter 2. These include providing an alternative standard for obtaining the reward. A lot of employers don't like this.

Let's say someone brings a doctor's note saying they're addicted to nicotine and just can't quit. You're legally bound to either waive your requirement or provide a different way to earn the reward, such as by completing a smoking cessation class. Some employers worry that this loophole will swallow the rule, but some employees probably won't want to bother with the class, so they'll pay the higher rate. Meanwhile, some employees who do go to the class may actually stop smoking.

Another requirement the employer must meet is providing the opportunity to earn the reward—in this case, the lower insurance rate—at least once a year. That would include your smoking cessation class, if you're using it for your alternative standard. But if you want to make your employees complete the class quarterly in order to get the reward, that's permissible.

> **TIP**
>
> **Style health-plan cost rewards as positive incentives.** Adviser Rae Lee Olson explains: "It's much better for employers to say, 'Your monthly insurance contribution is $50 but you get a $25 discount if you don't smoke,' rather than saying, 'The contribution is $25 but you have to pay an extra $25 if you smoke.' It's six of one and a half a dozen of the other from the employer's financial perspective, but the first feels a lot better to people."

Education: Why Quit Now?

As with all parts of your workplace wellness program, education is an important first step. Even while knowing that smoking is dangerous, many smokers remain in denial. Being confronted with both the facts and positive messages about their own power to change can be just what's needed. And if some of your smokers simply aren't ready to quit yet, you'll at least plant the seed.

Fortunately, a wealth of free information and resources are available to help you.

- **Bring in guest speakers.** Speakers are good for launching your efforts or keeping motivation high. A charismatic doctor or counselor, for example—or an exsmoker (perhaps from your own staff)—can give everyone a mental boost and encourage them to feel that, this time, they really can quit.
- **Include information in your newsletter or health library.** If you subscribe to a newsletter, it will probably regularly cover smoking. If not, put in a suggestion. Also, add informational pamphlets or fact sheets to your library or common area; many are available from the CDC and American Cancer Society (check their websites for instructions; in some cases, you can download the information, in others, you'll need to place an order). Be sure to include information on the dangers of secondhand smoke. Many people who can't quit for their own sake will do so in order to save their spouse, partner, or child from harm.

- **Encourage smokers to visit their doctors.** This is especially important if a personal consultation with a doctor wasn't part of the opening stages of your wellness program, or if some employees missed this opportunity. It's one thing to hear general messages about the risks of smoking, but another to have your doctor look you in the eye and say, "This habit is ruining your health, and if you don't stop, you'll die young." In fact, studies show that input from a physician can double a smoker's chances of successfully quitting. But don't expect the doctor to lead the patient through the entire quitting process—many of them aren't trained to do this.

- **Distribute a list of local restaurants with no-smoking policies.** This will encourage outings to places where smokers won't be tempted to light up. (No need to do this if you live in an area that has already prohibited smoking in public places. Such bans are catching on, but don't yet exist in the majority of U.S. states.)

- **Remind employees of any smoking cessation benefits offered as part of their health insurance.** Despite your best efforts, they may still have no idea.

- **Use informational posters.** These won't change anyone's behavior on the spot, but the facts on smoking are pretty stark and can be vividly conveyed in print, ideally with color images. Beyond the skull-and-bones messages, be sure to include posters with messages that remind people how energetic they'll feel and the things they could do if they quit tobacco. Free posters are available at www.notobacco.org/photos; the Centers for Disease Control (www.cdc.gov; click "More Publications," then "Smoking & Tobacco Use"; you'll need to request that copies be shipped to you); and from your local health department or nonprofits such as the American Cancer Society or American Lung Association. Swap out your posters occasionally, so that people will continue to notice them.

Reversing the Damage

Although no one can recover overnight from the effects of smoking, the healing process begins immediately and continues over the years, as follows:

- **One day after quitting:** The oxygen and carbon monoxide levels in the blood return to normal, and blood pressure should begin to drop.
- **Two days after quitting:** Senses of taste and smell sharpen.
- **Three to six months after quitting:** Lung function increases and circulation improves. The person doesn't feel as tired and short of breath.
- **One year after quitting:** The risk of heart attack is cut in half.
- **Two years after quitting:** In women, the risk of cervical cancer drops.
- **Ten years after quitting:** The risk of stroke and heart disease are closer to that of a nonsmoker. The risk of lung cancer and pancreatic cancer has fallen substantially.
- **Fifteen years after quitting:** The risk of heart disease or stroke is, at last, no more than that of a nonsmoker.
- **Long-term:** Ten or more years may be added to the person's life, depending on the age at which he or she quit.

Activities: Taking Action to Stop Smoking

Enough talk—it's time to take action. Here are some activities you can suggest, organize, or support to help your smoking employees kick the habit. Of course, we recommend not being too pushy about your offerings. The key is to encourage your employees and demonstrate that you have faith in their ability to quit smoking—not that you feel sorry for them or are impatient with their struggles. Most smokers by now understand that their habit isn't a completely private matter, but that it also affects the people around them. They'll welcome offers of help if their participation remains voluntary and their privacy is respected.

Your program is most likely to succeed if you view your workplace's antismoking activities as a long-term endeavor and a source of support for people who are either trying to quit smoking, have just relapsed, or are trying not to restart the habit.

- **Hold an on-site smoking cessation program.** If you have enough smokers on staff to warrant a group, bringing in outside experts to run such a program can be both convenient for the employees and a great way to build mutual support. For example, here's Dr. Foulds' description of the program he and his colleagues offer: "It's typically a six-session group, sometimes preceded by a presentation to the staff that describes what we do, why it's a good idea to quit, and what we can do to help. Those who sign up get an individual assessment at which we find out how motivated they are, how addicted they are, and what meds they might use. Then the group starts, typically with about 15 people. We meet once a week for six weeks. The second group meeting is 'quit day.' By the last meeting, they've quit for four weeks, which is about how long nicotine withdrawal lasts. The main purpose of the group is to get people through the hardest part, when the nicotine withdrawal symptoms are at their worst."

> **TIP**
>
> **They must commit to quit.** "Patient selection for a group is important," explains Dr. Foulds. "The group is effective, in part, because people support each other. Those who would otherwise have struggled see other people succeeding, and say 'Hey, I want to keep with the program, I don't want to be the only one smoking.' But if half the group members aren't really wanting to quit—maybe they just want to cut down on the number of cigarettes they smoke—it can have the opposite effect. Then those who wanted to quit see other people continuing to smoke, and they say, 'If it's okay for them to smoke, I'm going to smoke, too.'"

- **Join the Great American Smokeout—or start one of your own.**
  Every year on the third Thursday of November, the American
  Cancer Society sponsors The Great American Smokeout. The
  object is to challenge and support smokers in refraining—or at
  least reducing their cigarette consumption—for just 24 hours.
  Gathering your employees to participate in this event as a group
  is a great way to either jumpstart or reenergize your wellness
  program's antismoking activities. For information and ideas,
  including posters, an employer toolkit, suggested email blasts,
  and encouragement to serve "cold turkey" sandwiches for lunch,
  go to www.cancer.org (click "Guide to Quitting Smoking," then
  "Great American Smokeout"). You might also hold your own
  companywide "Smokeout" events or challenges at other times of
  the year—perhaps including incentives for those who participate.
- **Offer incentives.** Research at General Electric showed that
  smokers who earned financial incentives were three times more
  likely to quit smoking than others. They studied 900 employees
  who smoked, offering only some of them potential, incremental
  rewards that included $100 for completing a smoking cessation
  class, $250 for remaining smoke free after six months, and
  another $400 for being smoke free after a year. That's a $750
  total possible incentive. Among the people offered the incentives,
  15% succeeded in remaining smoke free after one year, while
  only 5% of the others achieved the same result. GE said the
  incentives paid for themselves in about three years. As an
  alternative to straight financial incentives, you can offer to pay
  a higher health insurance contribution to nonsmokers. (But see
  "How Hard Can You Push?" above.)
- **Recognize individual successes.** Newsletter stories (with advance
  permission) or accolades at a company meeting can create
  positive energy around employees' efforts to quit.

TIP

Wondering how to verify who has really quit? You can ask employees to sign statements, which will be enough to keep some honest. A more practical suggestion for employers who base their employees' health insurance contribution on whether they smoke, offered by adviser Rae Lee Olson, is "to allow employees to change their contribution amount on a monthly basis. In other words, instead of asking for verification of an entire year spent smoke free, let people change their status (from smoker to nonsmoker or vice versa) throughout the year, if necessary. That way as they're trying to make positive changes in their life, they can receive immediate rewards. Also, it allows them to be honest if they happen to slip back into smoking (rather than feeling dishonest about it for the remainder of the year). This can be a pain from an administrative standpoint, but the structure is much more supportive of employees who are really making an effort to quit."

Individual Treatment: Yum Yum, Nicotine Gum

Our suggestions up to this point have all been important, but with one significant limitation. As Dr. Foulds puts it:

> *Most of these workplace support measures are motivational—in other words, they increase the chances that someone will try to quit. That's a good start, but you still haven't provided an active ingredient for helping people to be successful when they try. Nicotine creates a physical addiction, and to think that giving employees a nice talk or asking them to sign a commitment statement is going to get them to quit is no more realistic than expecting the same from a heroin addict. Quitters really need the help of medical treatments, particularly those that have been evaluated and approved by the federal Food and Drug Administration (FDA).*

Various antismoking treatments, drugs, and devices have been around for years, and some can truly help. The U.S. Public Health Service recommends a combination of counseling and medication, which it found to be more powerful when used in combination than either is alone. (See *Treating Tobacco Use and Dependence* at www.

surgeongeneral.gov/tobacco.) So there's good reason for you to subsidize such treatment or take the additional measures described below:

- **Help employees access free or low-cost counseling services.**
  A great free resource is the helpline 1-800-QUIT-NOW (http://1800quitnow.cancer.gov). Anyone in the United States can call its counselors (from 7 a.m. to 9:30 p.m. on weekdays, and Saturdays from 9:30 a.m. to 1 p.m.) to discuss things like trigger situations that intensify cravings, steps toward quitting, and more. This service will also send free literature by mail. Both the printed literature and the website contain useful lists of local resources such as workshops, support groups, and treatments from hypnotherapy to acupuncture. These are offered at places like medical centers, health departments, nonprofit organizations (such as the American Lung Society), and private offices. The approximate prices of additional services are mentioned in the literature.

- **Subsidize enrollment in smoking cessation or counseling programs.**
  In an ideal world, your first stop would be your health insurance carrier. However, the truth is that only a minority of carriers provide smoking cessation coverage. What's more, as a small employer you've got very little leverage in negotiating added benefits to what's likely to be a cookie-cutter plan. Your time and resources will be better spent doing some research on locally available programs to decide which are worth subsidizing. (See "Evaluating Smoking Cessation Programs," below, and follow the privacy guidelines in Chapter 2.) According to studies, you're likely to spend less than the amount that the smoker's habit is currently costing your business. Counseling might include individual or group sessions, or even phone counseling. If the cost is impossibly high, offer to share it with the employee, or make coverage conditional on, at a minimum, the person completing the program or remaining smoke free for a set period of time. Having employees pitch in won't be a burden on them in the long run, given the already high costs of their tobacco habit.

Evaluating Smoking Cessation Programs

Start by getting program recommendations from doctors, staff at local nonprofits, and past smokers. You can also look for program reviews online. Then examine each likely sounding program to find out:

- **Price.** There's no need to take the quoted amount per employee at face value: Ask about group discounts, or whether the provider offers free or reduced reenrollment fees for enrollees who fail to quit.

- **Experience.** Look for an outfit that's been around for a few years, with highly trained or medically educated staff, and testimonials from other employers or respected physicians and organizations.

- **Scope of services.** Find out exactly how many hours of activity or services enrollees are entitled to and exactly what's included, for example: classes; advice on related topics like fitness, nutrition, and stress management; counseling (in person, by phone, or online); outreach to family members who'll be providing support; or other services.

- **Flexibility and ease of use.** You want a program that you or your employees can tailor to individual needs—for example, a choice of meeting at its facility or at your workplace, making late-night phone counseling appointments, talking with bilingual counselors, and more.

- **Use of breath tests to measure exhaled carbon monoxide.** As Dr. Foulds explains, "Smokers typically have at least ten times as much carbon monoxide in their blood as nonsmokers. It binds to the very red blood cells that should be carrying oxygen, thus making the heart work harder. As people reduce their smoking, however, the exhaled carbon-monoxide levels drop. Seeing these immediate results from the breath test boosts the smoker's motivation and also gives you, as the employer, a biochemical validation of the person's claim to have quit."

> ## Recommended Resources for Online Counseling and Peer Support
>
> Here are several other sources of good support for your employees:
>
> **www.becomeanex.org** Helps smokers create realistic plans to quit, reach out to others for support, and learn about fellow smokers'—or former smokers'—experiences via members' forums and blogs.
>
> **www.quitnet.com** Offers support from current smokers trying to quit, former smokers, and experts.
>
> **www.ffsonline.org** The American Lung Association's Freedom From Smoking message board is a peer network where smokers trying to quit offer mutual support at all hours of the day or night.
>
> **www.lungusa.org** The American Cancer Society provides this message board for smokers trying to quit. (Click "View all message boards," then "Quitting Smoking.")
>
> **www.smokefree.gov** The American Cancer Society offers counseling advice via instant messaging or telephone.

- **Subsidize costs of medications that help smokers quit.** While there's still no magic pill that will turn a smoker into a nonsmoker overnight, some worthwhile prescription, as well as over-the-counter (OTC), medications are available. Among the most widely used OTC medications are nicotine replacement therapy (NRT) gum, patches, and lozenges. These medications could make the difference in your employees' success at quitting. For details on what the medications are and how they work, see the table of "FDA-Approved Smoking Cessation Medications," below. Then figure out exactly what your health plan covers and consider filling in the gaps (again, following the privacy guidelines outlined in Chapter 2). Even if your plan covers smoking cessation, chances are it doesn't cover OTC remedies— which according to Dr. Foulds, "is a shame, given that the OTC remedies are both popular and medically useful." Unfortunately, the price may stop some people from trying NRTs on their

FDA-Approved Smoking Cessation Medications			
Medication Name	**How It Works**	**How It's Taken**	**Rx?**
Bupropion (Zyban or Wellbutrin)	An antidepressant that has been found to aid in smoking cessation as well, primarily by reducing withdrawal symptoms	Patients begin taking the pill while still smoking. They continue for seven to twelve weeks until they can, with the help of other treatment, create new habits that will help assure they don't return to smoking.	Yes
Varenicline (Chantix)	Lowers cravings and dampens the pleasure of smoking	Tablets of varying dosages are taken daily for 12 weeks, starting with a week when the patient is still smoking. Patients who are smoke free at the end of that time may continue taking for another 12 weeks, for maintenance purposes.	Yes
Nicotine Nasal Spray	Delivers a small dose of nicotine to a smoker, relieving withdrawal symptoms. Over time, the smoker is expected to wean off	Dispensed from a pump bottle up to 40 times a day at the beginning, less when weaning off	Yes
Nicotine Inhaler	Same as nicotine nasal spray	Dispensed from a plastic cylinder that people puff on when they have cravings; actually looks similar to a cigarette; to be used for up to 12 weeks	Yes
Nicotine Lozenges	Same as nicotine nasal spray	Similar to a hard candy, the lozenge releases nicotine as it dissolves in the mouth. Patients use a lozenge when they feel cravings, reducing usage over the 12-week weaning-off period.	No
Nicotine Gum	Same as nicotine nasal spray	When experiencing cravings, patients briefly chew a piece, then park the gum in their cheek. Up to 24 pieces per day are allowed, with patients gradually reducing the amount when weaning off.	No
Nicotine Patch	Same as nicotine nasal spray	Typically worn for 24 hours a day for a period of weeks, though one type is worn only during waking hours. Patients wear smaller and smaller patches as they wean off nicotine.	No

own, fearing that they'll turn out to be a waste of money—thus leaving them less to spend on cigarettes! NRT patches and gums typically cost from $35 to $55 for a two-week supply and $300 for a recommended course of treatment. If you can't afford to fill in any such gaps in coverage, you might share costs with the employee or condition your payment on employee action or results.

> ⓘ **TIP**
> **Haven't smokers heard of these treatments by now?** Yes, but myths and misinformation abound. Many smokers believe, for example, that NRTs are as harmful as cigarettes because they contain nicotine (which is far from the most harmful chemical in a cigarette) or that NRTs are dangerous for people with heart disease (also wrong).

The Link Between Low Income and Smoking

Experts say that the highest level of smoking occurs among people who earn less than $50,000 a year. (You know better than anyone how many of your employees that describes.) Within that same income bracket, people tend to avoid nonemergency medical care when there are costs or copayments involved. All the more reason for you, as an employer, to be generous in subsidizing smoking cessation benefits.

> ⓘ **TIP**
> **Don't give up on employees who relapse.** You may feel frustration that your program "didn't work," but that shouldn't affect your compassion as well as your support for the wellness program's continuing efforts to help smokers quit. It usually takes five to seven tries before a smoker quits. You can think of every relapse as one step closer to the goal!

Support: Where Have All the Smokers Gone?

The best way to reinforce the message that there are healthy alternatives to a smoking habit is to ban smoking from the workplace. If some people are still smoking, it makes it too easy for workers to feel left out of their own "club" if they don't join in, fall prey to temptation, or even bum a cigarette. Realize, however, that for the majority of smokers, a smoke free workplace policy isn't sufficient motivation by itself to quit— it may just create a distraction, as they wonder when they can get out for their next cigarette break. We'll discuss how to establish smoke free policies in Chapter 13.

Once an employee is taking active steps to quit, realize that the results are neither immediate nor guaranteed. Withdrawing smokers will need support from friends as well as the workplace. Here are some ways to offer that support.

- **Don't quibble with the withdrawing smokers' use of sick time.** They may need it to deal with withdrawal symptoms, such as irritability, anger, anxiety, restlessness, difficulty concentrating, insomnia, and even increased coughing as the lungs start to clear themselves. Dr. Foulds has talked to people who described quitting as feeling "bereaved," or like they'd turned into "a bear with a sore head." The person may also be dealing with side effects from the smoking cessation drugs, such as nausea.

- **Allow some program participation during working hours.** For example, Dr. Foulds explains, "When we do on-site programs at workplaces, we typically meet with the smokers as a group, over the lunch hour. This, however, requires that the employer allow time to attend, without feeling pressured by deadlines or other meetings. We've started asking for up-front help from the employer on this, to make sure that group members don't just work right through their lunch hour."

Helping the Addicted Worker

Meet Your Advisers

Renee Brown, M.A., LMFT, Executive and Clinical Director; and **Lisa Molbert,** Assessment Director; both at Sequoia Center, a drug and alcohol treatment and recovery center located in the San Francisco Bay Area.

What Renee does: She oversees all operational aspects of the business, such as staffing, program development, communications, marketing, and human resources. Renee also supervises clinicians working with clients receiving chemical dependency treatment.

What Lisa does: She assesses clients with substance abuse and mental health issues who are interested in coming into rehab treatment. Lisa has also been doing drug and alcohol interventions for three years for families and businesses.

Renee's favorite healthy food: "In the summer, I love fruit smoothies in the morning. A little fruit, plain soy milk, fat-free unflavored plain yogurt, some protein powder, and a teaspoon of vanilla in a quick blend. Protein in the morning really helps me get going."

Lisa's favorite healthy food: "Ryvita dark cracker bread with an almond date spread. I basically put a bunch of dates and almonds into a food processor, add a little water, and grind it up into a paste. I spread it on dark Ryvita, and it's so good!"

Renee's top tip for staying fit and healthy: "Like many, my job is very stressful. Other than the usual exercise and healthy food choices, I rely heavily on regular spiritual practices to keep my brain in 'calm' mode. I also believe that if we work hard, we must play hard! So, whatever you love to do after work, do it with gusto."

Lisa's top tip for staying fit and healthy: "I love to hike with my dogs on weekends and when I have time off."

Your employees' private lives are mostly just that—private. However, certain unhealthy or even illegal habits can spill over into their working lives, exposing them and other workers to harm and potentially putting your business at risk. In some cases, you'd want to intervene even if you weren't trying to implement a comprehensive workplace wellness program. But this isn't solely a discipline issue: In many cases, you're dealing with a valued worker who simply needs some support in getting life back on track.

In this chapter, we'll examine:

- the high price of addiction—particularly to drugs and alcohol—in the workplace
- cost-effective strategies you can implement as part of your general wellness program
- ways you can support individual treatment, including how to deal with employees who don't seek treatment on their own or whose behavior is having a serious effect on their job performance, and
- how to create a workplace environment that supports recovery rather than fostering addiction.

TIP

Get your policies in place. Your must undergird your actions with a workplace policy that prohibits use of drugs and alcohol at work and reminds people that they must show up "fit" to work. And you'll need to decide whether to require drug testing as a condition of employment. See Chapter 13 for details on making these and other policy decisions.

Addiction and Substance Abuse at Work: What You Need to Know

Let's start by defining what we mean by addiction. An addiction can involve any substance or activity that someone relies on and returns to up to the point where it controls his or her life. Abuse of drugs (legal or illegal), alcoholism, compulsive eating and other eating disorders, sex addiction, self-mutilation, workaholism, and tobacco smoking are all examples of addiction.

Other than tobacco (discussed in Chapter 8), the addictions you're most likely to come across in the workplace are drugs and alcohol. Although we tend to think of these problems as belonging to people on the margins of society, the truth is that most people who abuse alcohol or drugs—including 76% of illicit drug users and 80% of heavy drinkers—have jobs. Younger workers (between the ages of 18 and 25) are more likely than others to drink heavily, binge drink, use illicit drugs, and show up at work either under the influence or with a hangover, but older workers are far from exempt from such behavior. Given these numbers, even a small business may discover that one of its employees has a drug or alcohol problem.

This section discusses the many ways in which addiction harms both the health of your employees and the strength of your business. It will also help you stay alert to the signs of addiction in your workplace.

RESOURCE

Want to guesstimate how many of your employees are using alcohol? An online calculator by the George Washington University Medical Center will, based on your industry, location, and number of employees, give you the likely level of alcohol usage and what it's costing your business. See www. alcoholcostcalculator.org.

How Addiction Hurts Employees' Health

The key thing to understand before making any judgments or decisions about employees struggling with drug or alcohol addiction is that addiction is, scientifically speaking, a disease. In layperson's terms, drugs or alcohol hijack the motivational circuits of a person's brain, making continued usage the person's top priority. Adviser Renee Brown explains:

This is one of the most widely misunderstood aspects of addiction. But the medical authorities have established that addiction is a disease in the same way as are diabetes, cancer, heart disease—you name it. People don't invite addiction into their lives any more than they invite in any other disease, but because of diet, genetics, or other factors, they may be predisposed to it."

And, as we all know, addiction to alcohol or drugs has direct, often damaging impacts on the body. Depending on the exact substance, problems might include things like loss of coordination and self-control, addled judgment, changes in heart rate, slowed reflexes, distorted vision, hallucinations or delusions, lapses in memory, blackouts, and ultimately damage to organs, such as the kidneys, liver, and brain.

Addiction to drugs or alcohol can also complicate other health conditions. Excessive alcohol consumption suppresses the immune system and can reduce the drinker's ability to fight off infection. Drugs and alcohol may interact badly with various prescription drugs (a particular problem among older workers). And certain conditions, such as heart disease, high blood pressure, diabetes, or depression may be worsened through alcohol or other substance abuse.

Think Addiction Is None of Your Business? Think Again

Although the numbers of people who keep their jobs despite addictions suggest that many are "getting away with" substance abuse, businesses are clearly feeling the impact. Alcoholism results in approximately 500 million lost workdays per year. Drug abusers are nearly 13% more likely to have skipped one or more workdays in the past month. While they're at work, employees who abuse drugs or alcohol are more likely than others to show up late or with hangovers, take long breaks, leave early, sleep on the job, argue with coworkers, use poor judgment, and otherwise perform at a subpar level.

Substance Abuse and Domestic Violence: The Connection

Numerous studies have shown that many domestic violence incidents are committed while the perpetrator is under the influence of drugs or alcohol. Domestic violence is a serious health issue unto itself: It affects more women than diabetes, breast cancer, or cervical cancer. By addressing substance abuse as part of your workplace wellness program, you may save your employee's spouse or children—or the employee him- or herself—from severe emotional and/or physical danger.

Just what signs and behaviors your own employees exhibit depend on how far their disease has progressed, as explained by Renee Brown:

> There are three hallmarks of the disease of addiction. It's progressive, meaning it gets worse over time. It's chronic, meaning long-lasting and recurrent. And it's ultimately fatal, if left untreated. So as an employer, the signs and behaviors you might encounter in an addicted worker depend on where they are in the progression of their disease. It could be anything from showing up late with red eyes or a runny nose, losing weight, shaking, or looking hung over, to getting into an accident with the company truck.

Employer experience shows that untreated alcohol and drug addictions more than triple the risk of workplace accidents. If these are serious enough to warrant a hospital visit, the trauma staff won't be surprised—between 40% to 60% of all patients admitted to hospital trauma centers were injured while using alcohol or other drugs. Depending on the severity and long-term impact of such accidents in the workplace, they may lead to rises in insurance claims and workers' compensation costs. Drug abuse alone reportedly leads to a doubled rate of workers' compensation claims.

Substance abuse is also associated with increased employee theft and fraud. This can impact both your business and other employees—perhaps even your customers.

With all this bad news, you may think that the best way to deal with an addicted employee is to discipline or fire the person. But that's not necessarily so. Studies show that providing treatment to addicted employees costs less than either ignoring the problem or terminating the employee. (That said, we do discuss practical and legal grounds for termination a little later in this chapter.) Replacing an employee can be particularly expensive, given the costs of recruiting, HR staff time, training the new person, and more. Treatment, by contrast, has been shown to be both cost-efficient and medically effective. An analysis by the Chevron Corporation in the mid-1990s found that, by including treatment options within its workplace programs and policies, it saved $10 for every $1 spent.

Treatment for addiction may, therefore, be an important component of your wellness program. Below, we'll discuss some of the many ways to approach the issue. First, however, let's take a quick look at the question of how to recognize those among your staff who may need help.

How Can You Tell Who's Addicted?

Although substance abuse will be obvious in some employees' cases, others may be skilled at hiding the problem—and too far in denial to seek treatment on their own. As an employer, you probably already know that making inquiries in this area can be touchy. (For an analysis of whether and when to use drug testing as an objective way of finding out, see Chapter 13.)

Your workplace wellness program makes a good setting within which to help people identify problems within themselves or among coworkers. The HRAs and biometrics tests administered at the start of the program (described in Chapter 3) should ask about substance abuse issues and direct people—at least those honest enough to answer directly—toward treatment. Beyond this, your educational and other measures, as described below, should help employees and supervisors realize the signs.

Eventually, you're likely to realize that someone has a problem, even if you don't know exactly what it is. Renee Brown says:

Because the disease is progressive, some of the visible changes are going to be gradual rather than dramatic—for example, you're not going to see somebody losing 70 pounds in a week. But you are going to see an ongoing pattern.

Which Workers Use the Most Drugs and Alcohol?

A 2007 study by the Substance Abuse and Mental Health Services Administration (SAMHSA) found that:

- Workers using the most illicit drugs included food service workers (17%) and construction workers (15%).
- Workers using the most alcohol included construction, mining, excavation, and drilling workers (18%), and installation, maintenance, and repair workers (15%).

However, cautions Lisa Molbert:

Don't take these numbers to mean that you're unlikely to find drug addicts or alcoholics in other industries or types of work. I've done addiction assessments for software engineers, nurses and other health care professionals, people who run businesses, financial advisers, and stay-at-home parents. Addiction can happen anywhere.

Education: Getting the Facts About Addiction

Even if only one member of your workplace has—or appears to have—a problem with addiction, it's worth including an awareness component in your workplace wellness program. For one thing, education may help that person see the need for treatment. For another, it may help others to realize that they themselves have, or are on the way to developing, a substance abuse problem—or that the same is true for a family member. And finally, it will help everyone understand how to respond if they see that someone's work is being affected by addictive behavior.

Here are some things you can do to get the right information to your employees:

- **Make sure all employees know about your company's drug-free policy.** The policy you develop (based on the advice in Chapter 13) should be made clear to all employees, whether in a group setting or in one-on-one, new employee orientations. A model for group orientations can be found at the Department of Labor (DOL) Working Partners website at www.dol.gov/workingpartners. (Click "Drug-Free Workplace," then "Employee Education," then "Drug-Free Workplace Advisor Program Builder—Employee Education.")

- **Bring in speakers.** Likely topics include the signs of addiction, as well as options for local treatment. Local medical centers or treatment providers—for example, Sequoia—are good sources of speakers. Make sure your speakers emphasize that addiction is a treatable disease of the brain, not an indictment of the addicted person. Finish or follow up the talk with information from a human resources staff person on how your company supports addiction recovery—for instance, by subsidizing treatment or offering flex-time or leave time for attendance, as discussed below. Reassure employees that you will maintain confidentiality to the extent possible, if they choose to take advantage of these offerings.

- **Distribute relevant pamphlets.** Provide access to pamphlets, books, and other resources in your in-house health library (or bookshelf). You can choose from literally dozens of pamphlets by going to your local Alcoholics Anonymous central office. (See www.aa.org.) For books, Renee Brown recommends: *Drinking: a Love Story*, by Carolyn Knapp (Dial Press Trade Paperback); *Healing and Hope*, by Betty Ford (Putnam Adult); *Alcoholics Anonymous Big Book* (Benei Noaj); and *Narcotics Anonymous* (Hazelden Publishing & Educational Services).

- **Include information on addiction in your regular health newsletter.** Articles with positive news about treatment methods are particularly valuable. You can also suggest sources of online information. Renee Brown recommends the Alcoholics Anonymous website (www.aa.org, under the tab "Is A.A. for you?"), where people can find simple questions and answers concerning whether their drinking patterns constitute alcoholism, and how they can seek treatment without giving up their anonymity.

- **Put up posters.** Colorful, encouraging posters are available from the U.S. DOL at www.dol.gov/workingpartners. (Under the "Drug-Free Workplace" tab, click "Employee Education," then "Workplace Substance Abuse Posters.")

Individual Treatment: Helping Addicts Get Help

Finding out that one or more of your employees is addicted to drugs or alcohol—or even suspecting as much—may come as a shock. But as you by now know, addiction doesn't mean that the person is morally bankrupt. Providing effective treatment options within your workplace wellness program is, as we'll discuss below, both a compassionate and rational way to help some employees turn their lives around.

But what if the task is truly bigger than you can handle? We'll begin this discussion by taking a brief look at the legal landscape, then we'll recommend wellness program options for those employees you might be able to help.

Employment Law Considerations

If you discover that someone on your staff is abusing drugs or alcohol, or has another addiction, your gut reaction might be to show them the exit door. From a legal perspective, you'd probably be well within your rights. Most employees work at will, which means they can quit at any time, for any reason, and you can fire them at any time, for any reason that isn't illegal. (For example, even an at-will employee may not legally be fired for discriminatory reasons, in retaliation for reporting a health or safety violation, or for exercising a legal right.)

Of course, the fact that you can fire an employee without legal repercussions doesn't mean you should. As explained above, the costs of firing and replacing an employee are often far higher than the cost of helping the employee conquer a substance abuse problem. Savvy employers don't fire people in haste; instead, they try to retain and reward their valued employees, and coach those who aren't meeting company standards to help them improve performance. This approach builds morale and company loyalty, improves overall performance and productivity, and keeps the company on the safest possible legal ground.

When deciding how to approach an employee with a substance abuse problem, there are a few important legal facts to keep in mind. We introduce them here, then discuss them more fully below.

- **The employee may have a disability.** In some circumstances, addiction is considered a disability, meaning that the ADA applies and you have certain obligations as an employer. For example, your company must keep records relating to the disability confidential, must consider reasonable accommodations to help the employee perform the job, and must not make job decisions based on the employee's disability.

- **Your company may face liability.** Employers are liable for actions their employees take that fall within the course and scope of their jobs. Once your company is aware of an employee problem that creates a safety hazard, the risk of liability increases exponentially. If an employee's substance abuse problem poses a risk of harm to others, you must make sure that the employee can do the job safely.

- **You must apply rules consistently.** While you may be tempted to bend the rules for an employee with a substance abuse problem, this is rarely a good idea. It can lead to morale problems and accusations of unfairness and discrimination. It can also make it difficult to apply your policies once you decide that it's time to step in and impose discipline.

When Addiction Is a Disability

Because alcoholism and drug addiction are diseases, the ADA may come into play. Current abuse of illegal drugs is not a disability, but alcoholism and past drug abuse are. In addition, an employee's use of legal drugs might have ADA implications. Here are the rules:

- **Alcoholism.** You may not discipline or fire someone simply for being an alcoholic. For example, you may not fire an employee simply because he or she attends AA meetings or takes a prescription drug—such as antabuse, naltrexone, or campral—to fight alcohol abuse.

- **Prescription drugs.** Use of legal drugs (whether prescribed or over the counter) might also be covered by the ADA, if the drugs are prescribed for a disability. As with any disability, you may have to make reasonable accommodations to help the person perform the job—for example, allow breaks to self-administer injections. However, the employee must be able to do what the job requires. If the employee's performance is impaired by legal medication— perhaps due to perpetual dizziness or drowsiness—and no accommodation can help, you aren't required to retain him or her.

- **Illegal drugs.** Current illegal drug use, sale, or possession garners no ADA protection. This means you don't have to worry about violating the ADA if you discipline or fire an employee for selling drugs in the parking lot or shooting up in the bathroom during lunch. Of course, you should make sure you've got your facts straight—that is, that illegal drugs are really involved—before taking action. For example, you could get into legal trouble if you fire an employee based on slurred speech and lack of physical coordination if those symptoms were caused not by illegal drug use but by a disability such as Parkinson's disease or multiple sclerosis. Workers with past, not current, drug problems get a bit more legal protection. Someone who is no longer using illegal drugs and has successfully undergone treatment or is currently participating in a supervised drug rehabilitation program is protected from discrimination by the ADA.

If the ADA applies to an employee with a substance abuse problem, you have an obligation to provide a reasonable accommodation to help the employee perform the job's essential functions. For example, an employee might need occasional time off during the day to attend rehab or therapy meetings. Modifications to work schedules are also a possibility. For instance, if an employee's prescription medication causes drowsiness or nausea in the morning, you might adjust the employee's schedule to provide a later starting time.

You also have an obligation to keep the employee's medical records (including facts such as the employee's alcoholism or treatment for substance abuse) confidential—that is, on documents and in files that are separate from the rest of the employee's personnel records. Although the employee is of course free to share his or her situation with others, the company may make such confidential information available only to:

- the employee's supervisor, if the employee's disability requires restricted duties or a reasonable accommodation
- safety and first aid personnel, if the employee's disability may require medical treatment or special evacuation procedures
- insurance companies that require a medical exam, and
- government officials, if required by law.

When Your Business May Be Liable

As an employer, you are responsible for the costs of doing business, including costs associated with any carelessness or misconduct on the part of your employees. For example, if your pizza company promises delivery within 30 minutes, you would most likely be liable for injuries caused by an employee racing to meet the deadline.

Whether an employer is liable for accidents caused by an employee's use of drugs or alcohol depends on many facts, including:

- the circumstances of the accident
- whether the employee was on duty
- whether the employee was following the company's rules or acting independently, and
- whether the accident was foreseeable given the employee's job.

If the employer knows about the employee's use of drugs or alcohol before the harm occurs, the risk of liability goes way up. For example, if you hand over the keys of the delivery van to an employee who is obviously drunk, you'd have a very tough time arguing that your company wasn't responsible for a resulting accident.

Potential liability is something you must consider when deciding how to handle an employee with a substance abuse problem. If the employee's job has inherent safety risks—for example, driving, operating heavy or dangerous machinery, climbing ladders, or performing delicate medical procedures—you will want to make very sure that the employee can do the job safely before allowing the employee to work. For example, you may want to require periodic drug testing to make sure an employee is staying clean and sober.

Why You Need to Apply Consistent Rules

Often, employers are tempted to make exceptions to the usual work rules for certain employees. Although this is understandable, it can lead to problems if you don't think it through. When you make an exception, you treat one employee more favorably than others, which often results in resentment or claims of bias. This doesn't mean you should never give an employee a break or show some kindness, but you should consider how your decisions will affect other employees or limit your options for dealing with future problems.

For example, let's say your company's attendance policy calls for a warning if an employee is late three times in a month. Jane has been late more than three times and she's confided in you that her lateness is due to her drinking more heavily since she and her boyfriend broke up. You feel bad for her, refer her to the EAP program, and decide not to write her up. But what about the next employee who's late three times? What if it's due to depression following a parent's death, anxiety-related insomnia because a spouse is on active military duty, or trouble figuring out the right public transit to take after the employee's car is repossessed? What if the employee just doesn't tell you why he or she is arriving late?

As you can see, it gets tough to make distinctions once you start deviating from company policy. This doesn't mean you can never make exceptions, but you should be consistent. For example, if you let an employee take an extra month of leave for rehab, you'll probably want to make the same leave available to employees who need it for other health reasons. Or, if you decide to pay part of the cost of rehab for an employee's domestic partner, even though your company's policy doesn't cover it, you should make that your rule for other employees as well.

Often, it's a good idea to adopt a two-pronged approach to performance or conduct problems due to substance abuse:

- Handle the workplace problems caused by substance abuse through coaching and discipline as dictated by company policy.
- Offer assistance for the underlying problem.

Absent an unusually compelling reason to do otherwise, you should hold everyone to the same standards of performance and conduct, and discipline employees as required by company policy when they fail to meet those standards. At the end of the day, you are running a business, and the work needs to get done. And you don't want to get into a situation where you're treating employees with performance or attendance problems caused by drug abuse more favorably than employees whose problems stem from a different source.

Intervening With Employees Who Haven't Sought Treatment

Whether or not you decide to discipline the employee, you should also consider offering or proposing treatment to an employee who may have a substance abuse problem.

Don't ignore the problem. That's an all-too-common response among managers—even those who feel comfortable raising other health-related concerns with employees. Addiction issues are likely to escalate, perhaps to the point where a manager lets frustration push him or her to an overly forceful or ill-timed confrontation in response to an immediate problem like an employee's drunken state at a party. And you aren't going to solve the employee's work problem—for example, spotty attendance, low productivity, or inappropriate behavior—until the substance abuse problem is dealt with. If you have an EAP program, call for managerial support and ask about referrals or counseling for the employee.

Starting the Conversation

Employers often worry about how to approach an employee who may have a substance abuse problem. They don't want to accuse the employee or provoke a defensive response, yet the issue has to be dealt with. You should know that it's okay, from a legal perspective, for a manager to ask an employee about possible substance abuse. Often, however, it's better to focus on how the employee's problem is affecting his or her work.

That way, you can give tangible examples and demonstrate that your purpose isn't to engage in a personal attack or to accuse, but to help the employee get back on track.

The employee's supervisor should sit down with the employee to talk about the problem. This can happen in the context of a disciplinary meeting or simply as an informal chat. Renee Brown offers the following suggestions:

> First, it helps if the employer has created a workplace culture where there's a sense of safety and confidentiality, giving the message that, "We want to do everything we can to keep you as an employee because we value you, and we're willing to work with you." Then a supervisor might approach the person, opening the discussion with something performance based. You wouldn't come right out and say, "You look like hell," but you might say, "You've been showing up late on Mondays; can we talk about finding a way to manage that?"

The employee may or may not admit to having a drug or alcohol problem. Denial is a common response. There's no point trying to force an admission, but you should be clear about what performance is expected. For example, Renee Brown suggests the supervisor might say, "I need you not to be slurring your words when you're doing a sale, and I need you to show up on time." Talk through the changes that need to happen, and ask the employee what you can do to help him or her turn things around.

Deciding on the Next Steps

If the employee reveals a substance abuse problem or is concerned that one might be present, make sure the employee knows how to access all the offerings of your EAP or health insurance plan. Talk about what you can do to help.

You should also create a written action plan, outlining what steps you and the employee will take in the future. You might indicate what improvements you need to see, deadlines, any assistance you can offer the employee, and plans to check in later and see how things are going.

> ### If the Employee Doesn't Admit the Problem
>
> No matter how understanding and supportive you are, some employees may not be willing to admit to a substance abuse problem. There's not much you can do in this situation except to make clear that your door is always open and to talk about the offerings available. As an employer, you can't force an employee to accept treatment; all you can do is handle the problem through your regular disciplinary channels and hope that the employee is soon ready to take Step One: admitting that there's a problem.

RESOURCE

Learn more about workplace investigations, discipline, and other important legal topics for employers. Some excellent resources from Nolo include:

- *Dealing With Problem Employees: A Legal Guide*, by Amy DelPo and Lisa Guerin
- *The Essential Guide to Workplace Investigations: How to Handle Employee Complaints & Problems*, by Lisa Guerin, and
- *The Progressive Discipline Handbook: Smart Strategies for Coaching Employees*, by Margie Mader-Clark and Lisa Guerin.

Recommending and Supporting Treatment

A number of effective treatments have been developed for substance abuse; you'll find them listed below. The list is long—in part because different treatments are appropriate for different people, depending largely on how far their disease has progressed. As Renée Brown explains:

> *If someone has cancer and it's at Level One, the treatment will be different than if it's at Level Five. For some addicts, the treatment could be as simple as going to twelve-step meetings and learning how to abstain from drinking or using. Others may need one-on-one counseling or an inpatient treatment program.*

When considering how to help your employees and their families with addiction issues, you'll need to be thinking of two issues: what your workplace can offer (or already has available through its EAP and medical insurance plans) and what the individual employee (or family member) needs. The main treatment possibilities include:

- individual counseling
- group and family counseling
- twelve-step programs
- inpatient treatment (from a few days to a month or more, in a residential rehab center or hospital)
- medication, such as acamprosate for alcohol or methadone or suboxone for opiate drugs
- life-skills training
- follow-up care during recovery, and
- various combinations of these.

What Can You Offer?

If you have an EAP, start by checking to see what benefits if offers. As described in Chapter 12, an EAP can provide confidential services to workers with drug or alcohol problems, including education, conversations with a friendly EAP staff member, and referrals to professionals. Some companies have found that this reduces the amount of actual medical coverage that their substance-abusing employees must draw on. And they also report a high rate of success—ChevronTexaco, for example, found that 75% of employees who went to the EAP with alcohol problems were able to improve their performance and keep their jobs.

Next, find out what benefits are offered by your health insurance provider. Many states' laws actually mandate that health plans provide the same or similar levels of coverage for substance abuse and mental health as they do for other health care, a concept referred to as "parity." As of October 2009, federal law (The Mental Health Parity Act, 29 U.S.C. § 1185a) will require the same thing for companies with more than 50 employees. Assuming your plan offers coverage, you might want to create incentives for attendance that either offset or directly reimburse the cost of employees' copayments (subject to the privacy and other cautions described in Chapter 2).

If neither your EAP nor your health plan includes substance abuse treatment, you may want to add coverage at renewal time. (This should raise your health insurance premium by only about 1%.) In the meantime, however, you may need to look into alternative treatment programs, and possibly offer to help pay. (Again, see Chapter 2 for how to do this within your privacy obligations. Also, see Chapter 13 for more on how to make paying for treatment part of your employment policies.) Don't worry, there are plenty of options other than celebrity rehab spa-clinics. In fact, outpatient treatment is more popular than inpatient, because it costs less and minimizes the employee's time away from the job.

TIP

Unhappy about paying for treatment? We understand. The trouble is, your employee is probably equally, if not more reluctant. Lisa Molbert says, "The number one reason that people don't come in for treatment—especially men—is money." Renee Brown adds, "Denial and fear of losing their job are right behind that, but money is clearly the biggest hurdle." So if you can remove that hurdle, you can make a huge difference in the addict's chance of recovery.

One free option is a twelve-step program such as Alcoholics Anonymous (AA; www.aa.org), described under "Twelve-Step Programs," below. This shouldn't, however, be the only option you make available to employees. As explained below, twelve-step programs incorporate belief in a "higher power," which has given rise to some religious objections.

RESOURCE

Finding more treatment programs. For additional help locating local drug and alcohol abuse treatment programs (inpatient or outpatient), check the Substance Abuse and Mental Health Services Administration (SAMHSA) website at www.findtreatment.samhsa.gov.

Finally, if you're going pay for substance abuse treatment, you want to make sure you're sending people to the best facility for the money. One way to suss out the best option is to visit a few likely treatment facilities yourself—or at least call—and ask the questions listed under "Questions to Ask a Prospective Treatment Center," below. (These questions are also available as a worksheet you can take along with you if you visit a treatment facility. See the "Treatment Center Evaluation Form" on the CD-ROM.)

Give your employee a chance to visit the top facilities on your list, to make sure they don't sign up for one whose environment turns them off from the start. As Lisa Molbert explains:

Choosing the right treatment center is a big decision. The person is going to be spending a significant amount of time there. If I were the employee and had three to choose from, I'd probably go visit all three, paying attention to the ambience, what the team is like, and what kind of energy I get from the place.

What Does Your Employee Need?

The more options your health plan and your wellness program can offer, the greater the chances that one will suit a particular employee's temperament and needs. If, for example, your health plan offers only a six-week, full-time course of treatment, an employee may be reluctant to sign up because "everyone will know" why they're gone for six weeks. Besides, their disease may not have progressed to the point of needing that level of treatment.

But how do you figure out what's best for an employee? One good way, according to Lisa Molbert, is to have the person assessed by a professional. She should know, since she does these assessments herself. And it's not always because the person is necessarily seeking treatment at Sequoia. For example, says Lisa:

I've had employees come to me referred by their employer for getting drunk at the Christmas party, where the employer was facing lawsuits because of the person's flirty behavior. The employer conditioned the person's future employment on getting an assessment of whether the person has an alcohol or drug problem."

Such an assessment will detail what the person actually needs in terms of treatment.

Twelve-Step Programs

Twelve-step programs refer to themselves as fellowships, because, throughout the world, they're largely self-supporting and volunteer led. Local group members meet regularly (using only their first names) to share stories and experiences and help each other recover from addictions and compulsions using the twelve-step principles. They do not employ professional counselors or therapists.

The twelve steps themselves include admitting that an addiction has made one's life unmanageable, belief in a higher power (no specific religious affiliation is required, but this may conflict with some employees' beliefs nonetheless), taking a fearless self inventory, making amends to those whom one has hurt, and more.

Just how effective the program is depends largely on the quality of members who happen to be in the local group at the same time. Some people have recovered through twelve-step programs alone. Experts maintain, however, that they're not usually a complete substitute for professional help.

Among the many twelve-step programs now in existence are:
- Narcotics Anonymous (NA; www.na.org)
- Cocaine Anonymous (CA; www.ca.org)
- Crystal Meth Anonymous (www.crystalmeth.org)
- Marijuana Anonymous (www.marijuana-anonymous.org)
- Gamblers Anonymous (GA; www.gamblersanonymous.org)
- Sexaholics Anonymous (SA; www.sa.org)
- Overeaters Anonymous (OA; www.oa.org).

Questions to Ask a Prospective Treatment Center

Here are important questions to ask of any treatment center at which you might help an addicted employee enroll. (For a worksheet you can take along with you if you visit a treatment facility, see the "Treatment Center Evaluation Form" on the CD-ROM.)

- **What treatment methods do you use, and what's the evidence that they work?** Best answer: A cogent explanation of treatment methods, backed up by recommendations from widely recognized physicians or providers and by scholarly studies showing significant improvement made by patients undergoing the same type of treatment.

- **Does your program have state or other professional accreditation or licensing?** Only acceptable answer: Yes (in fact, you should see this mentioned on their website). At a minimum, the program should meet any state licensing requirements. It may also have received accreditation from a national program such as the Joint Commission (www.jointcommission.org) or the National Committee for Quality Assurance (www.ncqa.org).

- **Does your clinical and treatment staff hold licenses and other credentials?** Only acceptable answer: Yes. Ask for specifics, starting with state licensing, if required. Apart from medical doctors, other directly relevant credentialing might include LADC (licensed alcohol and drug counselor), LPC (licensed professional counselor), CAC (certified addictions counselor), and CCDP (certified co-occurring disorders counselor).

- **Aside from your core program, what supportive treatment do you provide?** Drugs or alcohol are rarely the only problem in addicts' lives. They may have so-called "co-occurring" or "dual" disorders—like depression or schizophrenia—that require expert psychological help. They might also benefit from nutrition, fitness, or even spiritual instruction. Of course, you'd want to check that any of these instructors are also licensed or credentialed.

- **What's your ratio of patients to counselors?** Best answer: One counselor for every five or fewer patients. Group activities can be great, but it's important that there also be opportunities for small-group as well as one-on-one attention or counseling.
- **During what hours are clinical staff members available on site?** If it's an inpatient facility, certain patients may need 24-hour care—in some cases, actual medical care.
- **Can you provide medical detoxification ("detox") to residential patients?** Best answer: Yes, if that's something your employee will require. For example, says Lisa Molbert, "An alcoholic with gastro-intestinal bleeding could need a hospital-type bed with an IV."
- **Do you include separate group treatment opportunities for men and women?** Best answer: Yes. Studies have shown that both men and women feel more comfortable discussing certain issues in front of, and receiving support from, groups composed of their own gender.
- **Do you provide additional support for the patients' families?** Best answer: Yes. Recovery doesn't happen in isolation, and it helps if the family understands the process and how to help.
- **Do you provide ongoing support after patients leave treatment?** Best answer: Yes. The success rate has been shown to double for people in recovery who receive some form of ongoing treatment. Remember that addiction is a chronic condition, so relapses are natural. They should be anticipated and averted whenever possible, with ongoing, if less intensive, follow-up support. Maintaining and celebrating the friendships and supportive relationships established while in care is also important, which is why some treatment facilities also plan reunions and other celebrations.
- **What insurance do you accept?** Best answer: Whatever insurer covers your employees or their family members! Find out which staff member takes care of insurance matters and talk to that person to make sure that he or she is knowledgeable and willing to be your advocate when it comes to getting coverage.

Creating a Supportive Workplace Environment for Recovery

An employee who has finished a treatment program is said to be in recovery—but never fully cured. Addiction isn't like the flu, where once it's over, it's over. Any expert will tell you that addiction recovery is a lifelong endeavor. Slipups sometimes happen, and aren't always disastrous—but can be.

As an employer, you can't be expected to monitor an employee's continued abstinence. In fact, you'd become very irritating if you tried. Below, however, are some constructive ways to create a supportive environment for a recovering addict. Note that many of these involve reining in the use of alcohol, which may not always be the addiction in question. However, exposure to alcohol use can be a trigger for other addictions. For example, if an office party turns into a beer-fest, then the general atmosphere and lack of restraint may trigger a recovering drug addict's cravings. (And while we're on the topic, a company that provides alcohol may be responsible for the behavior of inebriated employees. This is probably why company holiday parties often feature prominently in sexual harassment cases.)

 TIP

You can't remove all temptations from a recovering addict's path. The world will present enough obstacles without your help, and it's the addict's job to learn to resist. But you can avoid making that job extra difficult by following some of the suggestions below:

- **When an employee has been on leave for treatment, have a pre-return meeting.** This should be a confidential meeting between the supervisor or human resources staffer and the employee. It's a chance for both of them to ask and answer questions. The supervisor, for example, might want to ask the employee about any special requests—perhaps that his or her desk be moved farther away from a coworker who's always trying to talk people into visiting a bar after work. The employee might have questions such as whether everyone at work knows where he or she has been, and how quickly he or she will be expected to perform at full speed. Create or update and sign a performance agreement detailing a schedule of expectations.

- **Maintain confidentiality where possible.** Obviously, certain people at the company will have to know about an employee's addiction and treatment. And others may have heard through the grapevine. But don't use this as an excuse for open conversations, memos, unasked for efforts to help, or even teasing about the matter. Because the employee's past drug addiction qualifies as a disability under the ADA (as explained above), you must follow the confidentiality rules explained above.

- **Be flexible about work hours.** Whether an employee is seeking treatment or wants the option of visiting a counselor or participating in a long-term support group, you can offer flex time and similar alternatives to ease the way toward follow-through. In fact, even if a few of your employees are recovering addicts who decide to form a mini-support group, allowing them to take slightly long lunches off-site makes sense and avoids privacy concerns. Notice that we don't recommend creating such a support group—this itself would give rise to privacy issues. But, as Renee Brown says, "It usually isn't long before the people dealing with alcohol or drug addiction find each other."

- **Educate management about the needs of a recovering addict.** A common complaint among employees being treated for addiction treatment is that their supervisors or managers have no idea about what is and isn't appropriate behavior. (That's true of coworkers too, but privacy rules forbid you from telling them about the person's addiction.) For example, some colleagues, trying to be supportive, will stop inviting a recovering alcoholic to any event or party where they know alcohol is being served. (This is a hurtful approach and seemingly patronizing—the recovering alcoholic should be the one to decide whether he or she can handle this type of occasion.) And supervisors sometimes act like it's their job to not only encourage, but counsel or monitor the person. Provide information to supervisors, perhaps by emailing relevant written matter. Remind them to be discreet about printing these out. Your EAP can help with this, or you can find some good material about recovery by visiting the DOL website at www.dol.gov/workingpartners. (Click "Substance Abuse Basics," then "Recovery.")

- **Plan office events carefully.** What if you have regular company parties or picnics where you've always served beer or other alcoholic beverages, and one or more of your employees is a recovering addict? Cutting off the flow might be overkill. But include lots of other drink options (see the nutrition guidelines in Chapter 5), and don't make alcohol the center of your offerings. Also limit the amounts available, so that the party isn't overwhelmed by inebriated folks raising loud toasts. Next, think creatively about designing events that are naturally alcohol free, such as a fresh-smoothie breakfast rather than a champagne brunch. Events held during the workday never need to include alcohol. If you do serve it, remind all employees to exercise moderation (or total abstinence if they do risky jobs like welding or truck driving), and not to take drinks back to their desks or workstations afterward.

- **Remind your managers to exercise restraint at office events.** A top-level employee who drinks too much sets the stage for other nonwork-appropriate behavior. Have a talk with anyone who's prone to silly behavior like suggesting a drinking contest. (It's been known to happen.)

Reducing Obesity

Meet Your Adviser

Trina Histon, Ph.D., Senior Manager of Weight Management and Director of the Weight Management Initiative at Kaiser Permanente's Care Management Institute in Oakland, California.

What she does: Dr. Histon helps Kaiser Permanente implement a public-health-based approach to obesity that includes healthy eating and active living. She also works with Kaiser Permanente doctors across the country to optimize the prevention of obesity, as well as to address the needs of children, adolescents, adults, and anyone undergoing weight loss surgery.

Favorite healthy food: "Steamed brussels sprouts with fresh ground pepper—easy to make and so good for you."

Top tip for staying fit and healthy: "I work out five times a week and I don't drive, so I have to walk everywhere. I suggest trying to build some activity into your everyday routine. Get a pedometer and aim for 10,000 steps a day!"

The tabloids would have you believe that everyone needs to be model thin—but don't buy it. A little extra padding can be healthy. However, if the pounds keep piling on, a person will be considered medically overweight, and eventually obese. We'll discuss these distinctions in more detail below, but the basic idea is that someone who is overweight or obese has an abnormal—and in many cases, medically dangerous—accumulation of body fat.

People who are seriously overweight may need more help than can be addressed by the general nutrition and fitness components of your workplace wellness program—for example, they may also benefit from counseling services and pharmaceutical supplements. A separate weight management program may therefore be an important focus of your wellness efforts. As adviser Dr. Douglas Metz says:

> Given the fact that 68% of America is overweight or obese, every employer will probably have to deal with this issue. Maybe not in a three-person bicycle shop where they're all triathletes, but in most other workplaces.

The good news is that the workplace can be an optimal setting in which to tackle weight loss efforts, because of the documented effects of social networks on obesity. Simply put, when one friend loses a lot of weight, the odds improve that another one will, too. (For a real-life example, see "Sisters Lead Company Weight Loss Challenge," below.)

And a weight loss program may be appreciated by many of your workers—including those who aren't motivated by serious health concerns. Lots of us just want to look and feel better, which is why weight management programs are commonly requested by employees.

This chapter will address the health risks associated with obesity, as well as how your wellness program can provide effective—and even enjoyable—ways for overweight or obese employees to drop some pounds.

The Connection: Obesity and Health Problems

Being overweight, especially to the point of obesity, can lead to a host of health troubles for your employees and for your business. First, let's look at how obesity is defined and then, at how it can damage physical health.

How Much Weight Is Too Much?

For the sake of simplicity, the point at which a person is considered overweight or obese is usually determined by a calculation of their "body mass index" or BMI. This is a ratio of body weight compared to height. Someone with a BMI of 25 or higher is considered overweight, while someone with a BMI of 30 or higher is considered obese. To use a concrete example, a 5'9" person who weighs 169 pounds or more is said to be overweight, and if that same person reaches 203 pounds or more, he or she will be considered clinically obese. (For more heights and weights, see "Where the Scales Tip: Obesity at Various Heights," below.)

As we said, however, this ratio is all about simplicity—it's not perfect. Dr. Histon illustrates how the measure can occasionally fail:

> *The example is someone like Arnold Schwarzenegger, whose BMI is probably 35 or 36, which puts him in the obese range. But obviously he's very muscular—and muscle weighs more than fat. This reveals the downside of the BMI measure: It doesn't really take body composition or muscle tone into account."*

Unless your office is staffed with iron-pumping Arnold look-alikes, however, obsessing about the fine points of the BMI standard probably isn't worth the effort. Dr. Histon explains:

> *If you look around most public spaces, you won't see many people who are too muscular. You'll see more who are truly overweight or obese. If you're an employer and looking at your entire employee population, the BMI is a pretty good indicator of how healthy your population is. It also offers a simple way for your wellness providers to start the conversation about weight loss goals with individual workers.*

RESOURCE
Where to find BMI calculations. For a quick reference, use the
chart just below. For individual calculations, go to online calculators like the one
offered by the National Heart Lung and Blood Institute at www.nhlbisupport.
com/bmi.

Where the Scales Tip: Obesity at Various Heights

The following chart shows the weight at which adults at various
heights are considered clinically obese—that is, their BMI has hit 30.

Height (feet and inches)	Weight (pounds)	Height (feet and inches)	Weight (pounds)
4' 10"	143	5' 8"	197
4' 11"	148	5' 9"	203
5'	153	5' 10"	209
5' 1"	158	5' 11"	215
5' 2"	164	6'	221
5' 3"	169	6' 1"	227
5' 4"	174	6' 2"	233
5' 5"	180	6' 3"	240
5' 6"	186	6' 4"	246
5' 7"	191		

For purposes of your workplace wellness program, using BMI is a
useful way to decide whether focused weight loss efforts should be part
of your program. After that, however, you'll want to make sure that your
employees who need help losing weight receive more individualized body
fat assessments, most likely from the coach or trainer administering your
biometrics tests or assisting them with their weight loss efforts.

What Are the Health Effects of Obesity?

A wealth of scientific evidence shows that obesity can lead to any of these serious conditions:

- Type 2 diabetes
- coronary heart disease and stroke
- metabolic syndrome (a combination of factors like high blood pressure, high blood glucose level, large waistline, and high cholesterol that significantly increase one's risk of heart disease)
- cancer
- sleep apnea
- osteoarthritis
- gallbladder disease
- fatty liver disease (which can lead to cirrhosis scarring and liver damage), and
- pregnancy complications (such as gestational diabetes—high blood sugar during pregnancy), preeclampsia (high blood pressure during pregnancy), and the need for or complications during cesarean delivery. Also, babies born to obese mothers are at greater risk of brain and spinal cord defects, stillbirth, prematurity, and other problems.

Exactly why obesity leads to such severe health troubles isn't always clear. The pressure on the body of carrying around extra pounds, and the strain on organs caused by excess fatty tissue, appear partly to blame. Still, scientists haven't quite pinned down, for example, the causal link between obesity and diabetes. In the case of cancer, some theorize that part of the problem may be the poor diet and inactivity that lead to obesity, as well as the tendency of toxins to build up in fatty tissues.

What is clear is that obesity is bad for both the body and for business. When it comes to the workplace, the effects of obesity can be dramatic. For example, people dealing with obesity typically:

- miss work more often, about five workdays per year rather than the average three
- produce less than others on the job—in fact, obesity is cited as the Number One health reason for productivity losses

- need more medical care—resulting in higher medical costs (from one-quarter to one-third more than people at normal weight), and
- use more short-term disability.

When the same person is both obese and has diabetes (a common combination), the impact on productivity is particularly dire. A 2009 study showed that people who were obese and had Type 2 diabetes lost 11% to 15% of their work time (about 5.9 hours a week) to health troubles. (Source: M.D. Rodbard, et. al., "Impact of Obesity on Work Productivity and Role Disability in Individuals With and at Risk for Diabetes Mellitus," *American Journal of Health Promotion* (2009), Vol. 23, No. 5.)

Emotional Effects of Obesity

Medical researchers are becoming increasingly aware of the close mind-body connection surrounding obesity. For example, research suggests that people with a mental illness, such as depression or anxiety, or with emotional issues, such as feelings of anger or loneliness, are likely to console themselves with "comfort foods" that lead to weight gain.

Weight gain, in turn, can lead to emotional or mental difficulties. For one thing, overweight people miss out on the endorphin-boosting psychological benefits of exercise. They may also feel rejected, unattractive, or discriminated against. These responses often exacerbate the underlying psychological issues described above, or lead to lethargy and self-defeating thoughts. The person may start avoiding social situations or physical activities where their weight will be particularly obvious—but possibly turn to more food for comfort. It's a vicious cycle.

With the right approach, your workplace wellness program can break that cycle. The key is to offer understanding and hope, not to feed into the social stigma and self-blaming that overweight and obese people are already experiencing.

Fortunately, obesity is reversible. Losing weight isn't easy, as many Americans know—or could at least guess—from all the diet books and fads regularly rolled out. But it's not a mysterious process: The basic formula is, and always has been, to eat less and exercise more.

The benefits of achieving a normal weight are great. Losing 5% of one's body weight—for example, ten pounds off a 200-pound frame—may lower the risk for several diseases, including coronary heart disease and Type 2 diabetes. In fact, Trina Histon says:

> *A study we performed found that worker productivity increased even after modest weight losses of as little as six pounds. Weight loss seems to switch people's mindsets. When they start feeling like they're taking care of themselves, getting more active, and physically feeling better, they become happier about doing their job.*

How Much Do People Lose on "The Biggest Loser"?

As you might guess, contestants on the popular television show "The Biggest Loser" don't stick to the medically recommended maximum pace, which is three pounds a week. If they did, the show wouldn't finish in one season. Show contestants typically lose more like five, ten, or in extreme cases up to 20 pounds a week, under careful and constant supervision.

We caution against modeling workplace weight loss competitions on this show, but if it's something your employees really want, take care not to expect or reward unusually rapid results. Set rules about weight loss methods—for example, by prohibiting the use of laxatives, supplements, or dehydration right before weigh-in time.

Combating Obesity With Your Workplace Wellness Program

Although you can probably look around and see who among your employees could stand to lose some pounds—and they probably know it themselves—it's obviously better if they get the official word from a professional. Your initial HRAs or biometrics tests are tailor-made for opening the discussion. These may include not only BMI calculations, but individual body-fat assessments (which can be more accurate, since they show how much of a person's weight is muscle rather than fat). Even the scales that HRA professionals bring in are usually better than average and able to handle more than 250 pounds. Dr. Histon emphasizes, "If someone weighs 330 pounds and the scales can't reflect that, a weigh-in doesn't do much to help them make positive changes."

To follow up on the survey or test, the professional administering it can let people know they're at an unhealthy weight, suggest a target weight, and provide referrals and recommendations for other parts of your program. Ideally, this will include a number of options, as adviser Dr. Doug Metz explains:

> *Obesity is a multifaceted problem, and finding both the cause and the solution is a personal matter. Whether we're discussing pant sizes or obesity solutions, one size does not fit all."*

Should the person see a doctor as well? Trina Histon says:

> *We do advocate that if someone is overweight or obese, has been very sedentary and isn't eating well, that they consider visiting a doctor before embarking on a significant weight loss journey. On the other hand, if someone wants just to eat more healthfully or start making other small changes, there's not as much need for a doctor.*

As an employer, you can't directly tell someone to visit a doctor, but you can ask them to sign a waiver before beginning a workplace weight loss effort, and include in that waiver the person's promise to visit a doctor. (See Chapter 2 for a sample waiver.)

Unfortunately, desperation to lose weight—and lose it fast—leads many people to try risky or extreme measures, which you certainly don't want to promote in your wellness program. For safety's sake, most people should stick to a slow and steady pace of one-half to two pounds—and no more than three pounds—per week. That's why we've been clear that weight loss should not be the primary goal of the nutrition and fitness elements of your program. Those elements will help create healthy habits for people trying to lose weight, but you don't want them to turn into a group obsession with weight loss. You'll need carefully targeted efforts to reach employees who truly need to shed pounds.

No-Fat Diets Are Dangerous!

One of the extremes to which many dieters go is to eliminate all fats from their diet. However, recent research has shown this strategy to be both ineffective and downright dangerous. Certain fats—the so-called monounsaturated and polyunsaturated ones—are crucial to basic functioning of cells, nerves, the human brain, and all the rest. Without them, people can get dry hair and itchy skin, become infertile, and have difficulty fighting infection and healing from wounds.

Omega 3s (within the polyunsaturated group) are especially important, with benefits like a lower risk of heart disease, better blood pressure, improved brain function, and reduced instances of depression and dementia. Omega-3s are found in cold-water, fatty fish such as salmon, herring, mackerel, anchovies, and sardines and in plant foods such as walnuts, sunflower seeds, and flax seeds.

Yes, these foods are caloric, but they're also satisfying and can slow digestion, making people feel full longer so they may eat less. And, researchers note, the U.S. population has been progressively gaining weight during the very years when weight loss diets have focused on cutting out fats.

The fats that *aren't* healthy include trans fats and saturated fats. Trans fats have been twisted or deformed, usually due to high heat. They're found mostly in fried and processed foods, often in the form of "partially hydrogenated vegetable oil." They both raise the body's level of bad cholesterol (LDL) *and* decrease good cholesterol (HDL). Processed or fast food snacks, fried foods, and cookies are common foods in which trans fats are found. Fortunately, U.S. manufacturers are now required to list trans fat content on food labels.

Saturated fats, found mostly in meat products and tropical oils (coconut and palm) are also worth avoiding. You'll recognize these because they're solid at room temperature—think of the skin on chicken or turkey or the edging on a steak. Saturated animal fat contains cholesterol and promotes heart disease.

⚠ **CAUTION**

Courts are increasingly recognizing obesity as a disability that merits protection under the ADA. To protect your company, do the following: Maintain the employee's confidentiality, avoid making employment decisions based solely on a person's weight, and offer any reasonable accommodations that will help the employee do the necessary functions of his or her job.

Education: Beyond Fad Diets

People probably think they know a lot about weight loss, but myths and misinformation abound. The most rational, well-read people sometimes try the wackiest diets, from drinking gallons of water to subsisting mostly on carrots. Below are some ways to get your employees in touch with the latest weight loss news and practices. Unless otherwise indicated, these can be made available to all of your employees (if they're interested), not only to those whose weight levels are medically risky.

- **Bring in speakers.** Discussions of healthy ways to lose or maintain an appropriate weight will probably be popular among many of your employees. You may be able to find free speakers, for example through the local branch of a respected weight loss company.
- **Make sure weight loss is discussed in your employee newsletter.** If you're subscribing to a newsletter from an outside source, you can probably count on weight management being covered. If you're writing one in-house, look for inspirational material on websites such as www.sciencedaily.com. (Click "Health & Medicine," then under "Medical Topics," click "Diet and Weight Loss.")
- **Direct people toward online and community resources.** For example, the Spark People website, at http://sparkpeople.com, has weight loss recipes, blogs, and a chance to sign up for a personalized diet and fitness plan, with advice from dietitians—and all for free. The Living Strong website (www.livingstrong.org) has calculators for figuring out ideal weight and calorie count per day, and lists of average calories within different foods (on the homepage, click "Fitness Tools"). Even your own health plan (particularly if it's an

HMO) may offer webinars or other educational opportunities on maintaining a healthy weight.

- **See what educational resources come with weight loss treatment programs.** If you'll be offering to pay all or part of certain employees' enrollment in weight loss treatment programs, see whether the program comes with access to online or other educational materials.

- **Pass out healthy, low-calorie recipes.** According to Dr. Histon, "People particularly like to get instructions for preparing family favorites in healthier ways." This may require some research. Take into account the ethnic diversity of your staff: A healthy enchilada recipe may not interest someone who's used to fried rice. For ideas, check out www.tasteofhome.com and www. epicurious.com (under "Recipes & Menus," click "Healthy Recipes"). Also keep an eye on cooking magazines and newspapers, which often offer recipe "makeovers." (Note that you might not want to pass these out to your whole staff, but you could distribute them at topical seminars, or make them available on company bulletin boards.)

- **Put up posters.** Your existing workplace wellness posters, such as those promoting eating lots of vegetables, walking regularly, and reducing stress will be relevant here. But it's also helpful to include in your array of posters (which should be rotated regularly) some with healthy messages especially for people trying to lose weight, for example with information on food calorie counts, reminders about portion control, or encouragement to start with manageable changes like holding weight steady. Smaller postings, such as recipes or recent articles, may also draw your employees' attention. Your health insurer may be able to provide these. Also check out free posters from the National Institutes of Health at http:// win.niddk.nih.gov/publications. Put the posters in appropriate locations, such as your workplace wellness library, the employee lunchroom, or a dedicated bulletin board.

Get in the Game
Tips for Healthy Eating and Physical Activity

With all of life's commitments, it is easy to let your health and fitness slide. Below are a few tips on how you can get on track with healthy habits. Chances are, you will realize it is not as hard as you think.

- Try to avoid eating too many calories by keeping portion sizes under control.
- Sneak in fruits and vegetables by adding berries to your cereal or crunchy vegetables to your sandwich.
- Cut down on sugary sodas, sports drinks, and juices by drinking water and other low-calorie drinks. Alcohol can also be a major source of hidden calories.

- Try to do at least 30 minutes of moderate-intensity physical activity, like brisk walking, on most days of the week.
- To lose weight, aim for at least 60 minutes of moderate- to vigorous-intensity exercise on most days of the week. Try jogging or playing a fast-paced sport.

Want more information on healthy eating and exercise?

CONTACT
Weight-control Information Network: 1 WIN Way
Bethesda, MD 20892-3665
Toll-free Number: 1-877-946-4627
E-mail: WIN@info.niddk.nih.gov
Internet: http://www.win.niddk.nih.gov

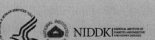
NIDDK NATIONAL INSTITUTE OF DIABETES AND DIGESTIVE AND KIDNEY DISEASES
NIH Publication No. 06-5578

Sisters Lead Company Weight Loss Challenge

Debby Tappan and Jackie Grabin are sisters as well as copresidents of Arrow Exterminating Company, in Lynbrook, New York. With a seasonal workforce of no more than 100 employees, the company has a warm, family atmosphere—which has its downsides when it comes to weight control. As Debby describes: "We have a party about anything that could possibly be partied about."

Jackie adds: "We celebrate everyone's birthday. In the past, that usually meant a cake, plus other goodies. On top of that, people often bring leftovers in from parties at home. It got to where you could easily gain 20 pounds in your first year here."

The sisters became concerned, and many employees openly talked about wanting to lose weight. So they came up with a plan in which employees could voluntarily chip in $50, making an agreement that they'd get their money back plus another $50 if they reached their goal weight. (The goal was a 7% reduction in weight for each participant.) All but three employees signed up.

What weight loss method did they use? Debby explains, "We got a reasonable rate at a local gym and went in halves with employees. We started buying fruit for parties instead of birthday cakes. And we brought in a personal trainer to privately weigh everyone once a week."

"Don't forget," says Jackie to her sister, "Each week you bought little gifts for everyone who had lost *any* weight that week—mostly party gifts from the dollar store, like a ball with a happy face or a yoyo." "That's right," says Debbie. "People really wanted those!"

The result: The employees, including Jackie and Debby, lost a combined 146 pounds the first time they ran the challenge, in 2007. And they've had continued success with subsequent challenges—in fact, they were about to launch another one as this book went to print.

Activities: Losers, Unite!

For the most part, we recommend that your wellness program promote healthy behaviors that will naturally lead to weight loss without focusing on the weight loss itself. If you follow our advice in the chapters on promoting fitness, reducing stress, and eating more healthy foods, you'll be doing just that. (For example, every 35 miles that someone walks can burn off a pound of fat, assuming caloric intake stays the same.)

Such an approach will help you avoid the mistakes made by other employers who, explains Dr. Histon:

> In the early days, tried to bring weight loss to the worksite and didn't succeed. People felt picked on, like they were being singled out. The employers who've ultimately been successful in helping people lose weight talk about total health, as opposed to just talking about weight.

Nevertheless, if it suits your office culture and many of your employees need to lose weight, including some well-organized, sensitively run group activities can be both effective and fun. Here are some ideas:

- **Hold a workplace weight loss contest.** Friendly competition among employees can spur weight loss like nothing else—but you need to approach it carefully. Be sure to provide guidance on setting personal goals and create a system that's fair for people starting at different weights; you can usually do this by basing goals on a percentage of body fat rather than on pound-for-pound losses. Dr. Metz suggests, "If you're going to base the contest on outcomes, such as amount of weight lost, it's safest to have this process overseen by a medical doctor to ensure that no participants put their health (or life) at risk. Having people sign a waiver saying they'll consult their doctor isn't enough." No matter who's running the program, be sure the contest rules make clear that no one will be rewarded for losing more than three pounds per week, which would be unhealthy.

- **Hold a holiday challenge.** Dr. Metz explains, "This is a safer sort of competition, because you're not actually asking anyone to lose weight—just to keep it off during one of the challenging times of year. People weigh in before Thanksgiving and then again after

January 1. All those who gained no more than three pounds during that period are rewarded."

- **Hold a potluck or recipe contest.** You may already be doing this within your nutrition program, but this time, the focus can be on not only healthy food, but healthy low-calorie food.

- **Offer incentives.** Either within the context of a contest or without, rewarding people for healthy weight loss can help keep them on track. Assuming your wellness program offers lots of ways to earn rewards (perhaps on a point basis), the fact that only those who are already overweight stand to win should not be a problem. However, if you sense that other employees might feel left out, another option is to reward people who are at a healthy weight for maintaining that weight, and reward underweight people for gaining weight.

- **Offer diaries to those who want them.** Dr. Histon says, "You can encourage employees to keep a food diary, preferably starting a week before altering anything in their diet so they can clearly see their current food choices and eating patterns. They might also keep a mood diary, describing how they felt and whether their day was stressful. Such diaries help people learn what the trigger points are for unhealthy eating and other behaviors. Evidence shows that keeping a food diary will increase the likelihood of successful weight loss and help maintain that weight loss. The longer you keep track of what you eat, the more likely you are to maintain healthy eating habits." (We've included a basic food and exercise diary on the CD-ROM at the back of this book. You can use it as is or modify it to suit your needs.)

- **Buy pedometers.** If you haven't provided pedometers to your wellness program participants already, consider doing so now. Walking is an easy and low-cost way for people of any weight to get moving and stay fit. In fact, those who are overweight may burn calories faster than others through walking (and similar exercise) because they're literally carrying around more weight.

- **Buy "GoWear fit" armbands for those serious about losing weight.** Got any gadget lovers among your employees? These high-tech toys, offered by BodyMedia (www.bodymedia.com), allow users to track how many calories they're burning at any moment as well as how efficiently they're sleeping. By uploading the recorded data to an Online Activity Manager, they get a precise tracking and goal-setting tool for managing weight loss through exercise. The armbands are not only recommended by Dr. Histon, but have garnered a good deal of positive media attention. The cost was between $160 and $300 when this book was printed, depending mostly on the length of subscription to accompanying online services.

Individual Treatment: Medical Options

Some of your employees may need more personalized, individual help in managing their weight than your general wellness activities can provide. They've probably tried to lose weight before and may be frustrated by complicating factors like a slow metabolism or the need for certain prescription medications that can cause weight gain as a side effect. Below are some ways to get those employees (or family members) beyond feeling guilty or hopeless, and to take active steps to control their weight. (In cases where you may be offering assistance with payments, see the privacy and fairness information in Chapter 2.)

- **Subsidize enrollment with a respected local weight loss company.** Look for an organization that, in the words of Dr. Histon, "addresses nutritional as well as behavioral aspects of weight loss and ideally also covers the importance of physical activity. Its programs should build knowledge on a weekly basis." For example, Weight Watchers (www.weightwatchers.com) has a 40-plus-year history of providing responsible approaches to weight loss based on flexible food planning (centered around good nutrition and calorie reduction), mutual support through regular meetings, and an emphasis on exercise and long-term lifestyle changes. You may be able to negotiate a group discount. Another good one is Take Off Pounds Sensibly (TOPS), a nonprofit whose members meet weekly in local chapters to receive positive reinforcement and motivation in adhering to their food and exercise plans. The annual dues were only $26 when this book went to print.

- **Find out whether a local gym has weight loss personal training packages.** If you're already paying for memberships, this might be a reasonably priced add-on, or you could split the cost with employees. Of course, you want to make sure that the program is safe, effective, and staffed with experienced people. Ask a lot of questions about who developed the weight loss program, what sort of community or medical recognition it has received, and what the qualifications of individual trainers are.

- **Encourage employees to attend a weight loss plan through your health insurer.** Particularly if your employees have an HMO, it's entirely possible that it offers a low-cost program or treatment option. The advantage to this is that you can be assured of medical supervision. Your insurance may also cover bariatric surgery, which adviser Dr. Histon says, "is risky, and certainly not appropriate for everybody. But for the right patient at the right time—usually one with a BMI of at least 40, or 35 if they have accompanying medical problems—it can be very effective. Many employers now cover the surgery for carefully selected patients and many hospitals are now accredited to conduct the surgery. Patients generally lose about 50% of their excess weight, and there's a good chance their diabetes will be resolved."

- **Arrange for in-person, email, or telephone coaching or counseling.** This service may be offered through your HMO, your wellness consultant, if you're using one, or other providers like Spark People (mentioned above) or the American Cancer Society. (The latter has a 24/7 telephone-based program in which trained counselors help employees uncover the obstacles that have kept them from making healthy choices and establish goals and a personal action plan—go to www.acsworkplacesolutions.com and click "Manage Weight," then "Choose to Change.") As with smoking cessation, counseling can be an important and effective tool in weight loss success.

- **Pay for obesity management medications.** These would have to be prescribed by a doctor, as such medication is appropriate only for someone in a structured weight loss program. If medication is appropriate for a particular employee, you might help with the copayment (as always, following the HIPAA privacy rules described in Chapter 2). There are two approved drugs on the marketplace for long-term use. One is an appetite suppressant, called Meridia. The other is a lipase inhibitor, called Xenical or Allī (over the counter, at one-half the prescription dose), which works in the gut to prevent absorption of fat and saves about 200–250 calories daily, thus helping patients lose an additional 3% to 5% of their weight. Both drugs are effective in helping patients lose weight. Dr. Histon notes that, "Like any drug however, the weight tends to come back on when the person stops taking it. Also, these drugs have side effects, and neither is suitable for pregnant women. Meridia can cause problems in people with high blood pressure. With a lipase inhibitor, eating too much fat at any given meal can lead to 'fecal urgency' which most people find very unpleasant. However, with careful regulation of fat intake, this won't be a problem. We're still waiting for a pill with acceptable side effects that's efficacious and safe for long-term use."

CAUTION

Don't pay for unapproved supplements. Dr. Histon warns, "You'll see ads in many women's magazines promoting the 'greatest solution' for weight loss, with pictures of someone who took off 100 pounds. Generally those are a waste of money. The weight loss industry knows that people are so desperate, they'll try anything. Some federal agencies are starting to clamp down on these companies, but people are still gullible. Whatever health strategy your workplace promotes, encourage participants to steer clear of these supplements."

Why Isn't Everyone Losing Weight at the Same Rate?

As your wellness program gets underway, and certain people enroll in weight management programs or efforts, you may notice that some are getting quicker results than others. Are the slow ones cheating on their diets? Not necessarily.

Trina Histon explains:

> Some people's metabolisms are faster than others. You'll see people losing weight at all rates. The TV show The Biggest Loser clearly shows that—some people lose ten pounds a week steadily, week after week, while others struggle to lose three or four pounds.
>
> Genetic and metabolic factors play a role, as well as gender factors. Men tend to have more muscle mass, therefore they can burn more calories. They also have fewer fat cells than women; women start out with more, making it more challenging to lose the same amount of weight.
>
> In terms of ethnicity, we do know that those who have an African American or Latino background tend to gain weight at faster rates. The average American will gain one to two pounds per year; that could be close to double that in those populations.

All of this adds up to another reason why your wellness program should not fixate on pounds lost, but on shared efforts to eat better, exercise more, and enjoy the benefits of improved health.

Support: It's Not Just Hiding the Candy

Again, losing weight should not become the central focus of your workplace wellness program. If you're already working to create a supportive workplace when it comes to good nutrition and fitness, you'll have done most of what's required to help those people trying to lose weight. However, for people who are openly trying to lose weight, it's appropriate to be encouraging—without nagging or giving them the evil eye every time you see them choosing a candy bar at the vending machine.

Keep in mind that, as Dr. Histon explains:

A lot of obese people have been victim to various forms of discrimination. By now, they've probably already been teased a lot, perhaps picked on when they were teenagers, with every name you can imagine. Even as adults, making fun of overweight people is the one remaining socially acceptable form of discrimination, as we see on television. In fact, we know that someone who's obese on average earns $10,000 less than others. So you need to be very respectful of how you set up your program, always setting the conversation in the context of health—and avoiding use of the word "fat," which people bristle against.

Some other ways to create a supportive environment include:

- **Make your fitness program inclusive.** For example, be sure to offer appropriate options for beginners or those who don't want to wear skimpy clothing. It's no fun being the only overweight person in a room full of yoga gods and goddesses.

- **Don't serve oversize portions at catered events.** Studies show that portion size in the United States has increased over the years, and that many people will eat whatever's put in front of them. For buffets, put out medium-sized, not large plates. If you offer temptations at meetings, such as a plate of pastries, put them on a side table where people won't mindlessly reach for second and third servings.

- **Find a manager willing to issue a challenge.** If someone high up in your company needs to lose a fair amount of weight and is willing to be the center of attention, telling employees "I'm going to lose 25 pounds, who wants to join me?" can be effective. This can help convince your overweight employees that they're not being singled out or picked on, and that your executives are really walking the talk. "Unless your employees are seeing their bosses and their superiors modifying their behavior," says Dr. Histon, "they're not likely to make changes themselves."

- **Create diet-conscious tips for eating at local restaurants.** Perhaps you're already creating a guide to healthy eating around your worksite, as described in Chapter 5. If so, it can be appropriate to include basic nutritional information, such as how many calories are in particular dishes or which local options are best if you have to grab lunch in a hurry. Trina Histon notes, "Most places now provide nutritional information. And even if someone is going to choose fast food for that day, it's worth pulling together information so that they at least choose the healthier options. This task doesn't have to be arduous—it can actually be fun, and you can engage employees in the discovery process. They can nominate their favorite places to have lunch, and then work with those various places to say, 'We're trying to be healthier. How can you support us in doing that?'"

Dealing With Chronic Illnesses

Meet Your Adviser

Dr. Janet Greenhut, Senior Medical Consultant at HealthMedia, a company that develops online coaching programs for health promotion, disease management, and behavioral health.

What she does: Dr. Greenhut makes sure that all HealthMedia's programs follow evidence-based guidelines and are medically accurate.

Favorite healthy food: "Carrots. (Really. I love carrots.)"

Top tip for staying fit and healthy: "Find something active you like to do and do it regularly with someone else."

The majority of U.S. workers have at least one chronic medical condition, and many have more. Chronic means long-lasting (three to six months) or recurrent, usually requiring ongoing medical treatment. Examples of chronic conditions include heart disease, hyptertension, asthma and other allergies, diabetes, arthritis, kidney disease, multiple sclerosis, osteoporosis, autoimmune disorders like lupus, mental illness such as depression, and cancer. As we discussed in Chapter 1, chronic conditions account for the majority of U.S. health care costs.

Some of these conditions may rise to the level of a disability. This doesn't mean that the person is completely incapacitated, but that, in legal terms, he or she has a physical or mental impairment that substantially limits a major life activity. So, for example, you may have workers who are legally blind, in a wheelchair, or (less obviously) unable to do things like climb stairs or hold heavy objects.

To some extent, chronic or disabling medical conditions are best addressed by your employees and their doctors. Lunchtime seminars probably aren't the best places to discuss dealing with serious illnesses, nor those shared by only a few people. Meanwhile, your general wellness program components can help to improve the health picture of employees with chronic conditions. For example, at the 35-employee office of the Metropolitan Milwaukee Association of Commerce (MMAC), Joline Woodward says, "One of our biggest program successes—in a program that focuses on fitness and nutrition—is that some people have gotten off medications for things like high cholesterol and chronic heartburn."

Still, there are a few other, more targeted ways your workplace wellness program can help, as we'll discuss in this chapter.

The Connection: How Chronic Illness Lowers Worker Productivity

You probably don't know how many of your workers are living with some sort of chronic condition. If well managed, their conditions may have only a small or irregular impact on their working day—or they may just keep quiet about what they're experiencing. Chronic conditions are considered to be a major source of workplace presenteeism—showing up despite being unable to work at full steam. The "big seven" conditions that consume the most health care dollars include cancer, diabetes, hypertension, stroke, heart disease, pulmonary disease (such as asthma and emphysema), and mental disorders.

Depending on the condition, even relatively healthy members of your workforce may be living with things like pain, hindered movement, allergy symptoms, or reactions to medications (such as dizziness, nausea, or drowsiness).

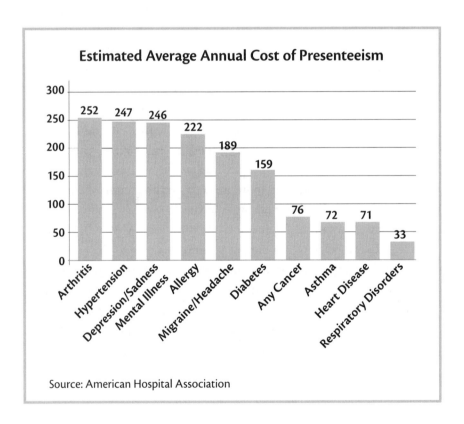

Source: American Hospital Association

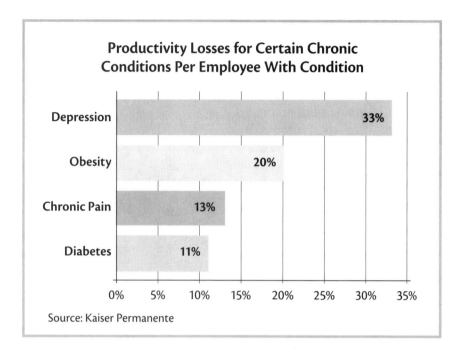

Productivity Losses for Certain Chronic Conditions Per Employee With Condition

Condition	Percentage
Depression	33%
Obesity	20%
Chronic Pain	13%
Diabetes	11%

Source: Kaiser Permanente

Chronic pain alone is reported to affect nearly one-third of American workers. Back and joint pain is common for both blue collar and office workers and, according to surveys by HealthMedia, leads to a self-reported 31% drop in productivity—both absenteeism and presenteeism. Other likely sources of pain include migraine headaches, fibromyalgia, endometriosis, and arthritis.

To make matters worse, fate doesn't always stop at one health condition per person. This may be a particular problem if you have an aging workforce. Two-thirds of people over the age of 65 are reported to have multiple chronic health conditions—and they probably didn't get them all on their 65th birthday. The complexities of simultaneously treating different, possibly unrelated health issues can lead to complications and adverse drug interactions, with no single doctor looking at the big picture.

Also, let's not forget that a worker may be a primary caregiver for a family member with a chronic condition and need to take days off for medical appointments or crises.

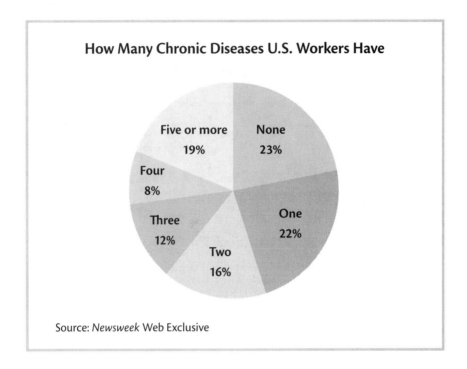

How Many Chronic Diseases U.S. Workers Have

Five or more 19%

None 23%

Four 8%

Three 12%

One 22%

Two 16%

Source: *Newsweek* Web Exclusive

Ongoing medical concerns are bound to give rise to emotional issues as well. Throughout the process of diagnosis and treatment, patients may experience fear, distraction, irritability, mood swings, insomnia, and depression (even if the primary condition isn't diagnosed as depression). These are not ideal mindsets for anyone trying to get through a busy workday.

What You Should Know Before Getting Involved

If you're already providing health insurance, you may wonder why employees with chronic conditions need any more help—especially given that your basic offerings toward better nutrition and fitness are likely to help them as well. This section takes a closer look at what employees with chronic conditions need—and what you'll want to know before stepping in with further assistance.

Understanding Employee Barriers to Optimal Self-Care

At a basic level, you want to be sure that your employees find satisfactory ways to treat their illnesses. Minimal care for chronic conditions means visiting the doctor, taking medications, and otherwise following up as recommended. Unfortunately, not everyone does these things. In fact, the field of health psychology makes a study of what's called "medical adherence." Researchers have found that between 25% and 50% of patients don't follow basic instructions for care, depending partly on the illness. The results of a failure to follow through can range from annoying—for example, when drug withdrawal creates side effects—to life threatening.

Why do people behave like this? In case you feel frustrated by the implication that you need to babysit your employees, let's look more closely at the underlying issues.

Taking prescribed medications on time and in the right way is among the biggest challenges for someone with a chronic illness. Treatment may require multiple medications, which may need to be taken at different times of the day or week, some with food, some without food, and so forth. Even remembering which pills to take can be difficult, especially if the condition or medications themselves make the person fuzzy-headed. Various medications may stop working or interact badly with other medications, leading to changes in prescriptions and trial periods before settling on a treatment plan. And copayment amounts can add up, sometimes causing patients to put off refilling their medications.

As Dr. Greenhut confirms:

A lot of people have trouble following all their doctors' directions all the time. That's especially true of people whose conditions have no obvious symptoms, like high blood pressure and high cholesterol. They may actually feel worse when they take the medication than when they don't, because of the side effects.

And, up to this point, we've just been talking about the pills. Depending on the condition, the person may also need to be responsible for physical therapy exercises or other self-treatments such as hot or cold packs, self-administered tests, making and attending appointments, and more. If you've ever had to do any of these things yourself, you know how easy it can be to let them slide.

You don't have to watch over this process for every employee with a chronic condition—but you can help make sure there's someone to give a little support, and you might find other ways to ease the person's efforts to maintain a healthy lifestyle. Like other parts of your wellness program, making the effort will help your bottom line in the end. Dr. Greenhut explains:

> *Studies have shown that people who don't adhere to their medication schedule are more likely to experience adverse effects, such as hospitalization, down the line. And that will eventually influence the employer's health insurance premiums. So it's really in the employer's best interests to help people stay on track.*

Guiding Employees Toward Existing Health Plan Offerings

Your health plan probably provides an important source of support to patients with chronic illnesses, in the form of what's often called a "disease management program." These programs provide a nurse or other expert to advise and encourage patients with chronic conditions—especially the big seven expensive chronic conditions and other high-risk issues, like complicated pregnancies. For example, adviser Dr. Doug Metz explains:

> *If you had diabetes and got a prescription at your regular doctor's appointment, a disease management nurse might call you two days later asking questions like, "Can I answer any questions about diabetes?," "Did you get your prescription filled?," "How was your appointment?," and "Did you remember to follow up on those other matters the doctor advised you about?"*

Your employees' health insurance plan, whether it's an HMO or a PPO, most likely has either its own disease management program or a contract with a separate company that provides disease management services (examples include Alere and ActiveHealth). Such programs actually help them keep their medical costs down. For example, adviser Doug Metz explains:

> *They don't want a member who has diabetes to have a foot amputated because of failure to take medications or have regular foot exams.*

As an employer, you don't really need to get involved in this process—just make sure that your employees know what's available to them. The services themselves are likely to be pretty good. Adviser Rae Lee Olson says:

> *Generally, they're sophisticated and well established. Twenty years ago it was a different story, but there's been a lot of research and standardization of disease management protocols since then. Disease management programs have become part of the fabric of today's health plans."*

Your job is simply to ask for details when choosing your health coverage (as described in Chapter 12) and highlight these offerings when presenting your health plan features to your employees.

Also check in with your EAP, if you have one. It may help employees find the right medical resources, classes, and support groups to help manage chronic diseases.

Promoting Healthy Responses to Chronic Conditions

Beyond the basic support described above, there are a few things you might consider implementing in your workplace to help employees (and their families, if they're included in your wellness program) with chronic conditions. We briefly discuss each of them here.

Education: Making Sure Employees Get the Message

If enough of your employees have certain chronic conditions in common, you may want to think about wellness program components that you can offer them as a group. As Dr. Kenneth R. Pelletier explains:

If you look at all the studies that have been done over the last 25 years, there are certain conditions that jump out, both as the biggest cost centers and the main causes of decreases in performance and productivity. High on the list are stress, cardiovascular disease, and pain, all of which can be addressed through a workplace wellness program. Although these people will be hopefully getting medical treatment, they could use the support in not just breaking even but actively managing their condition.

This doesn't necessarily mean holding full seminars on disease topics. But your knowledge of common chronic conditions may help inform your other wellness choices. If, for example, a substantial number of your employees have cardiovascular issues, holding a separate class on daily self-care or eating well for cardiovascular health might make sense. Or if many employees have neck or back pain, you could distribute sheets showing appropriate daily stretches, to be posted by people's workstations.

Is Back Pain Affecting Many of Your Workers?

One of the most widely offered and used wellness program components is classes in back care. With workers of all kinds prone to developing back pain or injuries, this may be a situation in which, rather than relying on individual treatment options you offer on-site lectures or classes.

A good back care class will cover topics like spinal anatomy, appropriate sitting and standing postures, sleep positioning, safe lifting techniques, stretching exercises, and injury prevention strategies. Check with your local hospital, occupational medicine center, and health plans to see whether you can arrange a class.

Activities: Dancing the Pain Away

As with your educational efforts, designing activities around chronic conditions will depend on how many employees and family members have common concerns. If, for example, a significant number have diabetes, you could organize a contest around creating the tastiest sugar-free dessert. If high blood pressure is problem for many employees, a potluck of salt-free dishes might be fun and educational. Activities like these wouldn't need to be restricted to people with the relevant illnesses; other employees might like to join in, for general health and prevention purposes.

Also, take a closer look at your roster of general fitness activities, to make sure it includes some options for people whose illnesses or disabilities prevent them from taking part in things like an office running club. For example, you might want to include, either on a one-time or ongoing basis, exercise or stretch classes for people with back trouble, carpal tunnel, or cardiovascular issues. Your local senior center is a likely source of instructors who are tuned into these issues. Also, a type of yoga called "restorative yoga" is especially designed for people who don't have the energy or ability to do challenging poses.

RESOURCE

Videos showing mild office stretches. Virtually everyone can benefit from simple stretches they can do in an office chair or cubicle. For free online videos, go to www.centre4activeliving.ca/workplace and click "videos."

First aid and cardiopulmonary resuscitation (CPR) classes are another good idea for any workplace. Everyone can benefit from learning how to respond to an emergency in the workplace or at home. The employees with heart or other problems will rest easier knowing that their coworkers will know what to do if they develop severe symptoms or lose consciousness.

Individual Treatment: Beyond Doctors

Your workplace wellness program can play an important role in helping individual employees with chronic conditions to cope with and manage their illnesses. Some wellness service providers will pick up where the disease management program leaves off. If you've hired an outside service provider to administer your workplace wellness program, it may, for example, offer personal or email reminders and coaching for certain conditions. (You may need to negotiate which conditions will be included, and with what type of follow up.)

Adviser Doug Metz explains the goal of the coaches at his company:

They try to help the participants stick with their course of health improvement. So for example, beyond dealing with basic adherence issues, they help with questions about how to practically implement the doctors' advice, like, "There's sugar in this ketchup, can I eat it without my diabetes acting up?" or "The doc said I should start exercising, but I haven't done that in 30 years. Should I walk or swim, and how much?," or "The doctor said I should manage my stress and not worry so much—I don't know how to do that!" Every issue around nutrition, exercise, stress management, and general lifestyle can be supported by a good wellness coach.

Your lowest-budget option in this realm may be a Web-based program, such as that developed by HealthMedia (but marketed indirectly, through other providers). Dr. Janet Greenhut, of HealthMedia, explains the advantages of this type of program:

Because it's Web-based, the employee can use it in the privacy of his or her own home. Even the employer doesn't need to know. The employer will probably find out that some employees have used the program, but through aggregate data, without names—it's completely confidential.

So, for example, if we're working with a person with diabetes, in our baseline assessment we'd ask about daily routine, including when the person takes any required medication. We want to find out how well the person is doing, how often he or she misses a dose, and whether he or she is getting refills when needed. If the medications are not being taken as directed, in our assessment we ask, "What things are standing in your way? Is it side effects, costs, or do you just forget? Do you have the medication with you when you need it? Are you embarrassed to inject insulin at work?" Things like that. And then in the online guide we make suggestions that are tailored to the person's motivations for taking the medication and whatever is standing in the way.

RESOURCE

No access to existing disease management or coaching? In the unlikely event that neither your health insurance plan nor wellness provider (if any) offers individual program options for disease management or complementary behavioral or lifestyle management, it may be worth separately subsidizing employee enrollment in an outside program. To identify online or local community resources, start with places like the American Cancer Society (www.cancer.org), the American Diabetes Association (www.diabetes.org), and the American Heart Association (www.americanheart.org). All offer—or can direct affected people toward—community support groups, activities, and other resources.

Support: Access and Flexibility

As Chapter 13 will address in more detail, employee policies that give people flexibility to attend doctors' appointments and deal with their medical issues ultimately benefit both the employee and employer. For example, a lot of medical offices don't have evening or Saturday appointments, and employees may need to take time off during the work day. Or, an employee managing an outbreak of symptoms may be more productive if allowed to work at home.

You can also take steps to ensure that your worksite itself makes your employees' lives more, not less comfortable or manageable. For example, it will help if you can provide parking to disabled employees and privacy for those who must give themselves injections. Most likely you'll take such measures in response to employees having made requests for "reasonable accommodations," as is their right under the ADA. But you will need to make sure employees are aware of their rights and know who to go to with their requests. And you need to be ready and able to take action: Try to avoid the common pattern observed at other workplaces, where accommodation requests get passed around ad infinitum because no one knows how to deal with them.

RESOURCE

More information on reasonable accommodations. You'll find lots of useful information on the website of the Job Accommodations Network (JAN), www.jan.wvu.edu. There, you can search for accommodations, download publications and guides, and review comprehensive and creative accommodation ideas using an alphabetical list of conditions from Addison's disease to wheelchair use.

Choosing Health Benefits

Meet Your Adviser

Matthew T. Sears, CEBS, CMS, Executive Vice President, the Jenkins Insurance Group, based in Northern California.

What he does: One of Matt Sears's most important tasks is putting the language of insurance into plain English, whether he's helping employers manage or choose their health benefits, leading workshops or trainings, or writing books and articles. Matt is the author of *The Benefits Performance Process, Maximizing the Performance of Your Employee Benefit Plan* (KSIE Press), which was named a "must read" by bookreview.com.

Favorite healthy food: "Seared Ahi tuna."

Top tip for staying fit and healthy: "Don't use email to communicate with people right in your building. Walk over and see them! And while you're at it, use the stairs. That's what I do, even when replying to an email someone sent me."

For many jobseekers, finding out whether an employer offers health benefits is as important as whether it offers a salary. The risks of going uninsured in America are high: One major illness or accident could bankrupt a person and lead to early death or disability. That makes providing health insurance, according to adviser Rae Lee Olson, "tantamount to a moral obligation."

Health insurance also affects who stays with your company. Adviser Matt Sears points out, "If your print shop doesn't offer health insurance but mine does, I can probably steal your best person." Unfortunately, not all employers get the message. A recent MetLife survey found a gap between the 81% of employees who say health benefits are important to workforce loyalty and the mere 59% of employers who think the same. (See "The 7th Annual MetLife Study of Employee Benefits Trends" at www.whymetlife.com.) Consider, for a moment, the importance of employee loyalty: It affects far more than retention; it also plays a role in day-to-day attitude, productivity, and willingness to put in exceptional effort.

However, as you know all too well, the costs of providing health insurance and other health-related benefits to your employees is high. (So far, no federal law requires you to provide them, though your state or city may—your broker can help you figure out the rules.) A slight majority of small businesses do offer health benefits, but that still leaves many who don't. In fact, in the very smallest businesses, with three to nine employees, the rate of health benefits coverage drops below 50%.

Deciding whether or not to offer health benefits is mostly a matter of balancing what your business can afford with its interest in recruiting and retaining the best employees and keeping them healthy. Yet, as you've been learning throughout this book, the very issue of what your business can afford is bound up with employee health. Unhealthy employees are less productive. Without health insurance, their health could deteriorate in ways that no fitness club membership or fruit bowl will cure.

The scenarios that could play out are stark. Imagine, for example, that one of your employees becomes critically ill with cancer and has to spend many hours each week shuttling between community clinics in search of free care. At a certain point, that person may be scarcely able to work—but will you be morally or legally able to let the employee go? More likely, you and your other employees will divide that person's work responsibilities until he or she becomes physically unable to continue working. If the person's income and assets are low enough to qualify for Medicaid or various state programs, some level of medical care will be available—but, as adviser Rae Lee Olson warns:

> *It's the people in the middle, who get crunched, those who make more than the threshold for support services, but not enough to provide their own insurance if it's not provided by their employer.*

So let's assume that you want to provide health insurance—and let's make it the best insurance available for the money. Your health benefits should also dovetail nicely with your workplace wellness program. This chapter will cover what you need to know, including:

- the types of insurance available
- choosing among insurance plans
- making sure your employees understand what's offered, and
- the role of an insurance broker in finding and implementing a workable health benefits solution.

 FORM

Keeping track of the details. You can use the Wellness Plan Worksheet on the CD-ROM at the back of this book to help you narrow down your options when choosing health insurance.

The Menu, Please: Health Coverage Options

Before you get overwhelmed by the glossy brochures, we'll look at the types of insurance options that are realistically available to your business. You may be looking for just one carrier or policy to cover all your employees—or you may want to offer a combo-platter of options for medical care, including some specialized types of coverage.

CAUTION
The majority of your employees may favor one insurance carrier.
If so, less popular carriers may remove themselves from the running, pointing to requirements that a certain percentage of your employees agree to sign up. For example, if most employees choose an HMO with a low employee contribution and reasonable copayments, a more expensive PPO won't want to get stuck with the small handful of employees whose illnesses are most likely serious enough to compel them to pay for greater freedom of access to doctors. Minimum participation requirements of 50% to 75% of benefit-eligible employees (typically those who work at least 20 or 30 hours a week) are common.

Health Maintenance Organizations (HMOs)

An HMO is group insurance that requires its members to use the services of participating hospitals, clinics, and physicians. As an employer, you'd normally make a fixed prepayment for each covered employee, probably lower than for other types of insurance (although the gap has been closing, and depends partly on factors like your employees' out-of-pocket obligations).

The exact structure and level of interconnectedness within the network varies, in some cases regionally. Some HMOs (like Kaiser Permanente) follow what's called an integrated staff or group model plan, in which the HMO owns its own facilities and makes all decisions on medical care internally—there's no distinction between who makes the decisions and who pays the bills.

Other HMOs, such as ones administered by Blue Cross, follow what's called an independent practice association (IPA) model. The insurance carrier basically rents the services of an existing medical group. All medical decisions—for example, referrals to specialists—rest with the medical group, not the insurance carrier.

Why employees like HMOs. Your employees may appreciate an HMO for its:
- easily navigated system
- low copayments
- minimal paperwork

- in some cases, broad enough staff pool to include multilingual doctors, nurses, and other staff, and
- emphasis on preventive care and health improvement.

Adviser Rae Lee Olson adds, "Employees appreciate knowing ahead of time what copayments will be—for example, they'll pay $15 for their copay and $20 for a lab test." (That ease of use helps you, too, because employees who get frustrated with their health plan sometimes ask the employer to step in and help.)

Potential downsides of HMOs. Critics complain of the following:

- the requirement to get a referral before seeing a specialist (even in-network)
- an inability to see an out-of-network specialist in the event of a serious illness or unusual condition (other than in cases where the HMO realizes it's a medical issue beyond its capacity to address)
- feelings of being "trapped within the system" after a bad experience with an HMO
- concerns that some HMOs pressure their doctors to save money by providing minimal care and holding back on referrals to specialists, and
- the reduced personal connection to one doctor, sometimes due to high turnover.

How Prevention Pays Off

The HMOs' emphasis on prevention isn't just talk; it's basic economics. HMOs have every incentive to nip their members' health problems in the bud. An HMO doctor gets virtually the same amount of money no matter how much treatment a particular patient receives, so it matters to them that their patients are healthy. By contrast, a doctor who's part of a PPO network gets to bill separately every time the patient shows up.

As an employer implementing a wellness program, you'll also gain from the emphasis on prevention. HMOs are becoming known for offering wellness benefits, such as behavioral classes, support groups, even fitness classes like yoga or tai chi. (For more on this, see "Step 3: Look for Services to Complement Your Wellness Program," below.)

Preferred Provider Organizations (PPOs)

The most widely available form of insurance is though a preferred provider organization, or PPO. This is more like traditional insurance in that, although you pay a set premium (usually more than you'd pay for an HMO), your employees must ordinarily submit claims for care (with the help of their doctors) as they receive it. PPOs also resemble HMOs in that the patients choose doctors from within a specified network of hospitals and doctors and receive the highest coverage for services within that network, often with preset copayments. If they visit doctors or hospitals outside the network, they'll have to pay more for services (as "coinsurance," which is usually based on a percentage of the provider's fee, rather than a fixed copayment) as well as increased deductibles.

Just how high your premiums are will depend on what you decide to include in your plan. For example, a PPO might lower your premiums in return for your employees paying a higher share of deductibles, copayments for in-network visits, or coinsurance.

Why some employees prefer PPOs. Your employees may appreciate:

- the freedom to make visits to out-of-network professionals
- the flexibility to self-refer to any provider in the network—even if it costs more
- an accompanying sense of autonomy, because employees aren't bound to a preselected group of people, and
- continuity, if an employee previously saw a certain doctor while under another PPO plan, perhaps with another employer.

Potential downsides of PPOs. PPOs have their downsides too, including:

- in some cases, more billing and other paperwork
- less advance certainty about coinsurance payments for out-of-network visits and other costs, and
- potentially high costs if the patient develops a serious condition and feels that the best care is available only outside of the network.

Insurance Plans Have Changed

What happened to traditional forms of health insurance, where you could see virtually anyone you wanted without the insurer creating group lists? HMOs and PPOs have pretty much taken over the field. Matt Sears says:

> Once-traditional fee-for-service or indemnity insurance is pretty much a thing of the past. It still exists for vision and dental, but that's about it.

Adviser Rae Lee Olson further explains:

> It's not that there was anything wrong with indemnity plans, but they were expensive for everyone. In most PPO plans today, incentives drive the vast majority of people toward using in-network, discounted care, which is less expensive for the insurer, the patient, and the employer.

Complementary Care Coverage: Acupuncture, Chiropractic, and More

Some people—often those with chronic conditions—regularly use alternative medicine, either in place of or in addition to traditional Western medicine. If that's true of a significant number of your employees, you can make their lives healthier and more affordable by buying coverage for such care—most likely chiropractic or acupuncture. Never tried it yourself? Ask around—even Western doctors are coming to realize that their focus on pharmaceutical drugs and surgery, while valuable for some conditions, doesn't work for certain things that complementary care does.

Dr. Kenneth R. Pelletier emphasizes that whether or not to offer complementary care coverage depends greatly on the needs of your employees:

> *If you can provide more than insurance for conventional medicine and you have a workforce where it makes sense to have an alternative benefit, then do it. For instance, if you have a lot of back injuries, you might have a back-saver program, chiropractic, or acupuncture. Or, if you have a large Asian population and acupuncture and Chinese herbs*

are preferred methods of treatment, it may make sense to develop a plan that covers that, because it's what your employees need. It's not an abstract decision; it really depends on your workers.

There are a few ways to insure complementary medical care. Sometimes it's available within an existing HMO or PPO system, though as Matt Sears cautions, "Your employee may have to really work the system to get it." In other cases, you may buy a rider, with the actual coverage most likely administered by a separate insurance company such as American Specialty Health or ASH. And under yet another model, you'd buy the insurance directly from a separate company.

Dental Coverage

Coverage for dental care, from regular checkups to root canals, occupies a separate insurance universe. You'll have a range of plans to choose from, with the most expensive offering your employees the widest array of dentists to visit and the lowest copayments, and vice versa.

Whether you decide to offer dental benefits is another matter. Although the coverage isn't terribly expensive for you or your employees, because dental costs tend to be fairly predictable, the risks to your employees if you don't offer benefits are low. But, adviser Rae Lee Olson notes:

> *Realize that dental insurance is a beloved benefit. There's something comforting about having someone else pay for that routine stuff that no one likes to get done anyway. It also causes people to take better care of their teeth, so from an employer's perspective, it's a feel-good thing to do.*

Besides promoting healthy teeth, she adds:

> *Dental insurance is a tax-advantaged benefit. The premiums are tax deductible to the employer, and the benefits are tax free to the recipient. So when your employee goes in and gets a crown that costs $800, you've already paid a premium that you were able to tax deduct, the insurance company pays the dentist $800, and the employee is never taxed on that $800. But if the employee just went to the dentist alone and had a crown that cost $800, he or she would (depending on tax bracket) have*

had to earn nearly $1,200 in order to net that $800 after taxes to pay the dentist. That's a big tax savings.

Vision Coverage

Yes, it's probably helpful if your employees can see what they're doing. The amount you'll pay for coverage is usually quite reasonable, and your employees will appreciate your help as they sport stylish eyewear that's carefully calibrated to their recent vision changes.

But how necessary is it for you to buy this for your employees? Matt Sears points out, "While vision benefits are popular, they actually don't protect people from any great risk, given that vision care costs are very low and predictable. That makes vision care ideally suited to self-insurance, or inclusion in an FSA or HSA program" (described below).

Most health insurance plans will cover treatment of more serious eye problems and diseases such as cataracts, retinal detachment, or glaucoma, because these are considered medical conditions rather than vision care.

Employee Assistance Programs (EAPs)

Employee assistance programs or EAPs have been around for decades, but have recently been gaining traction as a way to fill in the gaps in other health care coverage. In fact, most employers now offer EAPs.

First, what is an EAP? The range of offered services—to both the employer and the employee—is so broad that even the definition is still being worked out. For example, an EAP plan might help managers deal with employee behavioral issues, workplace accidents, emergencies, or major transitions like a merger. The plan might provide employees with coaching, counseling, or referrals for mental health treatment, violence prevention services, or wellness issues. Some EAPs also offer access to financial and legal advice.

The costs are lower than you might expect—depending, of course, on the range of services. A good plan can be purchased for less than $5 per employee per month.

The typical EAP operates on two different levels. The first level is phone support—employees can call an EAP representative, who will refer them to the services they need. For example an employee might call about a child who has an eating disorder or a spouse who is an alcoholic. The EAP will link that person with AA or Al-Anon, therapists, or other resources. (Limited programs offering phone referrals only may also be obtained as add-ons to long-term disability insurance.)

The second level provides in-person counseling—typically three to ten sessions per issue. This is different than the type of counseling most health insurers provide, which usually covers medical diagnoses like depression and anxiety. EAPs are designed to help employees cope with stress, so an EAP might counsel someone whose everyday life is strained by a difficult relationship with their teenager, an alcoholic spouse, or responsibility for an aging parent.

As a small employer, you may find an EAP particularly useful for providing or augmenting portions of your wellness program. In fact, Matt Sears says:

> Small employers may need full EAPs more than large employers, simply because the small ones have fewer resources with which to handle employee needs."

For example, if you recognize that seemingly intractable management-staff issues at your office are undercutting the success of your wellness program, being able to call on your EAP might be healthy for your business at a number of levels.

Rae Lee Olson adds:

> I recommend EAPs for employers of any size. Life is stressful, and most of the things that people need to call an EAP about are things that they wouldn't feel comfortable discussing with anyone else. The EAP can also give your managers a tool with which to avoid getting too engaged in employee's personal problems, while providing a meaningful solution and then redirecting people back to work. Employers train their managers to respond to employees with something like: "Jane, I'm really sorry that things are kind of rough at home. You know, there's this great EAP resource, I invite you to call them and make use of that it. Now, let's focus on how to get your job done here."

One Size Doesn't Fit All: Choosing Health Plans

Now that you know a little bit about the types of coverage you can offer, it's time for the tricky part: Which health-related benefits should you choose? There are a number of important factors to consider when making this decision, and you'll want to get help from a good insurance broker. But before you start making phone calls, take some time to think through your basic approach, including:

- whether you're inclined to offer just one insurance plan or a range of options, and
- whether you'd like to offer coverage for your employees' dependents—spouse, domestic partner, and kids.

As to the first point, we asked advisers Matt Sears and Rae Lee Olson whether small employers are best off choosing a single type of insurance for their employees or whether it's better to offer multiple options. Both agree that there's no right answer to this important question. You'll have to use your own experience and instincts to evaluate what's best for your business. Matt Sears says:

> *A number of personal, even emotional, factors go into this decision. Some employers, philosophically, want to give their employees lots of choices, while others want to keep it simple—or aren't big enough to have many choices. We always ask which insurance companies an employer has used before and liked or disliked. Some HMOs, for example, draw strong emotional reactions—people either love them or hate them.*

Adviser Rae Lee Olson adds:

> *The first thing the employer needs to define is their strategic philosophy around medical insurance. Do we want to have a Cadillac plan, a Ford, or a Pinto? If you decide, for example, that you can only afford a Pinto, then when your employees say, for example, "But we want acupuncture and lower copays!" you can say those are really important things, but our budget won't allow it. Our priority is putting as much as we can into employee salaries.*

When it comes to offering coverage for dependents, you'll have to think through the pros and cons. Providing insurance for spouses or domestic partners and children could make the difference between retaining and losing key employees. And it may reduce your employees' stress about family members' medical needs, thus increasing their focus and productivity.

But of course the benefits come at a cost. There's also an interesting fairness element when considered from the vantage point of unmarried or unattached employees. As Matt Sears points out:

> *Some employees look at employer contributions towards dependent coverage as unfair, because the employer spends more on colleagues who are married than on single employees who do the same job.*

If you can't actually pay for family benefits, you can offer employees the option to arrange care for their dependents through your workplace, but pay their own premiums. This has the advantage of keeping the family on the same plan.

> **CAUTION**
> **Know the law regarding domestic partners.** If you want to provide coverage for married couples, it's good practice to provide equal coverage for registered domestic partners. In fact, your state's law may require it. Check the law, keeping in mind that domestic partnership goes by different names from state to state—in northeastern states, registered partnerships are often called civil unions; in Hawaii, they're "reciprocal beneficiary relationships."

With so many options, how do you choose the medical insurance carrier and policy that will best serve your employees' health and wellness needs? We recommend four steps:

1. Find a good insurance broker.
2. Gather information about your employees.
3. Look for benefits that support your workplace wellness program.
4. Fine-tune your plans and make your final choices.

Regulatory Compliance Issues When Offering Health Benefits

Once you decide to offer health benefits to your employees, you must comply with a variety of state and federal laws and regulations. For example, you may need to provide your employees with:

- an ERISA (Employee Retirement Income Security Act) summary plan description and plan document (for all plans)
- annual informational 5500 filings to the Department of Labor (DOL) for plans with 100 or more participants, containing information on premiums, plan assets, and plan expenditures
- a Section 125 plan document to allow for pretax contributions and/or flexible spending accounts
- COBRA (Consolidated Omnibus Budget Reconciliation Act) compliance and notifications if you have more than 20 employees (federal law) or if your state has a parallel law covering employers with fewer than 20 employees
- HIPAA privacy and security documentation, compliance, and training, and
- disclosures about how your chosen health plans integrate with federal and state regulations, like the Medicare Part D notice, the Women's Health and Cancer Rights Act notice, and the Mental-Health Parity Act notice.

Adviser Rae Lee Olson cautions, "Some employers mistakenly think that their job is over when they've chosen a health insurance plan, but it's important to recognize that providing insurance comes with a whole package of obligations." But don't be overwhelmed. A health benefits broker can walk you through all of your compliance issues.

Step 1: Find a Good Insurance Broker

There's no reason not to get a broker on your side from the beginning. A common mistake employers make is thinking they're going to get a better price by asking for quotes from a number of different brokers. That doesn't work, because the prices for small group health insurance plans are set in advance and filed with the state, so the underwriters quote those prices. You're better off evaluating potential brokers, finding one that you trust who offers services that you need, and then asking that person to go to all the insurance companies on your behalf.

Note that this approach is different from the one you'd take for property or casualty insurance, in which not every insurance broker can secure quotes from every single insurance company. There, you'd have good reason to ask for quotes from different brokers.

What does the broker do for you? The basic services should include:
- gathering relevant information about your workforce and your preferences as employer
- getting proposals from insurance companies
- explaining the different proposals to you
- helping you pick an insurance company or combination of companies
- arranging the contracts, and
- educating your employees about the coverage.

As Matt Sears points out, however:

That's just the bare-bones service. You should look at what added services a broker offers, like assisting you with underwriting and rating calculations; helping you comply with federal and state laws; lending a hand with human resources work, all kinds of stuff. This is why there's a significant advantage to selecting a broker who specializes in employee benefits, rather than simply someone with an insurance license.

If you're tempted to go without a broker entirely, think again. It won't save you any money, and it may cause you some real headaches. Matt Sears explains:

While the broker is paid by a commission from the insurer, the premium calculations in a small- and midsized-employer market have the commission payment built in. So going directly to the insurers— assuming they'd even agree to deal with you directly—wouldn't lead to a lower price. And most insurance companies won't deal directly with employers, on the assumption they don't understand what they're doing.

So if someone were to call up an insurance company and say, "I own a small print shop and I want to buy insurance," most often they'll say "fine" and then refer the person to a broker.

You can see why finding the best broker is so important. Get referrals from human resources professionals in fellow businesses. Then contact your state insurance commissioner or check its website to make sure that any broker you're considering is licensed in your state and hasn't been the subject of complaints or disciplinary proceedings. (Licensing involves taking an exam, passing a background check, fulfilling continuing education requirements, and more.)

In addition, confirm that the broker is a member of a professional association, like the National Association of Insurance and Financial Advisors (www.naifa.org/consumer/advisor.cfm) or the National Association of Health Underwriters (www.nahu.org/consumer/findagent. cfm). Rae Lee Olson says:

Such memberships basically define the people who are in the business as opposed to doing it on the side. Professional organizations also keep brokers abreast of important legislative changes.

CAUTION
Switching from an existing insurance plan? Don't wait until two months before renewal time to find a good broker—or one you like better than your old one. This practically guarantees that you'll be hurrying to choose a health plan. You may end up with one that doesn't make your employees happy, meaning you'll have to switch next year.

Step 2: Gather Information About Your Employees

Depending on your approach, this step has one or two parts. At the very least, you must pull together some basic information about your employees. You may also want to ask them about their wishes and needs. We discuss each in turn.

Creating an Employee Census

Before your broker can approach insurance carriers for quotes, you should draw up a census of your employees. Your broker can help you with this. Expect to assemble information such as:

- gender
- marital status
- age
- how many hours each employee works per week (some plans don't cover part-time employees)
- any dependents who will be covered
- home zip code, and
- health risk factors among the employees or covered family members (reported to the insurers anonymously, with no names attached to health conditions).

If that last bullet point sounds too personal, realize that it's exactly what the insurers will ask after you choose a particular policy and submit an application. As Matt Sears explains:

Insurance companies more closely scrutinize smaller groups. If you know, for example, that one of your employees has had a heart attack, the insurance company will want to know about that, too.

○ TIP

There's no need to pry. You need only report health conditions that you know about. You don't have to survey your employees and you certainly shouldn't dig into their health insurance files—for a variety of HR reasons, among which is that you might be skating close to a violation of HIPAA's complex rules on privacy. But that doesn't mean you can lie. As Rae Lee Olson points out, "You won't be able to say, 'Gee, I didn't know about our employee being pregnant with triplets, never mind that we were in the process of finding a replacement for her when she went out on FMLA.' But you're also not going to be responsible for knowing that one employee's son is detoxing in the hospital while another's husband is having cancer therapy. You must report what you naturally know, but you don't need to dig."

What will the insurer do with this information? Every state has different laws governing rates but, in general, the insurance companies must publish their rates for every plan and age group. Insurers are then allowed to modify the rates based on a risk adjustment factor, depending on the risk level presented by a group. (For example, in California, the rates can change by plus or minus 10%, while in Illinois, the rates can be adjusted from zero to nearly 67%.) Matt Sears explains:

> *If you've got a lot of employees in poor health, you'll probably have to pay a surcharge. If they're all 25-year-old athletes in great shape, you'll probably get a discount. And in case you're curious, simply refusing to answer the underwriting questions won't get you a better price.*

The insurer can also add or subtract for the risk associated with your particular industry. For example, an industrial manufacturer may have to pay more than a consulting firm. The exact rating rules vary by state and type of business.

Addressing Your Employees' Needs and Wishes

In an ideal world, in addition to assembling facts, you'd also solicit input directly from your employees. If your employees could see for themselves the inevitable trade-offs involved in choosing a health insurance policy, they'd perhaps be less likely to complain to you about the details later. Transparency and good communication within the process of choosing benefits has been shown to raise employee satisfaction with their health plan from 22% to 76% (Watson Wyatt *World@Work Study*, 2004).

But there's one major caveat: This line of thinking works only in settings where the company culture is attuned to sharing information, with a lot of mutual trust. The more typical scenario, says adviser Rae Lee Olson, is that:

> *You get all your employees in the room and everyone starts creating a wish list. That makes it very hard to contain the discussion—and you're practically guaranteed to end up with disappointment when you later bring out the chosen policy. Even if you're just choosing between two policies, you may end up with 50-50 support, which means half*

the people in the room will be unhappy. I usually advise great caution when employers want to open up the discussion to their employees.

That said, if you've got an exceptional group of employees who are prepared to make a joint, difficult decision, you can gather their input in one of two ways. One is to put out an anonymous survey. (Better brokers will handle this on behalf of their clients.) Another is to literally gather people together for a discussion—including family, if appropriate. Among smaller employers in particular, Matt Sears says:

It can be appropriate, depending on the culture of your company, to take a kind of, "Susie uses acupuncture, so we need to make sure it covers acupuncture" approach. It can get very personal, especially when the managers know the health conditions of practically everyone in the room.

TIP
The policy costs how much? Expect to hear some shocked gasps if and when you present actual dollar amounts to your employees. Most assume that their own contribution covers a bigger part of the cost than it does. At a simple management/staff relations level, this will help them see the true value of this unseen part of their paycheck.

Regardless of company culture, you're asking for difficulties if you start a group discussion with an open-ended question like "What do you want in a health plan?" A better way to keep the discussion on track is to narrow down the options in advance, then solicit specific input on certain issues. Matt Sears says:

Often the decision of what type of insurance to buy is a series of compromises. A company can't afford to pay for everything that everyone wants. So they may come to the employees and say, "Given our budget limitations, would you rather pay a little bit more out of your paycheck, participating in the premiums every month, or would you rather pay more when you go to get a prescription filled?"

Make sure your employees can also follow up with anonymous input, if they wish. No one should have to reveal in front of their coworkers that they, for example, have a life-threatening illness or place priority on getting coverage for erectile dysfunction medication.

No matter what, you and your employees will have to recognize that not all of your employees' health needs can be anticipated. A bit of gambling is always involved in deciding what to cut in order to save money. These are difficult decisions for everyone.

> **CAUTION**
>
> **Switching plans isn't easy.** If you're considering dropping existing coverage—no matter how dissatisfied your employees are with it—expect some bumps in the road. Employees get used to a plan's administrative procedures and benefits—for example, having certain prescription drugs covered or visiting certain doctors. Some may have designed an ongoing course of treatment around a particular financial and coverage strategy. Your best bet is to find a plan you'll want to stick with.

Step 3. Look for Services to Complement Your Wellness Program

The more services your insurer offers that go beyond treating disease to actually promoting wellness, the less your workplace program has to do. That's why Buffalo Supply—a Colorado-based medical-equipment company with fewer than 25 employees—asks a lot of questions when evaluating its insurance plan options for the coming year. As Kara Parker, vice president of finance and human resources, explains:

> *We look at whether the benefit providers offer things like a weight coach, diabetes plan, or groups to keep people on track. That lets us utilize services that larger companies can afford to pay for separately. This year, we found a provider that offers voluntary signup for treatment programs for various conditions, in which a nurse helps coordinate your care, and talks to you at least once a month about your goals.*

Virtually all insurance plans offer the preventive basics: vaccinations, annual physicals, cholesterol tests, and early-diagnostic tests, such as mammograms, Pap smears, and colonoscopies. Your job will be to ensure that your employees take advantage of these.

But some insurers may offer even more. Some HMOs, for example, have done an excellent job of adding wellness components to their medical services. As you make your purchasing decisions, be sure to consider whether:

- the HMO is proactive about reaching out to its enrollees
- the wellness program is genuinely easy to access, and
- the program contains interesting program options that will change behavior and employee health, such as classes or individual attention for people with who need to make changes regarding nutrition, stress, and exercise.

 RESOURCE

Looking for independent ratings of health plans? The National Committee for Quality Assurance (NCQA) provides accreditation and assessment of the health plans and hospitals available in your state. They look into things like what percentage of the health plan's population gets preventive care, how many people get access to specialists, and more. See www.ncqa.org.

Step 4: Make Your Final Choices

With your broker's help, you should develop a list of health plan features that are most important to you and your employees. Your list might include items such as:

- deductible and copay amounts (either a set fee or a percentage of the service fee)
- prescription drug coverage (including copay levels for generic drugs, preferred brand-name drugs, and drugs that aren't on the insurer's preferred list)
- maximum annual coverage (if any)
- range of choices and locations of doctors and hospitals
- preventive benefits

- prenatal care
- mental health counseling
- experimental treatments, and
- anything else affecting your employees.

As you might guess, it's also important to discuss your budget with the broker at this point.

> ### TIP
>
> **Don't compromise on preventive services.** The more coverage you give your employees for vaccinations, cancer screenings, and other basic preventive measures, the more likely your employees are to use these services—thus reducing the likelihood of bigger medical problems down the road.

Your broker will work with the insurance companies, using the criteria you provided, and come back with specific quotes. The broker should bring you details on several specific proposals, illustrating how each best meets your desires and budget. The proposals will also reveal what additional services are included, either by the insurer or the broker.

This, says Matt Sears, "is where the 'art of the deal' comes in. A good broker understands the products offered by various insurers and HMOs and will work with the underwriter to find the plans that are a good fit, based on your criteria. For example, many insurers offer risk adjustment factor 'deals' to win new customers, so your broker should include those offers as part of the final report presented to you."

At this point, you may need to do some tweaking in order to meet your budget—for example, change an HMO copay from $10 to $30. Or, as discussed in Chapter 2, you could raise all the employee contributions—for example, from $50 to $150 or more—while offering rebates to employees who participate in your wellness program.

If all the quotes for standard medical insurance are way out of reach, you could switch to a high-deductible health plan or to catastrophic loss insurance, both of which kick in only after the patient has paid a certain amount out of pocket, say $1,000 or $2,000. "In this economy," says Matt Sears, "almost every client has to ask for some kind of tweaking."

TIP

Last resort: voluntary benefits. If a particular type of coverage is important to your employees, such as dental, vision, or complementary medicine, you may be able to offer an arrangement where they pay the premiums, on a monthly basis, as a pretax paycheck withdrawal. The insurance carrier may require that a certain number of people sign up for this, however. Talk to your broker for details.

Can Employees Opt Out of Your Coverage?

If you're not requiring an employee contribution, your employees will normally be happy to sign up for your health plan coverage. If you are asking them to pay, however, your employees have the right to opt out. Some of them may have separate insurance—for example, under a spouse's policy. (In fact, it's to your benefit if employees opt out in favor of a spouse's policy. What's more, according to Matt Sears, "It's entirely appropriate to offer a small payment to persons who waive coverage because of this.")

But you should refuse any requests from individual employees that you reimburse them for a separate insurance policy that they buy individually. This type of opting out can create trouble at renewal time for your group policy, because only the healthy employees will likely find cheaper coverage on an individual basis elsewhere.

Rae Lee Olson explains:

You've created adverse selection, where all the healthy risks take themselves elsewhere. That means your main group is an unduly risk-laden population, so over the long term your rates will increase. At your renewal cycle, your insurer is going to see that you don't have enough premiums to support the high level of claims, because a significant portion of your healthy people are off the plan. It's cleaner and easier just to say to your employees, "Here's our policy. If you want it, it's 50 bucks; if you don't, that's fine."

Helping Employees Get the Most From Their Coverage

It doesn't do you much good to provide health insurance if your employees don't know how to use it. Handing them a marketing brochure probably isn't enough; those are often written to make the plan sound good, not to help the employee make the most of their rights and benefits. Many businesses have learned the hard way that when employees have difficulty accessing the care they need, even if it's the health plan's "fault" for poor communication, the employer takes the heat. After the hard work of choosing and paying for health care for your employees, the last reaction you want is frustration.

Introducing Employees to Their Benefits

After signing up for a new or renewed policy, you should invite representatives of your health plan companies or your broker (who's more independent than the actual company rep) to meet with your staff, explain the plan in person, and answer questions. The in-person meeting is the method that most workers, young and old, prefer for learning about their health plan.

Your broker can also help with ongoing communications. Matt Sears says:

> We build a website for our clients that's related only to their benefits. It's a portal for employees that has all of their benefit information; legal and compliance information articles and newsletters; and a huge module on health and wellness that allows employees to find information about everything from "what is a migraine and how do I treat it" to ways to contact your doctor and get assistance from the insurance company.

CAUTION

Remind your employees to double-check their benefits before getting treatment. Lisa Molbert, an assessment director at Sequoia Center (you met her in Chapter 9), frequently encounters clients having trouble getting the health coverage they thought they deserved. She says, "For example, a person who comes to us seeking treatment for addiction might have already called their health plan's member services department and established that we're on its list of regular, contractual providers. But that doesn't mean that the person is actually preapproved for treatment. Perhaps, for instance, the person doesn't meet the insurer's criteria for the level of services needed. This can lead to unpleasant surprises when the person is asked to pay out of pocket." It's important that your employees are aware of potential snags like this one—and that they choose ethical treatment providers who will fully evaluate and explain the insurance situation, cost of treatment, and reason for recommending a certain level of care at the outset.

Keeping Tabs on Employee Satisfaction

With any luck, your health plan won't give rise to complaints—which is the usual way that small businesses learn about problems. Rather than sitting back and waiting to see what happens, it's best to be proactive about evaluating the plan after you've signed up. As Matt Sears explains:

Identify someone within the company who can best deal with complaints and concerns, and tell your employees who that is. Actively reach out and ask employees how things are working, before they complain. This highlights the value of the plan you provide and minimizes employee frustration when a problem occurs—after all, you've already demonstrated that you care. Employee surveys are an easy way to check on how things are going. Just be prepared to act on feedback if you request it.

Keep in mind that it's better that employees come to you before doing too much grumbling amongst themselves or spreading rumors on the order of, "They could have given us better health coverage if the boss didn't need to put his son through college next year."

Your broker can be a great help here. Adviser Rae Lee Olson explains:

The basic brokers might just sell you a policy and leave, but good brokers set the expectation that they'll get involved in employee problems with the insurer and that they'll help create solutions throughout the year. My team gives our business cards to every single employee. In fact, we encourage employees to call us directly, so that the HR person doesn't have to hear about the employee's health problems. For example, I'll get questions like, "I'm having trouble getting my antidepressant medication covered at the pharmacy." That's the kind of information the HR person really doesn't want to know, but the broker can perhaps clear up a misunderstanding about how to get preauthorization from the doctor.

Setting Up Flexible Spending or Health Savings Accounts

Even with health insurance, a reasonably healthy person can easily spend several hundred dollars a year on copayments, over-the-counter treatments, alternative treatments like acupuncture or chiropractic adjustments, and anything else required to fill the gaps in his or her coverage. To help ease the burden, you can arrange to have your employees participate in a tax-advantaged plan, namely:

- a flexible spending account (FSA), or
- a health savings account (HSA).

Flexible Spending Accounts (FSAs)

FSAs work as follows: You pick a company to administer your FSA. Then, your employees choose an amount of money to set aside from their paycheck over the course of the calendar year—such as $1,000—*before* you've withheld any tax from that paycheck. (You, not the IRS, decide the maximum amount employees may set aside, and decide whether to supplement those set-asides.) Employees then draw on that money to pay medical expenses, usually with a simple system of saving receipts and submitting claims to the plan administrator online or via fax. They may even be given a debit card with which to pay their expenses.

You'll pay a fee to the plan administrator, typically between $5 and $7 per employee per month. As Rae Lee Olson points out:

> *The amount your business saves by not having to pay FICA taxes on the amounts the employees set aside will typically be enough to more than cover these monthly fees.*

Your FSA administrator can be a good resource, helping you and your employees with nuances of eligibility not described in the IRS publications. However, your administrator may also set some special rules beyond the IRS regulations. For example, Rae Lee Olson explains:

> *Some FSA administrators will not allow mileage and parking expenses, even though these are on the IRS list. The reasoning is that such expenses are just too hard to document.*

TIP

Guess what happens if the employee doesn't use all the money in their FSA? It stays with you, as the employer. This is known as the "use it or lose it" rule. Of course, we know you won't be waiting and hoping for this to happen: The more on-the-ball employees, finding that they haven't used up all the money in their account, will make a mad, last-minute shopping trip for aspirin, diaper cream, and bandages, all of which can be claimed under an FSA. The catch, however, is that IRS regulations prohibit stockpiling, so a good FSA administrator won't allow people to claim reimbursement for more than one of each thing— one bottle of aspirin, one tube of diaper cream, one package of bandages, and so forth.

Setting up an FSA lets employees, in effect, get a tax discount on their health care expenditures. Just how much they'll save depends on what federal tax bracket they're in. But even in the 15% tax bracket, setting aside $1,000 a year will net the employee $150 in federal tax savings plus state tax savings. In addition, you as the employer save on FICA taxes (7.65% as of 2009).

The type of expenses your employees can pay from the FSA are broader than you might expect. They come from the IRS's rules for tax-deductible medical expenses, and include medical and dental expenses, such as copays, prescription drugs (including birth control pills), acupuncture, chiropractic adjustments, psychotherapy, eyeglasses, fertility treatments, lab fees, and more. Beneficiaries can also claim reimbursement for over-the-counter drugs like pain relievers and antacids (but not vitamins, unless doctor prescribed). Finally, FSAs cover medical expenses incurred by the employee's spouse and dependent children (but not domestic partners, except for the rare cases where the partner is tax qualified as a dependent).

Health Savings Accounts (HSAs)

Instead of FSAs, some employers offer another tax-saving option known as a "health savings account" (HSA). Contrary to widespread misunderstanding, this isn't a policy by itself, but a bank account that can be offered in combination with a qualifying high-deductible health plan (HDHP). These plans must meet various special requirements defined by the federal government. The HSA allows your employees (or you, on their behalf) to deposit money into an interest-bearing account managed by a bank or other financial trustee. The deposit entitles the employee to a tax deduction, and the interest is tax free, too. As with an FSA, the employee can later draw on this account to cover out-of-pocket medical costs.

The bad news for your employees is that, to be eligible, the health plan must require unusually high deductibles—for 2009, it was at least $1,150 for self-only coverage and $2,300 for family coverage. That can deter regular visits to the doctor. (On the other hand, as adviser Matt Sears points out, it also deters running to the doctor just because a TV ad promised that a "purple pill" would somehow change your life.)

If a high-deductible health plan (with correspondingly lower premiums) is the best your business can afford, the HSA at least offers a way to lessen the burden on your employees. In 2009, the employee can contribute up to $3,000 if he or she has individual coverage or $5,950 if it's family coverage. (The IRS resources mentioned below will give you the latest figures.)

Getting the money back typically involves either paying for medical expenses using an HSA debit card or checks, or requesting reimbursement after the fact. Unlike FSAs, your employees need not worry about end-of-year deadlines. The employee owns the account, so any unused amounts stay put and accumulate toward retirement or any future health care expenses. Once the employee reaches age 65, the money can be withdrawn from the account for any purpose, without penalty. However, the person will have to pay taxes on the money if the funds aren't used to pay for eligible health care expenses.

The types of expenses that qualify are the same as those that qualify for other medical and dental tax deductions.

RESOURCE

More information about FSAs and HSAs. For more details, download IRS Publication 502, *Medical and Dental Expenses*, and IRS Publication 969, *Health Savings Accounts and Other Tax-Favored Health Plans*, available at www.irs.gov.

Drafting Workplace Policies
That Promote Health

Meet Your Adviser

Kelly Kuglitsch, attorney with Drinker, Biddle & Reath (www.drinkerbiddle.com), in the Employee Benefits and Executive Compensation Practice Group in Milwaukee, Wisconsin.

What she does: Helps employers, in their role as sponsors, administrators, and fiduciaries of retirement and health plans, to comply with the complex standards of ERISA and the Internal Revenue Code, and to keep up to date with ever-changing benefits regulations and laws. In this capacity, she has also assisted clients in implementing HIPAA-compliant wellness programs, to promote employee health and reduce employee-related health costs. Among her other activities, she is a chapter editor for *Employee Benefits Law*, a treatise published by BNA books.

Favorite healthy food: "Sweet potatoes. On busy weekdays, I often microwave a sweet potato in the morning and take it with me as a portable breakfast. They contain great vitamins, low-glycemic complex carbs, and are very filling, because they contain more fiber than oatmeal when eaten with the skin."

Top tip for staying fit and healthy: "Portion control and making conscious, healthful food choices."

So far, we've talked about the benefits of having a wellness program, strategies for creating a program, and specific behaviors and activities to target, from smoking to fitness to chronic illness. But the best wellness programs aren't stand-alone operations: They work together with the company's culture and policies to create a consistent message. For example, if you've identified smoking as a significant problem for employees and you've educated employees on the dangers of smoking and secondhand smoke, you'll also want to consider developing workplace policies on smoking. Is your workplace smoke free? Does your company allow every employee the same amount of break time, or do you follow the somewhat common practice of allowing smokers to take a "cigarette break" whenever they feel the need? Will you pay all or part of the bill for employees who successfully complete a smoking cessation program?

This chapter will help you think through some of your policy options relating to your wellness program and goals—and we explain how to draft a general policy explaining the wellness program. After all, you're going to a lot of trouble to promote employee health, and you should let employees know what's available to them. We also cover specific workplace policies that will support your wellness initiatives, including policies on smoking, drugs and alcohol, and time off.

Before we delve into specific policies, however, it's important to take a step back and consider what information you should put in writing in your employee handbook and what information would be best left to other methods of communication.

The Purpose of Written Policies

If your company has been around for a while, you may already have written policies that you distribute to employees. You may have a complete employee handbook, or you may just have a few written guidelines for employees, such as a policy against sexual harassment or rules for using company cars.

We recommend that all but the smallest companies have an employee handbook—that is, a comprehensive written collection of policies. A handbook tells employees what the company expects from them and what they can expect from the company. It helps ensure that employees are treated consistently and fairly, because everyone goes by the same set of rules. The process of creating a handbook gives your company an opportunity to reflect on every aspect of its relationship with employees and to decide how it wants to handle issues going forward.

A handbook can also provide valuable legal protections. If ever a dispute develops, it helps you show that employees had notice of your company's policies. If your company is an at-will employer (as most are), putting that information in your handbook can help you protect your rights. And, certain types of policies—such as a policy prohibiting harassment and discrimination—can help your company defend itself in court.

This doesn't mean, however, that everything the company decides to do should be written down and distributed to employees, or that every company program or initiative should be included in the employee handbook. Once you put a policy in writing, employees will expect your company to follow it—and, if a legal dispute ever develops over a policy, a court may well require you to live up to your written commitment. The information that doesn't belong in an employee handbook includes:

- **Information that changes frequently.** A handbook or other written policy manual should be relatively stable. Although you may need to update or add a policy from time to time, you don't want to have to revise the handbook every few months. Nor do you want employees relying on policies that are out of date. Even if employees know that a policy is no longer current, it looks unprofessional to have stale information in a handbook. If your company used to provide a benefit it has discontinued, it can even make your company look cheap or insensitive to employee needs, exactly the opposite of what you're hoping to achieve with your wellness program. Information that is subject to change, such as employee rosters, reimbursement rates, a schedule of lunchtime discussion topics, or a list of approved vendors, should be provided in other ways.

- **Information that is provided in official documents.** For example, most companies don't include in their employee handbook a detailed description of the insurance benefits they provide. These benefits change, even if only slightly, from year to year, and employees typically receive brochures and other information directly from the insurance company that describes these plans and benefits. Including all this information in the handbook would make it impossibly long and require frequent updating; if you get it wrong or don't keep the handbook current, employees may believe they have benefits that are no longer available to them.

- **Topics on which you want some leeway.** Once you put a policy in writing, you need to follow it. Employees will expect you to adhere to what you've said in the handbook, and they may even have a legal right to require you to do so. That's why many employers don't put any policies in writing about things like pay raises or severance pay. If your company decides, for example, to divert money to wellness program incentives that it would otherwise have spent on the annual raises promised in its handbook, employees may claim that you breached a contract.

Some of your wellness initiatives will fit into one of these categories. For example, the particular counseling options available from your health insurance provider may change over time, or the prices for those programs may change. Your company may want to allow itself some wiggle room on issues like how much it will reimburse employees who join a gym, participate in a smoking cessation program, or meet a particular fitness goal. Similarly, you may not want to commit the company to activities or benefits that it may not continue or that haven't yet begun. For example, if you're considering having a weekly on-site class on yoga or stress reduction, but don't yet know whether enough employees will participate to make it worth the expense, don't talk about the class in your handbook.

So how can you tout and publicize your wellness initiatives without making commitments your company might not be able to keep? Keep these tips in mind:

- **Focus on the goals of your program, not on the specific ways you hope to achieve them.** Talk about employee health and fitness, productivity, living a balanced life, and so on, not about offering a $25 gift certificate to employees who lower their resting pulse rate by five points.

- **Provide details in other ways.** You might use any number of methods to convey your specific plans, including official documents from your insurance carrier and other service providers, documents generated for particular events or drives (for example, you could hand out or post written rules for your company's stair-walking challenge, or send an email telling employees what on-site activities you'll offer that year or quarter, such as yoga or stress reduction classes), and in-person conversations between employees and the person who oversees your wellness efforts, such as your human resources department.

- **Tell employees where to get more information.** This will help you make sure employees find out everything they need to know without having to include it all in the handbook.

CAUTION

Avoid mentioning rewards or incentives for meeting certain health standards. As was discussed in Chapter 2, if you reward people for reaching certain personal health goals (as opposed to giving rewards for completing certain activities) and if the rewards or incentives are tied to your health plan, you'll have to comply with HIPAA—meaning you must also indicate that a reasonable alternative standard is available. For example, says Kelly Kuglitsch, "If you offer lower health care premiums to everyone who loses a certain percentage of their extra weight, you'll need to mention that people medically unable to lose weight can win the award in some other way—though you don't have to go so far as describing what the alternative is." This legal requirement applies to any written materials that describe the terms of your wellness program and mention a health standard.

Drafting a Basic Wellness Policy

It's a good idea to include a statement in your handbook explaining your company's commitment to employee health. This lets employees know about the efforts you're making on their behalf, and tells them how to access all of the information and activities your company provides.

For the reasons discussed above, we suggest giving yourself some leeway when describing your wellness program in an employee handbook. You might adopt a general policy explaining your company's commitment to employee health and describing some of the goals of the program in broad strokes, then divulge the specifics using some of the tips in the previous section.

Let's say that, after reading this book, your company decides to begin a wellness program. Your employees complete HRAs and, after reviewing them, you target smoking, obesity, and stress as the most pressing health problems for your workforce. Your health insurance provider offers some programs in stress reduction, proper nutrition, and smoking cessation. You also plan to offer healthy snacks in company vending machines, make your workplace smoke free, and start a club for employees who want to walk during lunchtime.

In its wellness policy, your company might say something like this:

> Our company is committed to the health and well-being of its employees. We have created a wellness program to support employee efforts to improve their fitness and nutrition, quit smoking, and enjoy better health in a variety of other ways. Ask the benefits manager for information about our wellness offerings and be sure to check out the Wellness Bulletin Board, just inside the Main Street entrance, for upcoming events, classes, and more.

You can then write a separate policy to address smoking in the workplace (we discuss that next). You can also provide documents from your insurance broker—and perhaps an in-person presentation—to be sure your employees understand its range of wellness offerings. Finally, you'll be able to consider other changes, such as new time-off programs to help employees reduce stress. Drafting a general statement about your wellness policy gives you flexibility and buys you time to decide exactly what you want to do.

Policies Relating to Smoking

There are a number of practical issues to consider when developing smoking policies. Will you prohibit smoking altogether or allow smoking in designated areas, if your state and local governments allow you to? Will you adopt an official smoking cessation policy? Will you address the often thorny issue of "smoking breaks"? And what about workers who smoke or use other tobacco products off the job: Will you take the extra step of trying not to hire smokers?

This section will help you think through these issues. After you've made some preliminary decisions, you'll need to make sure the policies you want to put in place don't violate federal laws or the laws of your state, city, or county.

As you probably know, plenty of laws regulate smoking. If your business is open to the public, like a store, restaurant, or office space where clients visit, you already have to follow the state and local rules for public accommodations. Most states also regulate smoking in the workplace, and some states protect smokers from discrimination. Local governments may impose more restrictions. A quick consultation with a lawyer—in particular, an employee benefits or labor and employment lawyer who can provide advice about the interaction of the proposed program with the relevant state and federal laws—will help you make sure your smoking policies pass legal muster.

Workplace Smoking

Your options regarding the most basic decision you'll need to make—whether to allow smoking at work—may be legally restricted. A growing number of states prohibit smoking in all public and private workplaces. If you do business in one of them, your company must ban workplace smoking.

If you aren't required to maintain a smoke-free workplace, you may still have to comply with other state and local restrictions, such as laws that require employers to create separately ventilated smoking areas, to erect physical barriers between smoking and nonsmoking areas, or to prohibit smoking in areas employees must use, such as the only break room or a locker room.

Regardless of whether you are legally required to ban smoking, there are many sound practical reasons to do so. Creating a smoke-free workplace is the easiest policy to adopt, as well as the least expensive and the most health conscious.

The Benefits of a Smoking Ban

A smoking ban will best support your wellness program goals of:
- helping employees quit smoking, and
- protecting nonsmokers from the harmful effects of secondhand smoke.

Consider these benefits of banning workplace smoking:
- **Less smoking.** It sounds obvious, but the effects are more far-reaching than you might think. Workplace smoking bans not only result in less smoking at work; they change smokers' habits off the job, too, and even lead some to stop smoking altogether. The Surgeon General has reported that prohibiting smoking in the workplace leads smokers to have fewer cigarettes each day, make more attempts to quit smoking, and have more success in quitting for good.
- **More support for those who are trying to quit smoking.** Those who have tried to—or successfully—quit smoking will tell you that it's hardest to stay on the wagon when they are around

others who are smoking. Workplace smoking bans take away this temptation, at least on the job. One study has shown that complete prohibitions on smoking at work lead to a 4% drop in the percentage of workers who smoke.

- **Better health for those who don't smoke.** The health risks of secondhand smoke are clearly established. There are more than 50 cancer-causing chemicals in secondhand smoke. Secondhand smoke in the workplace creates an increased risk of lung cancer and heart disease for nonsmokers.

- **Less expense for employers.** As explained above, states that allow smoking in private workplaces often impose restrictions on smoking areas, which may have to be a certain distance from nonsmoking areas, have separate ventilation systems, and/or have structural barriers. All of these requirements cost money, which you can save by simply banning smoking outright, not to mention the money you can save on health insurance premiums, cleaning and maintenance, and even fire insurance.

- **Higher productivity.** Because a workplace smoking ban leads employees to smoke less or even quit smoking altogether, it also leads to fewer smoking breaks and fewer absences for smoking-related illness.

- **Fewer potential legal claims.** If you allow smoking in the workplace, nonsmokers may make a number of health-related legal claims. Because secondhand smoke is a known carcinogen and exacerbates a number of existing health conditions, employees exposed to smoke may make claims for workers' compensation benefits, request accommodations for disabilities aggravated by smoke, or even claim a violation of the Occupational Safety and Health Act (OSHA).

- **Improved company image.** Do you want customers to associate your company with good health, cleanliness, and vitality? Employees who smoke can undermine this image. Customers may not be interested in advice on nutritional supplements, proper workout techniques, or organic products from an employee who reeks of tobacco smoke. They may not want to order food from someone with a hacking cough.

When you consider that all of these benefits come at virtually no cost, it's easy to see why so many private employers have adopted smoking bans. Even employers concerned about how smokers will respond to a ban have little need to worry: Smokers and nonsmokers alike recognize that no-smoking policies make sense. A Gallup poll taken after California's law banning workplace smoking went into effect revealed that 83% of smokers thought employees should be protected from secondhand smoke at work, and almost 70% of smokers thought the California ban was positive.

Still, you know the culture of your local area and workplace better than anyone else, and as adviser Kelly Kuglitsch notes:

> *Employers who are perceived as taking too hard a line against tobacco use risk negative employee and public relations and raise questions about how far down the slippery slope the employer will go—will they ban overweight employees next?*

Such considerations may not change your ultimate policy decision, but they should make you think about how best to communicate your decision to employees, as a matter of internal relations.

Drafting a Smoke-Free Workplace Policy

It's easy to draft a "no smoking" policy. If you want to keep it very simple, you can draft a policy that says, "Smoking is not allowed on company property." Or, you can explain why you've chosen to ban smoking, perhaps linking the policy to your wellness goals.

No matter how you decide to word your policy, you should put it in writing and distribute it to employees. This is a legal requirement in some states. Beyond the legalities, however, having a written policy ensures that every employee knows the rules. This means employees are more likely to observe the ban—and those who don't won't be able to argue that they were unaware of it.

Helping Employees Kick the Habit

As explained in Chapter 8, most smokers say they would like to quit, but the addictive power of nicotine is a formidable foe. If you've decided to pursue any of the options described in Chapter 8 to help employees stop smoking, you should outline them in your written policy. If someone at your company will handle these efforts, your policy can direct employees to that person. For example, your policy might state:

> Our company supports employee efforts to quit smoking. If you want to quit smoking and need help, ask the human resources director for information on smoking cessation programs.

Smoking Breaks

Even if your efforts to help employees quit smoking are successful, you'll probably still have a few smokers on staff. If you adopt a smoke-free workplace policy, they'll have to leave the premises to light up. Which leads us to a continuing source of workplace tension: the cigarette break.

According to a survey by the National Business Group on Health, almost half of the smokers surveyed reported that they took three to six smoking breaks a day, and most of those who took breaks said they lasted from five to 15 minutes each. If you do the math, you can see that smokers are spending anywhere from 15 minutes to an hour and a half each day on cigarette breaks—which is probably not what you had in mind when you set their salary. You're not the only one noticing, either: Nonsmoking coworkers often resent these extra breaks or even feel entitled to take more time off themselves.

Some employers try to get a handle on this problem by adding language to their smoking policies reminding employees that they may smoke during scheduled or authorized breaks only. For example, your policy might state:

> You may smoke during meal or rest breaks only. Employees
> may not take "smoking breaks" in addition to the regular breaks
> provided to every employee under our policies.

Employees Who Smoke Off Duty

In the last few years, there have been a number of news stories about
companies that have taken their smoke-free *workplace* policies to
the limit by turning them into smoke-free *workforce* policies. These
companies refuse to hire—or threaten to fire—employees who smoke.
One famous example is the Weyco Company, an insurance consulting
firm in Michigan that told employees they would have to quit smoking
within the next fifteen months or face termination. When the deadline
came, 20 employees had quit smoking to save their jobs; four others were
fired. Kelly Kuglitsch notes:

> *While such a policy might have given rise to lawsuits in some states
> (for reasons described below), it was legal under the laws of the state of
> Michigan.*

Supporters of policies like these point out that banning smoking
at work doesn't keep employees from smoking on their own time,
which still adds the costs of increased health insurance premiums and
absenteeism to the company's bottom line. Also, those who smoke at
home or during breaks often still smell of smoke, which may bother
customers and coworkers. The only way to truly eliminate the downside
of smoking employees, these advocates say, is to get rid of them, either
by firing them or by turning them into nonsmokers.

Policies like these carry risks, however, which in our opinion far
outweigh the possible rewards. For starters, a policy that prohibits
smoking off the job would be illegal in a number of states. More than
half of the states have laws that explicitly prohibit discrimination against
those who smoke or use tobacco products or more broadly prohibit job
discrimination based on off-duty legal activities. In states that have these

"lifestyle discrimination" statutes, an employer who fired or refused to hire those who smoke would be violating the law.

Even in states that don't prohibit lifestyle discrimination, trying to regulate what employees do on their own time can quickly lead to trouble. (At the time this book was written, some lawsuits were starting their way through the system.) For starters, these policies are nearly impossible to enforce. Kelly Kuglitsch notes, "Plenty of employees will bristle at being told what they may or may not do during their off hours." And, many employers don't relish the thought of being seen—by employees or by the public—as Big Brother. Does your company brand involve fun, freedom, independence, or some variant of "doing your own thing"? Good luck with that if you become known for policing your employees' private lives.

What's more, the evidence indicates that punitive policies like these—which threaten employees who fail to shape up—don't work as well as rewards-based programs. For more on the value of rewards-based programs and how to implement them effectively, see Chapter 2.

Policies Relating to Drugs and Alcohol

As explained in Chapter 9, substance abuse by employees can lead to numerous workplace problems, from absenteeism and low productivity to on-the-job accidents, workers' compensation claims, and even lawsuits by outsiders harmed by an impaired employee's actions. That's why every employer, regardless of size and industry, should have a written policy prohibiting drug and alcohol use at work.

Beyond this basic guideline, there are a few additional policy questions to consider. Will your company serve alcohol at company functions? Will your company require drug testing? If so, who will be subject to testing and what procedures will be followed? Will your company support employees who are trying to get sober? This section describes some of your options for handling these issues.

Drugs and Alcohol at Work

Your policy should tell employees that drug and alcohol use at work is prohibited, including:

- use of illegal drugs
- misuse of legal drugs (such as over-the-counter medications or drugs that have been prescribed to the employee), and
- drinking alcohol.

Your policy should also prohibit employees from showing up at work inebriated. If any employees have access to company cars or other vehicles, your policy should expressly state that employees may not drive under the influence.

Make sure you consider—and address in your policy—issues your employees might consider to be grey areas, particularly when it comes to alcohol. As Kelly Kuglitsch explains, "Because social drinking is common in our culture, employees may not be aware of your company's expectations here." For example, if your company requires service technicians to be on call for weekend emergencies, should these employees refrain from drinking entirely, or is it okay for them to have alcohol as long as they are well under the legal limit for driving? What are the rules for sales representatives who routinely take clients out to dinner? You may want to have a lawyer help you come up with rules that are both legally sound and practical in this area.

Another issue you'll need to tackle is work-related events. Many companies have barbecues, holiday parties, or even happy hours that involve drinking. Given how many stories everyone's heard or seen about events like these ending badly, it's not surprising that some employers have opted for alcohol-free celebrations. If yours is one of them, make that clear in your policy. If your company allows alcohol at certain company functions, your policy should make clear that employees are expected to act appropriately and responsibly at these events, and that drinking to the point of intoxication is not allowed.

Drug Testing

Some companies, including those in certain transportation fields (such as aviation or trucking) and some government contractors, are legally required to test employees for illegal drugs. For the most part, however, your company probably has the right to decide—within very proscribed legal limits—whether to require drug testing.

State and local law dictates whether, how, and of whom a company may require drug tests. For example, some states require employers to provide a certain amount of advance notice, some allow testing only for particular occupations or in certain situations (for instance, after the employee is in an accident that causes injury or completes a drug rehabilitation program), and some require employers to follow prescribed protocols, such as using a licensed laboratory or allowing employees to request a retest. Employers also have to make sure that the way they conduct the test doesn't violate employee privacy. These rules can make it difficult to design a legally sound drug testing program.

> CAUTION
>
> **The most protective law is the one that rules.** The field of employment law is heavily regulated by federal, state, and even local authorities. Because drug testing is hotly contested, you can expect to find layers of laws on the topic. Where this type of overlap occurs, employers must follow the law that provides the most protections for employees; in the case of drug testing, this may be a local ordinance, particularly if you do business in a city known for its liberal views. This is another good reason why companies that wish to drug test employees should consult a lawyer.

There's no doubt that drug tests are controversial. Many employees find them invasive and believe they demonstrate a lack of trust. Because drug tests detect residues from drug use that occurred days, or even weeks, prior to the test, there's also the issue of relevance: If an employee occasionally smokes pot on the weekend, but has a stellar performance record, should that be a firing offense? Drug tests can also turn up legally prescribed drugs, which can lead to a different set of problems. There's also the issue of false positives: Everything from antibiotics to vitamins to herbal supplements and even certain types of food can generate an incorrect test result.

For all these reasons, many employers wisely choose to forego drug tests. If your company is considering drug testing, you should consult an experienced attorney to learn the rules you'll need to follow. And, if you decide to require drug tests, you must develop a written policy explaining the testing process to employees. Many states require drug-testing employers to adopt a written policy, often with particular information, such as when drug tests may be required, the consequences of refusing to take a test, and the consequences of testing positive.

What About Medical Marijuana?

In some states, it's legal to use marijuana for medical purposes. Typically, medical marijuana laws provide that possession and cultivation of a limited amount of marijuana for personal use, as prescribed by a doctor, is not a crime. This raises a question for drug testing employers: If an employee tests positive for marijuana, but uses the drug in accordance with a valid medical prescription, may you discipline or fire the employee?

In California, at least, the answer is "yes." In a recent case, the California Supreme Court found that a company may fire a recently hired employee who tested positive for marijuana, even though the employee didn't show up at work under the influence and had a valid prescription to use the drug for back pain. The employee, Gary Ross, argued that his employer, Ragingwire Telecommunications, fired him illegally; he claimed the company should have instead been required to accommodate his disability by allowing him to use marijuana for pain management while off duty. The Court disagreed, finding that the company didn't have a duty to accommodate drug use that is illegal under federal law. *Ross v. Ragingwire Telecommunications Inc.*, 42 Cal.4th 920 (2008).

Rehabilitation Programs

As explained in Chapter 9, it often makes more sense for employers to support employee efforts to recover from drug or alcohol abuse than to adopt a zero-tolerance approach. If your company will assist employees who want to kick the habit, you should say so in a written policy. Be careful, however: This is one of those areas where you will want to leave yourself some leeway to decide how to handle individual situations as they come up. There's a world of difference between, for example, an employee with excellent performance who is finding it difficult to wean herself from pain medication prescribed following a car accident and an employee who is arrested selling heroin in the company parking lot.

Support for Rehabilitation

If your company is committed to helping employees with substance abuse problems, you should say so in your policy—without locking yourself in to a particular course of action for every employee. For example, you might make a general statement like this:

> Our company believes that employees who have substance abuse problems can help themselves by enrolling in a rehabilitation program. Overcoming difficulties with drugs and/or alcohol will not only help these employees in their personal lives, but will also help them to be more effective and productive workers.

Performance Standards

Your policy should also make clear that employees must meet the requirements of their jobs, whether or not they have a substance abuse problem. This will help you keep your options open in the future. If you don't explicitly reserve your company's right to enforce its performance and conduct standards, an employee might point to your support for rehabilitation as an implicit promise that problems stemming from substance abuse won't result in discipline. Here's an example of the language you might use:

> Please note that even as you might be seeking assistance for your substance abuse problem, we still expect you to meet the same standards of performance, productivity, and conduct that we expect of all employees, including our prohibition on alcohol and illegal drug use at work. Failing to meet these standards for any reason, including a substance abuse problem, may result in discipline or termination.

Leave for Rehabilitation

Some companies offer employees time off for substance abuse treatment. In fact, in some states and localities, employers *must* offer leave for an employee to participate in a rehabilitation program. The federal Family and Medical Leave Act also allows time off for rehab.

If you are required or choose to offer leave for rehabilitation, you'll need to make some decisions about the details, including:

- **Who is eligible for leave.** For example, will you have a length-of-service requirement? Will only full-time employees qualify? Will you require employees to provide medical proof of a substance abuse problem? Must rehab be prescribed by a doctor?
- **How much leave you will allow.** When making this decision, you might consult your health insurance provider and rehab programs in your area to find out what is reasonable.
- **Whether leave will be paid, partially paid, or unpaid.** You should also consider whether employees on leave will continue to accrue benefits, such as vacation time.
- **Whether you will impose any requirements for an employee's return to work.** For example, you might ask employees to provide proof that they successfully completed a program, require a fitness-for-duty exam, or even impose a drug test requirement, if the law allows it in your state and locality.

When making these decisions, you will probably have a lot of flexibility. However, if your state or local government requires employees to offer rehabilitation leave, it may also set procedural rules for that leave. Check with an attorney who specializes in employment law to make sure your program will meet all applicable legal requirements.

Telecommuting and Flexible Schedules

Does your company allow employees to work from home? If so, you're not alone: In 2007, more than 12 million employees were teleworking more than eight hours per week, and these numbers are steadily increasing. Many employers also allow employees to work a flexible schedule, so they can have time off when they need to attend to other things. All of these options allow employees to meet their commitments and personal needs—perhaps including exercise and other healthy activities—while still getting their work done.

Telecommuting

Especially these days, when more and more companies are trying to come up with ways to save money, telecommuting has grown in popularity. When employees work remotely, employers need less space and equipment. Because employees place tremendous value on being able to work from home, telecommuting is a much-desired job benefit; in tough economic times, allowing employees to work from home can help ease the pain of other cuts, such as a reduction in hours or pay. Employees who work from home save time and money by avoiding the commute. They can also fit errands, chores, and other home-based tasks into their workday.

Not every industry, position, or employee is right for teleworking, however. Although technology has made remote work much easier, there are still some positions for which regular attendance is crucial. Even if a job lends itself well to remote work, the employee filling the job might need more interaction, supervision, or structure to perform well. If you find the right fit, however, allowing employees to work from home at least some of the time significantly boosts morale; cements employee loyalty to the company; saves everyone time and money; allows employees to better juggle their work and private lives; and helps them maintain good health.

Remote work raises a number of important legal concerns, all stemming from the fact that the employer remains responsible for the employee but has far less actual control over the employee's work and work environment. If you allow employees to work from home, you'll need to decide how to handle these issues:

- **Safety.** Employers have a legal obligation to provide a safe workplace, even if employees don't work on site. An employee who is working from home is still protected by OSHA and workers' compensation insurance. The employer might also be liable to an outsider who is injured at the employee's home, such as a delivery person who trips on the front steps while handing over work-related documents. For these reasons, employers who allow remote work should always provide appropriate safety equipment, make sure their insurance covers potential problems, and perhaps even inspect the employee's workspace.

- **Wage and hour concerns.** Technological advances make it possible—even necessary, it seems—to work any time, anywhere. This creates problems if the employees doing all of that work are entitled to earn overtime, especially if those employees work from home, where employers don't necessarily learn of their extra hours. Employers are legally responsible to pay eligible employees for all overtime that the employer "suffers or permits" them to work, whether the employer knows about it or not. Employees who work from home may do work that isn't recorded, and for which they aren't properly paid. You must be particularly cautious when allowing hourly employees to work from home— and you should have a policy that requires employees to get permission, in advance, before putting in any overtime.

- **Fairness issues.** Because working from home is such a desired benefit, it's important to be evenhanded and consistent in deciding who gets to do it. Determine ahead of time the positions for which working from home is appropriate, as well as what you will require or expect of employees who want to work from home. Be mindful of laws that prohibit discrimination; gender discrimination can be a particular problem here. For example, some employers ask female employees who have children to demonstrate that they have childcare for the hours during which they are expected to work, but don't think to ask the same questions of male employees.

Flexible Schedules

If your company's needs allow it, flexible scheduling is one of the cheapest and most effective ways to improve employee morale, productivity, and give the employees the ability to integrate their work with staying healthy and other aspects of their lives. Flexible scheduling allows employees to make time for the activities that are important to them, such as caring for children or other family members, exercising, going to school, or doing volunteer work, while still getting their work done. It's no wonder that the majority of employers now allow their employees some form of flexibility in scheduling.

Flexible scheduling is essentially any way of getting a job done other than a standard Monday through Friday, 9-to-5 schedule. An employee could work a compressed schedule, putting in four ten-hour days rather than five eight-hour days. An employee could work an early morning schedule, or even take a long break in the middle of the day and make up the hours by coming in early or staying late. Employees can even share a job: For example, two new parents who each want to work part time could split the hours, responsibilities, pay, and benefits of a single position. Flexible scheduling costs the employer nothing more than some additional supervision, and can really boost morale and attendance.

When deciding who is eligible for flexible scheduling, you'll have to consider the needs and culture of your workplace. Often, some positions in a company lend themselves well to flexibility, while others require more regular hours and attendance. Some companies require employees to put in a certain amount of time before they can ask for a flexible schedule, so the company can make sure that the employee is integrated into the company and performs well. You'll also have to decide what options you'll offer and how you'll make sure the work is getting done. For ideas, see *The Work From Home Handbook*, by Diana Fitzpatrick and Stephen Fishman (Nolo); although it's written for employees, it's full of great information and tips on which jobs—and which workers—are best suited for flexible scheduling, how to make sure the arrangement is working, and much more.

Time-Off Policies

Your company's time-off policies can directly support employee health. Paid leave allows employees to stay home when they are ill, to obtain preventive care when needed, to better care for both work and family, and to recharge their batteries with the occasional vacation. Most companies offer employees at least some paid time off: Even though paid leave isn't legally required in most places, it's become a nationwide standard.

In addition to paid time off, your company may be required to offer unpaid leave in certain circumstances. For example, the FMLA requires employers with at least 50 employees to provide 12 weeks of unpaid leave per year for employees to recuperate from a serious health condition, care for a seriously ill family member, bond with a new child, or handle practical matters relating to a family member's call to active military duty. The FMLA also allows employees to take up to 26 weeks off to care for a family member who returns from military duty with a serious illness or injury.

Among the questions you'll need to consider here are how much leave to offer, which employees may use it, what it may be used for, and what rules employees must follow—for example, whether employees will have to give a certain amount of notice in advance of taking vacation time.

The Family and Medical Leave Act

If your company is covered by the FMLA, you must provide written information to employees about the law's requirements. You should also have an FMLA policy in your handbook explaining who may use FMLA leave, what situations are covered by the FMLA, how employees may request leave, and so on. The notice and procedural requirements of the FMLA are fairly complex; if you need to know more, check out *The Essential Guide to Family and Medical Leave*, by Lisa Guerin and Deborah C. England (Nolo), which provides all of the information, guidance, and forms you'll need to comply with the law.

Vacation

According to the Bureau of Labor Statistics, 75% of employees in private industry in this country have at least some paid vacation benefits. Our country is unique in the developed world in not requiring private employers to offer paid vacation time, and U.S. employers typically provide fewer vacation days than employers in other countries. Employers in this country provide nine days of paid vacation per year, on average, in addition to six paid holidays.

Even with this comparatively minimal amount of vacation, your employees are unlikely to take full advantage of it. A study by Hudson, a worldwide recruitment service, found that over half of U.S. workers don't use all of their vacation time, and a full 30% take less than half of their days off.

We hope your company offers at least some paid vacation—and encourages your employees to use it. It's a proven stress reducer that helps employees rest, restore their energy, spend time with their families, and balance their jobs with their other commitments and interests.

If your company does offer paid vacation, you'll need to consider these issues:

- **How much time off will you offer?** Many employers provide more vacation days to employees who stay with the company over time. For example, you might offer ten days of vacation during the first year or two of employment, then bump up to 15 days per year after that. Or, you could offer the same number of days to everyone. Another issue here is whether you will cap the total amount of time an employee may accrue. Many employers do. A cap requires employees to occasionally take some vacation to avoid burning out; it also prevents employees from accruing so much vacation that they can take months off at a time—or require the employer to pay out all that saved time when employment ends.

> **CAUTION**
>
> **"Use it or lose it" policies may be illegal.** Employers are legally entitled to limit how much vacation time an employee may earn. However, some states forbid "use it or lose it" policies, by which an employee must forfeit accrued vacation time that he or she doesn't use by a certain date (typically, the end of the year). Because these states view vacation time as a form of compensation that the employee has earned, a policy that takes away accrued vacation time is seen as refusing to pay employees money that they are owed, which is against the law. Although the difference may seem fairly technical, a cap on accrual is legal in these states because it prohibits the employee from earning vacation time in the first place, rather than taking it away after the employee has earned it.

- **How will time off accrue?** Many employers allow employees to earn paid vacation as they go—for example, employees might earn eight hours of paid vacation every month, which is then added to their total available vacation time. Other companies give employees their full allotment of annual vacation days at the beginning of each year.

- **Who is eligible for vacation days?** If you have part-time employees, will you offer them paid vacation too? Many employers simply prorate earned vacation time. For example, if a full-time employee earns ten vacation days per year, or 80 hours off, an employee who works half time would earn half that amount of vacation time. Some companies don't allow employees to take any paid vacation until they've been with the company for a certain amount of time.

- **What happens to unused vacation days?** Some states require employers to cash out accrued vacation time that an employee hasn't used when the employee quits or is fired. If your company does business in one of these states, or chooses to pay out unused vacation, you should say so in your policy.

- **How must employees request and schedule vacation?** If your company will require employees to give advance notice, submit a vacation request to their supervisors, or follow other procedures in order to take vacation time, your policy should explain the rules. Many employers impose some kind of notice requirement, if only to prevent having too many employees out at the same time.

Sick Leave

The Bureau of Labor Statistics reports that 60% of employees in private industry have access to paid sick leave. No state currently requires employers to offer paid sick leave, but some cities and the District of Columbia do have such requirements. These jurisdictions recognize that forcing employees to choose between their health and their jobs is both unfair and unkind.

Allowing employees to take time off when they are sick is also sound from a policy perspective. Paid sick days encourage employees to stay home when they're ill, rather than coming to work to infect their coworkers or perform at a substandard level. Providing paid sick leave needn't come with a big price tag: A 2004 survey showed that employees take an average of only 3.9 sick days for their own illnesses or injuries each year and another 1.3 days to care for ill family members (if permitted by the employer's sick leave policy).

If your company provides paid sick leave, you'll need to consider the same issues that apply to vacation leave: How much time will you offer, which employees will be eligible, and so on. You should also consider what employees may do with their sick leave. For example, may employees use sick leave for routine preventive care? To care for ill family members or take them for check-ups and other appointments? To avoid exposure to germs during a major pandemic? To attend other activities associated with your wellness program, such as health screenings, nutrition classes, meetings for a weight loss group, or a smoking cessation program? Some states require employers who provide sick leave to allow employees to use it for family members or preventive care; even if your state doesn't, policies like these go a long way toward promoting employee wellness and reducing stress.

Special Concerns for Communicable Diseases

As we go to press, the H1N1 flu virus is sweeping a number of countries, leaving school closures, bans on public gatherings, and general panic in its wake. Health officials fear that this is only the first outbreak. If this virus follows the pattern of other pandemics, the worst could still be ahead of us. As the weather turns colder again, all of us spend more time inside, exposing ourselves to the germs of others.

What can employers do, policy wise, to minimize employee exposure and protect their companies from massive absences? The key is to keep sick employees out of the workplace and encourage measures at work to halt the spread of the virus—while remaining a voice of calm authority. Here are some tips from the experts:

- **Tell sick employees to stay home—and send them home if they come in anyway.** In your sick leave policy, state that employees should not come in to work if they have been diagnosed with or exposed to a communicable disease or are suffering its symptoms. Also, warn employees that anyone who arrives at work with obvious signs of communicable disease, such as a fever, weakness, or cough, will be sent home immediately.

- **Develop a response plan *before* any crisis.** Your company should be prepared for the possibility that a number of employees will be out simultaneously. Who are the key employees your company needs to keep its doors open, and what will you do if they are ill or otherwise unable to come to work? How will you communicate with employees who are off-site—for example, to tell everyone not to come in the next day, because there's been a large-scale outbreak?

- **Encourage telecommuting during the pandemic.** If employees have already become sick, allow others to work from home, if possible. This will prevent unnecessary infection.

Paying Employees Who Don't Use Sick Leave

Some employers create incentives for employees who don't use their sick leave. For example, an employee might be eligible for an "attendance bonus" for not taking any sick days for a year, or the company might cash out unused sick days or convert at least some of them to vacation days at the end of each year.

If your company has attendance problems and really needs to cut down on unscheduled absences, this type of award program might be effective. But it has a real downside. The point of offering paid sick days is to encourage employees to stay home when they are sick or need to care for a family member, so they can be fresh, focused, and healthy while they are at work. A bonus system provides the opposite incentive: It encourages employees to come to work regardless of their health, to get the award. According to a survey conducted in 2007, employers ranked attendance bonuses as only the fourth most effective way to cut down on unwanted absences. What was ranked number one? Creating a "paid leave bank": a paid time-off program that lumps all paid leave together, as described below.

Paid Time-Off (PTO) Programs

Rather than adopting separate policies on vacation, sick leave, and other types of time off, many employers now adopt a single policy to give employees a certain number of paid days off per year, which employees may use as they wish. There are many benefits to adopting a unified PTO policy rather than offering different types of leave. A PTO program reduces paperwork and recordkeeping hassles. It also cuts back on unscheduled absences: Because employees can use PTO for any reason, there's no need to call in "sick" at the last minute and much less incentive to take "mental health" days. A PTO policy allows employees to manage their own time off as best suits their own needs.

There are some drawbacks to offering PTO, however. For those employees who use sick leave only when they really are sick, PTO provides more time off overall, which creates higher costs for employers. Also, in states where employers are required to cash out unused vacation days when an employee leaves, employers will have to pay out the employee's entire allotment of PTO, even if some of it was intended to be used for illness. PTO programs also make it difficult to track reasons for an employee's absence. Although this is a benefit from a paperwork and management perspective, it may create problems if, for example, an employee is using time off for a reason that's covered by the FMLA (for which your company must give certain notices and count the time against the employee's FMLA entitlement), and your company doesn't find out about it because the employee doesn't have to give any reason for being absent.

When developing a PTO program, you'll need to consider the issues covered above for sick and vacation policies, including how much time off to provide, which employees are eligible, how leave will accrue, and the like.

RESOURCE

Get your policies in writing, with help from Nolo. You can draft an effective, legally sound handbook quickly with *Create Your Own Employee Handbook*, by Lisa Guerin and Amy DelPo (Nolo); it includes a CD-ROM that lets you cut and paste policies to easily create a handbook that works for your business.

How to Use the CD-ROM

The CD-ROM included with this book can be used with Windows computers. It installs files that use software programs that need to be on your computer already. It is not a standalone software program.

In accordance with U.S. copyright laws, the CD-ROM and its files are for your personal use only.

Please read this appendix and the "Readme.htm" file included on the CD-ROM for instructions on using the CD-ROM. For a list of files and their file names, see the end of this appendix.

Note to Macintosh users: This CD-ROM and its files should also work on Macintosh computers. Please note, however, that Nolo cannot provide technical support for non-Windows users.

Note to eBook users: You can access the CD-ROM files mentioned here from the bookmarked section of the eBook, located on the left hand side.

How to View the README File

To view the "Readme.htm" file, insert the CD-ROM into your computer's CD-ROM drive and follow these instructions:

Windows XP and Vista

1. On your PC's desktop, double-click the **My Computer** icon.

2. Double-click the icon for the CD-ROM drive into which the CD-ROM was inserted.

3. Double-click the file "Readme.htm."

Macintosh

1. On your Mac desktop, double-click the icon for the CD-ROM that you inserted

2. Double-click the file "Readme.htm."

Installing the Files Onto Your Computer

To work with the files on the CD-ROM, you first need to install them onto your hard disk. Here's how:

Windows XP and Vista

Follow the CD-ROM's instructions that appear on the screen. If nothing happens when you insert the CD-ROM, then:

1. Double-click the **My Computer** icon.
2. Double-click the icon for the CD-ROM drive into which the CD-ROM was inserted.
3. Double-click the file "Welcome.exe."

Macintosh

If the **Health Program CD** window is not open, double-click the **Health Program CD** icon. Then:

1. Select the **Health Program Forms** folder icon.
2. Drag and drop the folder icon onto your computer.

Where Are the Files Installed?

Windows

By default, all the files are installed to the **Health Program Resources** folder in the **Program Files** folder of your computer and added to the **Programs** folder of the **Start** menu.

Macintosh

All the files are located in the **Health Program Resources** folder.

Using the Word Processing Files to Create Documents

The CD-ROM includes word processing files that you can open, complete, print, and save with your word processing program. All word processing files come in rich text format and have the extension ".rtf." For example, the file for the Wellness Plan Worksheet discussed in Chapter 2 is on the file "worksheet.rtf." RTF files can be read by most recent word processing programs including Microsoft *Word*, Windows *WordPad*, and recent versions of *WordPerfect*.

The following are general instructions. Because each word processor uses different commands to open, format, save, and print documents, refer to your word processor's help file for specific instructions.

Do not call Nolo's technical support if you have questions on how to use your word processor or your computer.

Opening a File

You can open word processing files with any of the three following ways:
1. Windows users can open a file by selecting its "shortcut."
   - Click the Windows **Start** button.
   - Open the **Programs** folder.
   - Open the **Forms** folder.
   - Open the **Health Program Resources** folder.
   - Click the shortcut to the file you want to work with.
2. Both Windows and Macintosh users can open a file by double-clicking it.
   - Use **My Computer** or Windows **Explorer** (Windows XP or Vista) or the **Finder** (Macintosh) to go to the **Health Program Resources** folder.
   - Open the **Forms** folder.
   - Double-click the file you want to open.
3. Windows and Macintosh users can open a file from within their word processor.

- Open your word processor.
- Go to the **File** menu and choose the **Open** command. This opens a dialog box.
- Select the location and name of the file. (You will navigate to the version of the **Health Program Resources** folder that you've installed on your computer.)

Editing Your Document

Here are tips for working on your document.
- Refer to the book's instructions and sample agreements for help.
- Underlines indicate where to enter information, frequently including bracketed instructions. Delete the underlines and instructions before finishing your document.
- Signature lines should appear on a page with at least some text from the document itself.

Editing Files That Have Optional or Alternative Text

Some files have check boxes that appear before text. Check boxes indicate:
- Optional text that you can choose to include or exclude.
- Alternative text that you select to include, excluding the other alternatives.

We recommend doing the following:

Optional text

Delete optional text you do not want to include and keep that you do. In either case, delete the check box and the italicized instructions. If you choose to delete an optional numbered clause, renumber the subsequent clauses after deleting it.

Alternative text

Delete the alternatives that you do not want to include first. Then delete the remaining check boxes, as well as the italicized instructions that you need to select one of the alternatives provided.

Printing Out the Document

Use your word processor's or text editor's **Print** command to print out your document.

Saving Your Document

Use the **Save As** command to save and rename your document. You will be unable to use the **Save** command because the files are "read-only." If you save the file without renaming it, the underlines that indicate where you need to enter your information will be lost, and you will be unable to create a new document with this file without recopying the original file from the CD-ROM.

Using Print-Only Files

The CD-ROM includes useful files in Adobe PDF format. To use them, you need Adobe *Reader* installed on your computer. If you don't already have this software, you can download it for free at www.adobe.com.

Opening PDF Files

PDF files, like word processing files, can be opened in one of three ways.

1. Windows users can open a file by selecting its "shortcut."
   - Click the **Windows Start** button.
   - Open the **Programs** folder.
   - Open the **Health Program Resources** folder.
   - Open the **Forms** subfolder.
   - Click the shortcut to the file you want to work with.
2. Both Windows and Macintosh users can open a file directly by double-clicking on it.
   - Use **My Computer** or Windows **Explorer** (Windows XP or Vista) or the **Finder** (Macintosh) to go to the **Health Program Resources** folder.
   - Open the **Forms** subfolder.
   - Double-click the specific file you want to open.

3. Windows and Macintosh users can open a file from within Adobe *Reader*.
   - Open Adobe *Reader*.
   - Go to the **File** menu and choose the **Open** command. This opens a dialog box.
   - Select the location and name of the file. (You will navigate to the version of the **Health Program Resources** folder that you've installed on your computer.)

Filling in PDF files

The PDF files cannot be filled out using your computer. To create your document using one of these files, print it out and then complete it by hand or typewriter.

Listening to the Audio Files

This section explains how to play the audio files using your computer. All audio files are in MP3 format. For example, Why Walking Makes a Great Activity Within Any Workplace Wellness Program is on the file "Walking.mp3." At the end of this appendix, you'll find a list of the audio files and their file names.

Most computers come with a media player that plays MP3 files. You can listen to files that you have installed on your computer or directly from the CD-ROM. See below for further information on both.

The following are general instructions. Because every media player is different, refer to your media player's help files for more specific instructions. Please do not contact Nolo's technical support if you are having difficulty using your media player.

Playing the Audio Files Without Installing

If you don't want to copy 27MB of audio files to your computer, you can play the CD-ROM on your computer. Here's how:

Windows

1. Insert the CD-ROM to view the "Welcome to Health Program Resources CD" window.
2. Click "Listen to Audio."

If nothing happens when you insert the CD-ROM,

1. Double-click the **My Computer** icon.
2. Double-click the icon for the CD-ROM drive you inserted the CD-ROM into.
3. Double-click the file "Welcome.exe."

Macintosh

1. Insert the CD-ROM. (If the **Health Program Resources CD** window does not open, double-click the **Health Program Resources CD** icon).
2. Double-click the **Health Program Resources** folder.
3. Open the **Audio** subfolder.
4. Double-click the audio file you want to hear.

Listening to Audio Files You've Installed on Your Computer

There are two ways to listen to the audio files that you have installed on your computer.

1. Windows users can open a file by selecting its shortcut.
   - Click the Windows **Start** button.
   - Open the **Programs** folder.
   - Open the **Health Program Resources CD** folder.
   - Open the **Audio** subfolder.
   - Click the shortcut to the file you want to work with.
2. Both Windows and Macintosh users can open a file by double-clicking it.
   - Use **My Computer** or Windows **Explorer** (Windows XP or Vista) or the **Finder** (Macintosh) to go to the **Health Program Resources CD** folder.
   - Open the **Audio** subfolder.
   - Double-click the file you want to open.

Files on the CD-ROM

The following forms are in Rich Text Format (RTF):

Form Title	File Name
Wellness Plan Worksheet	worksheet.rtf
Wellness Program Waiver and Release of Liability	waiver.rtf
Wellness Program Interest Survey	survey.rtf
Wellness Program Announcement Letter	letter.rtf
Wellness Program Newsletter Announcement	announcement.rtf
Treatment Center Evaluation Form	form.rtf
Food and Exercise Diary	diary.rtf

The following forms are in Portable Document Format (PDF):

Form Title	File Name
Checklist for a Successful Wellness Program	checklist.pdf
Wellness Program Interest Survey	survey.pdf
Your Wellness Program's Baseline Data	data.pdf
Treatment Center Evaluation Form	form.pdf
Food and Exercise Diary	diary.pdf

The following forms are audio (MP3):

Form Title	File Name
Why Create a Wellness Program?	WhyWellness.mp3
Wellness Program Incentives	Incentives.mp3
Wellness Program—Walking	Walking.mp3

Index

A

E

EAPs (Employee Assistance Programs), 163, 170, 213–214, 220, 253, 268–269

Early detection. *See* Prevention and early detection

E-communications, wellness information via, 28, 30, 46

Economic downturn, effect on wellness, 156, 164, 180

Education. *See* Health education, information, self-help tools

EEOC (Equal Employment Opportunity Commission), 53

Emotions, 229, 238, 250

Employee Assistance Programs (EAPs), 163, 170, 220, 268–269

Employee census, for health insurance quotes, 275–276

Employee confidentiality, 53–55, 83, 84, 206, 207–208, 220

Employee feedback, on wellness program, 89, 90

Employee field trips, 44

Employee handbook, 77, 292–293. *See also* Workplace policies

Employee loyalty, 14–15, 261

Employee participation, wellness program, 40, 50, 52–53, 82, 84, 89

Employee privacy, 46, 51, 53–55, 220, 275, 304–305

Employee recognition, 46, 55

Employee Retirement Income Security Act (ERISA), 272

Employees' interests, assessing your, 61–66

Equal Employment Opportunity Commission (EEOC), 53

Ergonomic awareness, 105, 169

ERISA (Employee Retirement Income Security Act), 272

Evaluating your worksite. *See* Worksite evaluation and program launch

Evaluations, seminar, 89

Events. *See* Office events

Exercise. *See* Fitness and exercise

F

Family
    and FSAs, 286
    health insurance coverage for, 271
    including in wellness program, 45, 56–57
    smoking cessation assistance to, 180
    spouses, 45, 56–57, 271, 281, 286
    using sick leave for illness in, 315

Family and Medical Leave Act (FMLA), 165, 307, 311, 312, 317

"Fat tax" legislation, 52

Federal laws
    Age Discrimination in Employment Act (ADEA), 51
    Family and Medical Leave Act (FMLA), 165, 307, 311, 312, 317

NOLO® *Keep Up to Date*

1 Go to **Nolo.com/newsletters/index.html** to sign up for free newsletters and discounts on Nolo products.

- **Nolo Briefs.** Our monthly email newsletter with great deals and free information.

- **Nolo's Special Offer.** A monthly newsletter with the biggest Nolo discounts around.

- **BizBriefs.** Tips and discounts on Nolo products for business owners and managers.

- **Landlord's Quarterly.** Deals and free tips just for landlords and property managers, too.

2 Don't forget to check for updates at **Nolo.com**. Under "Products," find this book and click "Legal Updates."

Let Us Hear From You

3 Comments on this book? We want to hear 'em. Email us at feedback@nolo.com.

HLTH1

NOLO *and* USA TODAY

Cutting-Edge Content, Unparalleled Expertise

The Busy Family's Guide to Money

by Sandra Block, Kathy Chu & John Waggoner • $19.99

The Busy Family's Guide to Money will help you make the most of your income, handle major one-time expenses, figure children into the budget—and much more.

The Work From Home Handbook

Flex Your Time, Improve Your Life

by Diana Fitzpatrick & Stephen Fishman • $19.99

If you're one of those people who need to (or simply want to) work from home, let this book help you come up with a plan that both you and your boss can embrace!

Retire Happy

What You Can Do NOW to Guarantee a Great Retirement

by Richard Stim & Ralph Warner • $19.99

You don't need a million dollars to retire well, but you do need friends, hobbies and an active lifestyle. This book shows how to make retirement the best time of your life.

The Essential Guide for First-Time Homeowners

Maximize Your Investment & Enjoy Your New Home

by Ilona Bray & Alayna Schroeder • $19.99

This reassuring resource is filled with crucial financial advice, real solutions and easy-to-implement ideas that can save you thousands of dollars.

Easy Ways to Lower Your Taxes

Simple Strategies Every Taxpayer Should Know

by Sandra Block & Stephen Fishman • $19.99

Provides useful insights and tactics to help lower your taxes. Learn how to boost tax-free income, get a lower tax rate, defer paying taxes, make the most of deductions—and more!

First-Time Landlord

Your Guide to Renting Out a Single-Family Home

by Attorney Janet Portman, Marcia Stewart & Michael Molinski • $19.99

From choosing tenants to handling repairs to avoiding legal trouble, this book provides the information new landlords need to make a profit and follow the law.

Stopping Identity Theft

10 Easy Steps to Security

by Scott Mitic, CEO, TrustedID, Inc. • $19.99

Don't let an emptied bank account be your first warning sign. This book offers ten strategies to help prevent the theft of personal information.

ORDER ANYTIME AT WWW.NOLO.COM OR CALL 800-728-3555

Prices subject to change.

NOLO® *Online Legal Forms*

Nolo offers a large library of legal solutions and forms, created by Nolo's in-house legal staff. These reliable documents can be prepared in minutes.

Online Legal Solutions

- **Incorporation.** Incorporate your business in any state.
- **LLC Formations.** Gain asset protection and pass-through tax status in any state.
- **Wills.** Nolo has helped people make over 2 million wills. Is it time to make or revise yours?
- **Living Trust (avoid probate).** Plan now to save your family the cost, delays, and hassle of probate.
- **Trademark.** Protect the name of your business or product.
- **Provisional Patent.** Preserve your rights under patent law and claim "patent pending" status.

Online Legal Forms

Nolo.com has hundreds of top quality legal forms available for download—bills of sale, promissory notes, nondisclosure agreements, LLC operating agreements, corporate minutes, commercial lease and sublease, motor vehicle bill of sale, consignment agreements and many, many more.

Review Your Documents

Many lawyers in Nolo's consumer-friendly lawyer directory will review Nolo documents for a very reasonable fee. Check their detailed profiles at **lawyers.nolo.com**.